Sounding Good

Sounding Good

Advancing Cultural Sustainability and Social Justice through Music

Catherine Grant

with

José Bonifácio da Luz ("Bengala")
José Jorge de Carvalho
Arn Chorn-Pond
Jessie Lloyd
Saurav Moni
Violeta Ruano Posada
Mohamed Sleiman Labat
Sandy Sur
Seyma Thorn

OXFORD
UNIVERSITY PRESS

Oxford University Press is a department of the University of Oxford.
It furthers the University's objective of excellence in research, scholarship,
and education by publishing worldwide. Oxford is a registered trade mark of
Oxford University Press in the UK and certain other countries.

Published in the United States of America by Oxford University Press
198 Madison Avenue, New York, NY 10016, United States of America.

Library of Congress Cataloging-in-Publication Data
Names: Grant, Catherine, 1977– author
Title: Sounding good : advancing cultural sustainability and social justice
through music / Catherine Grant.
Description: [1]. | New York : Oxford University Press, 2025. |
Includes bibliographical references and index. |
Identifiers: LCCN 2025037584 (print) | LCCN 2025037585 (ebook) |
ISBN 9780197698440 paperback | ISBN 9780197698433 hardback |
ISBN 9780197698471 | ISBN 9780197698457 epub
Subjects: LCSH: Cultural property—Protection | Music—Social
aspects—Cambodia | Music—Social aspects—Algeria | Music—Social
aspects—Brazil | Music—Social aspects—Vanuatu | Music—Social
aspects—India | Music—Social aspects—Australia
Classification: LCC ML3916 .G73 2025 (print) | LCC ML3916 (ebook) |
DDC 306.4/842—dc23/eng/20250827
LC record available at https://lccn.loc.gov/2025037584
LC ebook record available at https://lccn.loc.gov/2025037585

DOI: 10.1093/oso/9780197698433.001.0001

Paperback printed by Marquis Book Printing, Canada
Hardback printed by Lightning Source, Inc., United States of America

The manufacturer's authorized representative in the EU for product safety is
Oxford University Press España S.A. of Parque Empresarial San Fernando de Henares,
Avenida de Castilla, 2 – 28830 Madrid (www.oup.es/en or product.safety@oup.com).
OUP España S.A. also acts as importer into Spain of products made by the manufacturer.

Contents

Preface

In 2003, UNESCO—the specialized agency of the United Nations whose global mandate includes culture—warned of "grave threats of deterioration, disappearance and destruction" of cultural practices around the world, including musical ones.[1] UNESCO primarily attributed this situation to deep and rapid social transformations of recent decades, including mass migration, urbanization, technological advances, modernization, and globalization. This idea largely persists in certain cultural and scholarly circles: that the global phenomenon of cultural loss is predominantly due to large-scale, perhaps inevitable, processes of social change. In many ways, this is fair enough: these processes have certainly irrevocably transformed the cultural landscape for many people around the world, and although some cultural practices have thrived or emerged anew as a result, others have undoubtedly suffered.

Not all situations of cultural endangerment or loss can be attributed to social change, though: sometimes, social injustices are the primary cause. People facing social injustices are less likely to be able to enjoy vibrant musical and cultural lives than those living in equitable and just conditions. Around the world, repressive political regimes and narrow societal attitudes to ethnicity, race, gender, sexuality, religion, ability, and freedom of expression are restricting the ability of certain groups of people to participate in the musical and broader cultural lives of their communities. Racially discriminatory policies and practices continue to constrain the cultural expression of many First Nations and minority (or minoritized) groups. Exclusionary educational policies are determining which musical and cultural knowledge systems children can learn, and which ones they can't. The climate crisis is forcing local communities to radically change their ways of life or even disperse altogether, drastically limiting their capacity for shared musical and cultural expression. All these matters of social justice affect cultural sustainability. Recognizing the connections between social injustice and cultural loss can be uncomfortable: it compels us to acknowledge the role that power and privilege play in the viable futures of cultural expressions around the world. Yet it is also empowering, reminding us that social justice and cultural sustainability can work in the service of each other, too.

With a focus on music, this book explores the positive potential of the relationship between social justice and cultural sustainability, a potential that holds important implications for musicians, activists, researchers, and all those with an interest in promoting healthy, diverse cultures in a socially just world. After an introductory chapter, the book has six core chapters (which can be read non-sequentially), authored in partnership with "Story Holders"—individuals who have first-hand knowledge of the social and cultural contexts at hand. Each of these core chapters explores a specific local musical practice or initiative in relation to one or more matters of social justice—from cultural, racial, educational, economic, and climate justice to forced displacement and freedom of expression. These case study chapters demonstrate the considerable depth, diversity, complexities, and possibilities inherent in the links between social justice and cultural sustainability.

In the closing chapter, I reflect on what these earlier chapters tell us about pathways in pursuit of a better world. At the heart of this chapter is the concept of *future justice*—achieving social, cultural, and economic wellbeing for present generations, while also securing and strengthening the lives of future generations. Social justice is more than the absence of social injustice, just as cultural vitality is more than the absence of threats to cultural practices. This closing chapter reflects on what a fully socially just world would mean for the future of music, cultural practices, and peoples across the planet. It is an exciting thought.

Acknowledgments

I am a fourth-generation settler of Irish and English heritage, who grew up on the land of the Ngunnawal people and wrote this book on the land of the Jagera and Turrbal people. With deep gratitude for their enduring custodianship and care for the country I call home, I pay my respects to the First Peoples of the unceded lands and waters now known as Australia, and acknowledge the ongoing vitality and richness of their cultural knowledge and practices.

This book is enabled and strengthened by the contributions of José Jorge de Carvalho, Arn Chorn-Pond, José Bonifácio da Luz ("Bengala"), Jessie Lloyd, Saurav Moni, Violeta Ruano Posada, Mohamed Sleiman Labat, Sandy Sur, and Seyma Thorn. Hailing from Australia, Brazil, Cambodia, India, Spain, Vanuatu, and Western Sahara, these Story Holders are artists, activists, advocates, thought leaders, and bearers of the magnificent cultural knowledge and practices of their communities. Despite widely varied personal and professional backgrounds, they share a deep, sustained commitment to advancing cultural sustainability and social justice through music. They are shaping the present and the future of their musical, social, and cultural worlds, and their perspectives on the topic of this book have vastly expanded and enriched my own. Friends, I am humbled by your generosity in partnering with me and sharing your stories in this way. Thank you.

Many further people have provided invaluable assistance relating to the case studies. For the chapter on the Khmer Magic Music Bus, I am especially grateful to Phloeun Prim, Frances Rudgard, Thon Dika, Phary Phacdey, and all the team at Cambodian Living Arts, for so warmly welcoming me into your exceptional community over a decade ago, for our various musical and research collaborations since then, and for practical advice on this chapter. For the chapter on the Rural Craft and Cultural Hubs, thanks to Debalina Bhowmick and the team at Contact Base (Banglanatak), who first connected me with Story Holder Saurav Moni and generously provided information and resources. For the chapter on *Portraits of Saharawi Music*, thanks to Danielle Smith, founding director of the UK-based charity Sandblast, and to Kamal Fadel, Lesley Osborne, and Barbara Glass of the Australian Western Sahara Association, for pointing me toward wonderful people and resources. For the chapter on the Leweton Cultural Village, thank you to Margaret Lonolun for research and interpreting assistance, and to all the people of Leweton village for your hospitality and kindness during my field visit some years ago. I am also grateful to Australian researchers Leah Barclay, Ashley Burgess, and Thomas Dick, who first facilitated my connections with ni-Vanuatu cultural leader Sandy Sur several years ago, and whose long-term research collaborations with the people of Leweton paved the way for my own.

I have had many stimulating conversations over the years about the topic of this book, and I am grateful to everyone whose perspectives have informed, enriched, and (especially) challenged my own. That includes my erstwhile doctoral supervisor and now colleague Huib Schippers, whose drive to better understand the dynamics of music sustainability first sparked my interest in the topic, and whose ways of thinking about cultural sustainability continue to inform my own. This text is strengthened by the critical feedback of anonymous peer reviewers, and of those friends and colleagues who read parts of the text: Brydie-Leigh Bartleet, Debalina Bhowmick, Kamal Fadel, Emma Heard, Malay Mandal, Katarzyna (Kasia) Sobczak, and Chris Stover. Special thanks to Barry Gorman, who tackled the whole manuscript. Eden Annesley, Mathew Klotz, and Teresa Kunaeva provided helpful research assistance. Ashley Burgess, Thon Dika, Pedro Aspahan, Roldan Muradian, Debalina Bhowmick, and Tim Cole kindly gave permission to use multimedia materials for the book and associated website; and for parts of Chapters 4 and 6, Springer Nature and Taylor & Francis respectively gave permission to adapt text of mine already published. Finally, thank you to the team at Oxford University Press, especially Lauralee Yeary and Rachel Ruisard: this book is better off for your guidance.

The Creative Arts Research Institute, Griffith University, contributed funding toward the honoraria for the Story Holders. The Vanuatu chapter draws on research funded by an Arts Education Law New Researcher Grant, Griffith University (2017). The Cambodia chapter draws on around eleven months' fieldwork conducted between 2013 and 2020, partly funded by an Australian Academy of the Humanities Travelling Fellowship (2013), a Reg and Molly Buck Award of the Society for Education and Music Psychology Research (2015), and an Endeavour Australia Cheung Kong Research Fellowship of the Australian Government (2015).

Acronyms

ABC	Australian Broadcasting Corporation
AFL	Art for Life
AHRC	Australian Human Rights Commission
AIATSIS	Australian Institute of Aboriginal and Torres Strait Islander Studies
ANIM	Afghanistan National Institute of Music
CFCH	Center for Folklife and Cultural Heritage, Smithsonian Institution
CLA	Cambodian Living Arts
COP	Conference of the Parties to the United Nations Framework Convention on Climate Change
ECFR	European Council on Foreign Relations
HIPAMS	Heritage-Sensitive Intellectual Property & Marketing Strategies
ICH	Intangible Cultural Heritage
ICOMOS	International Council on Monuments and Sites
ICTM	International Council for Traditional Music
IFACCA	International Federation of Arts Councils and Culture Agencies
IP	Intellectual Property
IPCC	Intergovernmental Panel on Climate Change
ISME	International Society for Music Education
KMMB	Khmer Magic Music Bus
MINURSO	United Nations Mission for the Referendum in Western Sahara
MSME&T	Department of Micro, Small & Medium Enterprises and Textiles, Government of West Bengal
NGO	Non-Government Organization
NITV	National Indigenous Television, Australia
NRPIPA	National Recording Project for Indigenous Performance in Australia
OCHA	United Nations Office for the Coordination of Humanitarian Affairs
OHCHR	United Nations Office of the High Commissioner for Human Rights
RCCH	Rural Craft & Cultural Hubs, West Bengal
SADR	Saharawi Arab Democratic Republic
SDGs	United Nations Sustainable Development Goals
SEM	Society for Ethnomusicology
SOAS	School of Oriental and African Studies, University of London
UN	United Nations
UNDP	United Nations Development Programme
UNESCO	United Nations Educational, Scientific and Cultural Organization
UNHCR	United Nations High Commissioner for Refugees
UNICEF	United Nations Children's Fund
UNWTO	United Nations World Tourism Organization
WIPO	World Intellectual Property Organization

Note to the Reader

The Story Holders, whose remarkable work is represented in the six core chapters, received an honorarium for their contributions to this book.

Royalties from the sale of this book will be donated to the charitable non-profit organization Terralingua.

Terralingua recognizes and respects the longstanding relationships that Indigenous Peoples all around the world have had from time immemorial with the lands from which they hail—the lands that they have cared for over generations, the lands from which stem their lives and livelihoods, their languages, cultures, identities, and dignity, and their rights and responsibilities as sovereign nations.

Terralingua is keenly aware of the historical and ongoing injustices and often atrocities that Indigenous Peoples have endured and still endure, and is staunchly committed to being of service by educating a wider public about the inextricable link between land, language, and culture and by helping expose and redress misperceptions and misinformation, in efforts to foster respectful and supportive relationships with Indigenous communities worldwide.

Visit https://terralingua.org/.

About the Companion Website

www.oup.com/us/SoundingGood

Oxford has created a companion website to this book. We encourage readers to visit the site to access websites, videos, photos, and other supplementary materials that illustrate and elucidate the text. Examples that are located on the companion website are signaled in the text by Oxford's symbol ▶.

Introduction

Sometime in the mid-twentieth century, a small seaside community started to industrialize the way it gathered food. The fishing songs once heard on the waters started to become redundant. Some of the younger inhabitants moved away to the cities to find their fortunes, and the usual life celebrations and old rituals no longer happened quite as much. The older members of the community noticed some time-honored musical practices falling out of favor, as younger generations turned to personal digital devices to enjoy a wider diversity of musics and began to prefer performances over participatory forms of music-making. Some community members regretted these cultural shifts and wished to take steps to prevent or at least retard them. Others, though, believed that the old cultural practices had largely run their course, and that apart from documenting their final throes for the sake of posterity, little could or should be done to maintain them.

For much of the twentieth century, this was a common trope in Western stories about cultural endangerment and loss. Cultural loss (it was said) was attributable to changing ways of life; it was inevitable; it lacked human agents and human agency: no-one (or no group) was really at fault, and in any case, no-one (or no group) would be able to stem the inexorable tides of global change, even if they wanted to. However, this story of cultural loss, while perhaps convenient, is not the full story. Around the world, it is often injustice—not (or not merely) inescapable change—that constrains the cultural lives of individuals and groups of people. War, conflict, racism, extremism, and other social ills repress freedom of cultural expression. Cultural colonialism inhibits the cultural agency and self-determination of certain groups. Neoliberal and capitalist forces that benefit some groups undermine the cultural rights of others, usually of those who find themselves on the less privileged end of global distributions of power and wealth. In short, the strength and sustainability of cultural practices are often jeopardized by social injustices, not only by changing lifeways.

This book is about the intersection of these two matters: what might be done, locally and globally, to ensure viable futures for cultural practices;

Sounding Good. Catherine Grant, Oxford University Press. © Oxford University Press 2025.
DOI: 10.1093/oso/9780197698433.003.0001

and what more might be done, locally and globally, to advance social justice. Music provides fertile ground for exploring the overlap of these topics, as recent ethnomusicological studies suggest. Jeff Todd Titon's long-running blog *Sustainable Music* deliberates on the intersections of music sustainability with environmental, economic, cultural, and social concerns,[1] and several authors in the edited volume *Sustainable Futures for Music Cultures* refer to the consequences for music sustainability of local injustices, including racist educational policies, repressive political regimes, and unequal distributions of resources.[2] Various other scholars explore specific musical cases where matters of cultural sustainability and social justice collide. Cultural, racial, and economic justice are themes of Santiago Alfaro Rotondo's and Henry Stobart's studies (in Peru and Bolivia, respectively) of music piracy, a widespread practice across the Global South that holds complex political, economic, social, and cultural ramifications for musicians and entrepreneurs.[3] The first part of Meike Lettau, Christopher Yusufu Mtaku, and Eric Debrah Otchere's edited book explores the ramifications for cultural (including musical) sustainability of forced displacement in West Africa, such as the internal displacement caused by the Boko Haram insurgency in Northeast Nigeria.[4] Kirsty Gillespie's research strongly implicates matters of environmental, economic, and distributive justice in problematizing relationships between music documentation, cultural sustainability, and the mining of Indigenous land in Lihir, Papua New Guinea.[5] Many further examples exist, exploring contexts from Rapanui (Easter Island) to the Brazilian backlands to The Gambia.[6]

Alongside this extensive body of music-related literature on the social justice aspects of cultural sustainability, scholars have recently intensified their efforts to understand music's relationship to social justice more generally, including its role in addressing contemporary social, political, economic, health, cultural and ecological challenges and crises.[7] Researchers in the area of community music are attending to the social justice, peacemaking, and political potential of their activities.[8] Those in music education have stepped up calls for cultural equity in that field, citing the moral and ethical imperative for decolonizing educational practices as well as the practical, social, and educational benefits of developing in learners a fuller understanding of the global diversity of musics.[9] Those in applied ethnomusicology are increasingly aspiring to contribute to social and political transformation through their work.[10] Ethnomusicologists Andrew Snyder and Katelyn Best even bid their disciplinary colleagues to try to remove altogether the need to point out when ethnomusicological research is justice-oriented, since that "ethical exigency should already be embedded within our practices, shape the currents of our thoughts, and guide the course of our actions in every aspect of ethnomusicological life."[11]

Building on these bodies of scholarship, this book explores relationships between cultural sustainability and social justice through music. It presents six case studies of current and recent music initiatives that illustrate how cultural sustainability and social justice can work in the service of each other. This positive correlation between cultural sustainability and social justice is admittedly not their only one. Cultural sustainability and social justice sometimes work in conflict—a matter I return to in the conclusion to this book—and these negatively correlated cases are emphatically worthy of investigation.[12] However, like Mark Pedelty (in his book on musical performance as environmental activism), here I attend to "positive examples that might supply us with new ideas, a secret or two, and new ways forward"—cases that are neither "necessarily typical" nor "completely unique," but that represent "an exemplary story."[13] Positive examples indicate possible pathways forward, and arguably carry the best odds of motivating real-world action.

Innumerable music-related initiatives around the world demonstrate how the sustainability of cultural practices and matters of social justice productively intertwine. I selected the six for this book based on four key considerations: the availability of existing foundational research; my own research networks and experience (which lie mostly in the Asia-Pacific region, especially Cambodia, Vanuatu, and Australia); the possibility to collaborate with someone with first-hand knowledge of the local context; and geographical, social, and cultural diversity across the case studies. This led me to the following selection: (1) Khmer Magic Music Bus, a project situated in a developing, post-conflict Southeast Asian country (Cambodia); (2) Mission Songs Project, set in a wealthy Western country with a fraught colonial settler history (Australia); (3) Meeting of Knowledges, situated in a large, multicultural, ethnically diverse country in the Global South (Brazil); (4) Rural Craft and Cultural Hubs, located in a populous, pluralistic country with a fast-growing economy (India); (5) *Portraits of Saharawi Music*, an externally-led project situated in a refugee camp whose residents remain forcibly displaced from their North and West African homeland (Western Sahara) following its invasion by a neighboring power; and (6) Leweton Cultural Village, an initiative located within a small-island Oceanic nation (Vanuatu) with vast cultural and linguistic diversity. (Appendix 1 summarizes the case study initiatives, locations, musical practices, and themes; Appendix 2 is a map of the case study locations.)

In the now-famous words of Black American feminist and civil rights activist Audre Lorde, "There is no such thing as a single-issue struggle because we do not live single-issue lives."[14] Boundaries blur between matters that are relevant to social justice and those that are not, and between any one social justice concern and the next. Cultural policy expert Arlene Golbard observes that all social challenges and crises are intersectional, "with overlapping impacts connecting race, gender, religion, orientation, ability, and every other characteristic that has been targeted for oppression."[15] The intersectionality of matters of social justice presents practical challenges in writing a book like this, since pulling at any thread tends to unravel the whole. Take the forced displacement of people (the "global refugee crisis"), a theme of Chapter 5 of this book. Thinking about any situation of forced displacement compels us to consider the social, economic, cultural, political, and historical processes and circumstances that precipitated it. Inevitably, a swarm of other social justice-related issues then tumble to attention: war and conflict, legacies of colonization, racism and xenophobia, fundamentalism and extremism, capitalism and consumerism, unequal distributions of power and wealth, and the climate crisis, among others. Or consider the climate justice focus of Chapter 6: it too raises a slew of other social justice considerations, including food security, economic security, stable employment, environmental management, gender equality, access to education and health services, and political agency.[16] Similar entanglements manifest within and across the six case studies in this book.

Thus, while each of the following six chapters brings to prominence one aspect of social justice, each one inevitably veers into the territory of other chapters, and into the territory of social justice issues that are not explicitly represented in this book at all. Prominent themes do emerge for each chapter: cultural justice through the Khmer Magic Music Bus in Cambodia (Chapter 1); racial justice with regard to the Mission Songs Project in Australia (Chapter 2); educational and epistemic justice through Meeting of Knowledges in Brazil (Chapter 3); economic justice through the social enterprises known as Rural Craft and Cultural Hubs in India (Chapter 4); political justice for those forcibly displaced from their homeland, with regard to the *Portraits of Saharawi Music* project (Chapter 5); and climate justice through the Leweton Cultural Village in Vanuatu (Chapter 6). Yet in highlighting these themes in the respective case study chapters and demarcating them here (and in Appendix 1), I recognize that this represents an imperfect attempt to make sense of a reality in which these and all other matters of social justice intertwine—with each other, with the global diversity of cultures and cultural practices, and with the human experience of the world.

No single volume could hope to cover all social concerns, and many matters of social justice do not feature as explicit themes of this book, though they may be implied at certain points. Disability and gender justice are two examples. As a social justice concern that is touched on in several case studies in this book, gender justice is perhaps most present in the chapter about the cultural practice *etëtung* (Chapter 6), which has economically empowered its ni-Vanuatu girl and women practitioners and enabled their greater participation in cultural and climate advocacy.[17] Equity for people with disability is especially relevant to the discussions in Chapters 1 and 4 about economic opportunity, meaningful livelihoods, and cultural participation in rural Cambodia and India, respectively.[18] A third example is health equity, or everyone having the opportunity to achieve their best health—a social justice issue that interweaves with people's capacity to lead and sustain fulfilling cultural lives.[19] Since health equity intersects with individual and collective wellbeing, it is arguably implicated across all six case studies in this book, with recent research across diverse cultural and geographical contexts suggesting that wellbeing increases as cultural rights, cultural vitality, and social equity increase.[20] I hope that the few cases and themes presented in this book stimulate further enquiry into the relationship of cultural sustainability to a wider range of social justice concerns, across a wider range of geographical contexts.

*

What is cultural sustainability? For this book, I define it as the circumstance of individuals and groups of people having the freedom and agency to make their own choices about which cultural practices[21] they engage in (and don't engage in), in which ways, and to which degree. Threats to cultural sustainability, then, are whatever inhibits those choices. Perhaps surprisingly, nothing in this definition suggests that cultural sustainability necessitates the secure future of specific cultural practices. Rather, conceiving of cultural sustainability in terms of human agencies and freedoms interlocks cultural sustainability with social justice: since matters of social justice affect people's ability to decide when and how to engage in cultural practices, those matters of social justice are matters of cultural sustainability too. (I explore this definitional interlocking and its ramifications in Chapter 1, a case study from Cambodia that centers on cultural justice and cultural sustainability.)

This definition contrasts with common twentieth-century attitudes to cultural sustainability, when anthropologists and ethnomusicologists preoccupied themselves with situations of cultural endangerment that interested them, but that sometimes presented no particular concern to the practitioners or communities[22] in question. Given the scope and speed of social changes throughout the twentieth century, such situations of cultural endangerment were relatively common. In the 1990s, for example, scholar of Māori music Mervyn McLean wrote of entire corpuses of paddling, rowing, and food-gathering songs that died out as Māori people of Aotearoa (New Zealand) modernized those practices.[23] At the turn of the twenty-first century, cultural heritage scholar Rajeev Sethi observed, "For millennia in India, women have gone to the well, and they have invented many songs to lessen the drudgery of carrying a water pot. . . . Now, there's a tap in the back yard. . . . So the songs will die."[24] I do not wish to argue that cultural sustainability measures are only ever justified in instances of social injustices: safeguarding may sometimes be warranted on other grounds, like aesthetic or pragmatic ones, or for reasons of maintaining cultural memories, histories, and identities.[25] However, my definition of cultural sustainability delimits the scope of this book to situations where practitioners and their communities perceive cultural loss as a cause for concern. In my view, such situations should emphatically receive priority in cultural sustainability research and action. Musical practices, it could be argued, are only important in that they are important to people—especially to those who practice them, or who call them their own.[26]

In these convictions, I launch my arguments in this book from three related premises. The first is that musical processes are at least as important as musical artifacts, that cultural processes are at least as important as their products. The second is that cultural practitioners and their communities are more important than their traditions, instruments, or repertoires (at least to the extent that these are separable); and the third is that human lives are more important than musical (or cultural) ones (again, to the extent that these are in fact distinct). These three premises, alongside my human-centered definition of cultural sustainability, shape the questions I explore in this book. Overriding any concern about the sustainability of specific music practices, for example, is my curiosity about what vibrant musical futures could mean for human lives. What influences people's ability and agency to make music? How can vibrant musical and cultural practices improve people's social circumstances? And how might musical and cultural participation help individuals and societies flourish, now and into the future?

The most common twentieth-century response to circumstances of music endangerment was to document and archive the musical practices affected. More recently, the ethnomusicological toolkit has expanded to encompass a range of cultural sustainability approaches that lie across cultural, social, educational, and economic domains, and that aim to maintain or revitalize cultural practices in living form too.[27] One characteristic of cultural sustainability efforts that has remained fairly consistent over time is a focus on supporting specific musical practices, whether by documenting and archiving them, celebrating and promoting them through media and performances, teaching them through educational programs, and so on. While this tack has proven successful in certain cases (at least in the short to medium term), it risks treating symptoms rather than causes, often failing to sufficiently consider or address the social factors that may have precipitated the demise of the cultural practice in the first place. In mitigating harms but failing to tackle the root of the problem, this approach to supporting cultural sustainability also risks reinscribing global power inequalities: those with funds and resources can be seen to be doing something about the problem, while avoiding taking more substantive steps to prevent cultural losses.

At the 2022 symposium *Communicating Sustainability: An International Conversation with Sustainability Activists*, Sámi- and Finnish-American scholar Tim Frandy implored delegates to recognize that one-dimensional conceptualizations of sustainability (such as those Western ones that isolate cultural practices from their wider social contexts) further entrench colonial power structures:

> Sustainability does not exist as a monolithic concept, a distinct agent of good in the world, and something that we ought to uncritically strive for. Rather, "sustainabilities" exist as pluralistic and culturally constructed phenomena, with deep, deep epistemological roots that differ widely across cultures. The belief that sustainability is new, that it is more science than belief, than culture, than ideology, that it's a universal concept, is a horrific act of ethnocentric erasure and one that actively harms Indigenous peoples today.[28]

In recognition of this, some contemporary cultural scholars are advocating for more human-centered, process-oriented, and Indigenous understandings of cultural sustainability. In his introduction to *Cultural Sustainabilities* (note the plural), Timothy Cooley is careful to point out that that edited volume "does not mean that we [authors and editor] believe all human cultural practices are sustainable or even should be sustained."[29] Folklorists Michael Mason and Rory Turner describe the research practice of cultural sustainability not as one that safeguards dying traditions, but rather as one that "fosters relationships, engenders knowledge about the sociocultural ecology, and guides diverse, ethical interventions that enhance the vitality and well-being of specific communities and cherished aspects of their expressive lives."[30]

Perceiving cultural practices relationally and holistically, within their sociocultural ecosystems, compels consideration of matters of social justice. Like cultural sustainability, social justice can be understood in various ways. By one common framing, social justice is concerned with whether and how benefits (and burdens) are fairly distributed among members of a social group (including between individuals belonging to different groups within a society). "Benefits" in this sense may be many things: income and wealth, education and employment opportunities, economic and social status, political rights, health care, housing, autonomy, and basic freedoms (including cultural freedoms), among others.[31] Historical and social constructions of race, class, gender, sexuality, ability, religion, and other markers of identity affect the ways such benefits are distributed in any given society. For this reason, matters concerning the equality and dignity of individuals and social groups are central concerns in this distributive framing of social justice, as are matters of power and privilege.

That framing of social justice might already seem vast, but others are even more encompassing. According to ethnographer Robert Rinehart and colleagues, social justice is not (only) about equitable sharing of resources, equality of opportunity, or how those with less power are treated by those with more: it is also about "the simple acceptance of another's humanness" and instances of "everyday kindness or unfairness."[32] Along these lines, some scholars argue that it is a matter of social justice that social policies and services enable every person and group of people to achieve their fullest potential, and that each individual "be treated with decency and humanity" along the way.[33] By this line of thinking, social justice is about individuals and communities at least as much as it is about policies and institutions, or the distribution of rights, resources, and opportunities.[34] Sociologist Kathy Charmaz's appraisal of the scope of social justice embraces humanistic, psychological, and moral dimensions:

> An interest in social justice means attentiveness to ideas and actions concerning fairness, equity, equality, democratic process, status and hierarchy, and individual and collective rights and obligations. It signifies thinking about being human, creating good societies and a better world, and what national and world citizenship means. It involves exploring tensions between complicity and consciousness, choice and constraint, indifference and compassion, inclusion and exclusion, poverty and privilege, and barriers and opportunities. It also means taking a critical stance toward actions, organizations, and social institutions.[35]

This expansive framing of social justice, which moves beyond concerns about the equitable distribution of benefits to "a way of seeing and acting,"[36] is the one I adopt for this book. This holds three key implications for this text. First, if the conditions that enable social justice are personal as well as institutional, psychological as well as political, then all these dimensions should be considered in efforts to achieve social justice—and in this book, inasmuch as it is concerned with advancing social justice. Second, this broad framing suggests that socioeconomic and political perspectives on social justice may need to be balanced with those that recognize and explore the particularities of how matters of social justice affect people's lives—especially, in this book, the lives of musicians and their communities.[37] And third, the more expansive the framing of social justice, the more likely it is that its meanings must vary across time and place, that people and social groups will differ in their interpretations, values, ideologies, and aspirations in relation to it.[38]

On this last point: not all societies (or nations) explicitly engage with the concept of social justice, at least as it is understood in the West.[39] Until relatively recently, most scholarly English-language sources on the topic promulgated the classic distributive notion of social justice: they promoted equality of opportunity and rights for individuals, fairness and equity in the allocation of social benefits, and dignity for individuals and for social classes. These Western notions about social justice have a materialist basis. They chiefly aim to benefit the individual, and to do so in mainly economic ways. They often lead to social policies and practices that aim to ensure individuals have equal opportunities and resources ("equality"), or that seek to understand and provide what individuals need to enjoy full, rich lives ("equity"). In focusing on the individual, they often de-emphasize the matter of equity between groups of people—for example, between races or genders.[40] Unsurprisingly, Western materialist conceptualizations of social justice may be held in rather less esteem in societies with different histories, values, political outlooks, religious beliefs, and cultural standpoints on solidarity and social obligation. In academic and policy discourse, a strong case can therefore be made for de-centering Western perspectives in favor of more nuanced and pluralistic framings of social justice—something that much recent social justice research aims to do.[41]

Social justice and human rights closely intersect, and critiques of Western notions of social justice dovetail with critiques of Western notions of human rights. Like social justice, human rights can be understood narrowly or expansively. On the one hand, human rights can be viewed as the global system of laws, mechanisms, courts, norms, and organizations that uphold the rights laid out in the United Nations' Universal Declaration of Human Rights of 1948; on the other, they can be understood as devolved local and transnational social networks and movements whose end-goal is that people are treated with respect, decency, and integrity.[42] (In practice, these binaries emmesh.) In both these framings, but especially the latter, matters of human rights overlap with many (if not all) of the social justice issues explored in this book, from the right to education (Article 26 of the UN's Declaration; Chapter 3 of this book), to the right to freedom of expression (Article 19; Chapter 1), to the right to seek and receive asylum from persecution (Article 14; Chapter 5). Even the very condition of cultural sustainability can be interpreted as a human right (especially according to the human-centric definition of cultural sustainability laid out earlier): Article 27 of the Declaration states, "Everyone has the right freely to participate in the cultural life of the community [and] to enjoy the arts."

Yet in the seventy years or so since the Universal Declaration of Human Rights, scholarly and political differences of opinion have surfaced regarding whether the concept of human rights is, or should be, universal. One point of contention has been the extent to which the Declaration propounds Western social norms, overlooking or altogether disregarding less globally dominant interpretations of what it is to live a good or just human life.[43] (The COVID-19 pandemic, for instance, underscored national governments' widely divergent and culturally specific views on how to balance the priorities, rights, and freedoms of the individual with the wellbeing of society at large: contrast the public health responses of the Chinese and British governments.) Music and cultural rights scholar Andrew Weintraub notes that the "universalist and moralistic tone" of the Universal Declaration has been criticized for being "Western-centric, prescriptive, imperialistic, and antithetical to the aims and practices of cultural relativism and pluralism."[44] Ethnomusicologist Helen Rees notes, too, how prescriptive attempts to explain and promote human rights (including cultural rights), arguably like the Universal Declaration, are confounded by "cultural change and the fuzziness of cultural boundaries."[45] Conceptualizations about human rights, like those about social justice, need to negotiate dissimilar worldviews if they are to hold purchase across diverse cultural settings.

All this has implications for my approach to writing this book. Canadian First Nations (Stó:lō) sound studies scholar Dylan Robinson urges us all to adopt a "critical listening positionality," self-reflexively interrogating "how race, class, gender, sexuality, ability, and cultural background intersect and influence the way we are able to hear sound, music, and the world around us."[46] Adopting a critical listening positionality requires me to recognize that my own ever-changing worldview affects how I think about social justice, as well as about music, culture, and everything else. My views on what constitutes an equitable society are fashioned by my upbringing, my society, my culture, my gender, and my evolving life experiences, including the years I have spent living and working in locations where social and cultural paradigms are quite different from my own. They are also shaped by my layers of unearned privilege as a White,[47] educated, middle-class, abled, cisgender, heterosexual, resident-citizen of a stable and affluent country (Australia), among other markers of my identity. While the perspectives on social justice in this book are informed and enriched by the knowledge contributions of the nine Story Holder's (who come from widely varying backgrounds and orientations), the conception of social justice presented by this book is chiefly mine—moreover, mine only at the time of writing. And yet, as social justice theorists Loretta Capeheart and Dragan Milovanovic point out, social justice develops and changes just as societies do, and "no single conception or practice of justice is adequate for all points in history or for all forms of society."[48] This is perhaps what political theorist Michael Walzer meant when he wrote that social justice does not exist in any abstract theoretical sense, but only in terms of culturally specific, socially constructed notions of what constitutes a good society.[49] I encourage you, the reader, to bring your own ideas about the latter to your interpretation and critique of this book.

*

Fieldwork has long been considered a non-negotiable for ethnographic research. Through the twentieth century, it was typically carried out by an outsider to those being studied—often a White researcher studying Black, Indigenous, or People of Color. When combined with power and privilege, fieldwork was seen to bestow the outsider-researcher with a level of authority regarding the group of people under study, a level exceeding even that of the people themselves. Fieldworkers ended up as "gatekeepers of knowledge,"[50] taking "findings" away to represent people without their direct involvement, sometimes even without their knowledge, and in ways that reinforced vastly uneven distributions of power. In recent decades, a growing scholarly discomfort with these extractive approaches—markers of the "colonial and imperial moorings"[51] of ethnomusicology and cognate disciplines—has led to more ethical research practices. Decolonizing methodologies, observes ethnomusicologist Deborah Wong, are now "all over our discipline, evidenced by oral life histories, autoethnography, collaborative research, and the sustained presence of native ethnographers."[52]

As researchers reflect on their positionality in what ethnomusicologist Oliver Shao calls "interlocking systems of oppression and inequality based on race, citizenship, nationality, gender, and class" in research,[53] some are questioning the ethics of outsider-led fieldwork altogether. The grounds are various, but one is the environmental cost, especially the hefty carbon emissions generated by air travel to fieldwork locations. Environmental psychologists Lorraine Whitmarsh and Agnes Kreil observe that especially in scholarly disciplines such as ethnomusicology and anthropology, environmentally unsustainable fieldwork practices are self-defeating: "The more the polluter elite maintains their high-carbon practices, including flying to demonstrably value other cultures", they write, "the more they contribute to destroying these cultures."[54] Acutely aware of this irony in relation to my own research on music endangerment and music sustainability, in 2018 I made (and published) a commitment to significantly reduce my academic flying for reasons of climate justice.[55] (Prior to that time, fieldwork had predominated in my research designs; in particular, the Cambodia and Vanuatu case studies in this book are informed by fieldwork I conducted for earlier projects.) Thus, I chose not to undertake ethnographic fieldwork for this book.

What alternatives are there? Some music scholars are choosing to integrally involve, in the research and/or writing processes, one or more (non-scholar) culture-bearers whose cultural practices or communities are represented in their research.[56] Done well, this collaborative approach contributes to dismantling systems of domination in music research: mitigating the risk of extractivism, ensuring the fullest possible representation in research outputs of these individuals and their communities, and generally "advancing a justice-oriented restructuring that listens with, rather than speaks for, colonized, excluded, and other historically marginalized peoples."[57] All research approaches raise ethical considerations, however, and this is no exception. Among other things, it necessitates an investment of energy and time in the research and/or writing processes by non-scholars, and assumes of them a level of interest in those processes—indeed, in the academic endeavor at large—that is arguably unreasonable to expect (though of course it can and sometimes does exist). Especially in cases where those individuals are cultural leaders or community elders with substantial cultural and social responsibilities, or where a range of publicly available sources already exists about their cultural and social contributions, experiences, and perspectives, this approach may be an unreasonable ask—as it was, I felt, for this book.

Believing in the ethical imperative (and many benefits) of a "coalitional"[58] approach to this project, I invited the involvement of nine individuals with deep first-hand understanding of the musical practices and social settings represented in the chapters that follow. Each of these individuals leads, or is involved in a major capacity, in one of the case study initiatives.[59] Each has also created and/or made substantial contributions to materials already in the public domain that promote awareness of that initiative, such as project websites, news media articles, blog posts, social media posts, recordings, other creative products, archival documentation, and multimedia resources. These remarkable individuals hail from a range of backgrounds and orientations: they are cultural knowledge-holders and educators, artists and social activists, peacemakers and community leaders. While all are fervently committed to the social justice and cultural sustainability agendas of this book, only one holds an academic role and is research-active; José Jorge de Carvalho opted to co-author with me Chapter 3 (that relating to the educational justice project he founded).

In conceptualizing the nature of our respective roles in producing this book, I take inspiration from the work of Our Race, an Australian organization that seeks to address exploitative and extractive storytelling practices through a shared commitment to safe and ethical storytelling.[60] By its terminology, all nine of my collaborators are *Story Holders*, people with lived experience of a Story—that is, "an idea, action, imagination, experience" or combination thereof—who own that Story and may choose to share it or not.[61] I am a *Story Caretaker*, whose responsibilities include creating a safe and supported way for Story Holders to share their stories, ensuring that Story Holders are able to make informed decisions about whether and on what terms their Story is told, and sharing their Stories with respect, sensitivity, and appreciation of the Story Holders' lived experiences. I take these responsibilities seriously and have done my best to meet them.

Except for the co-authored Chapter 3, then, the words you read in these pages are my own. For transparency, I retain authorial voice throughout the case study chapters, referring to the Story Holders in the third person and drawing on existing sources, including theirs, to the extent possible. Each Story Holder determined how, and to what extent, they provided me with new insights for this book. Their preferences varied, from engaging in one or more semi-structured discussions, to exchanging emails and texts over some months, to providing oral or written input into the relevant chapter draft, to some combination of these. Our communications took place in 2022 and 2023 by Zoom, WhatsApp, and email. All were in English except those with Bengala (José Bonifácio da Luz) (Chapter 3), for which José Jorge de Carvalho provided Portuguese–English interpretation.

Again, every research approach has its limitations and complexities. One here is the positive bias that arises from my partnering with individuals who are inevitably invested in the success of the case study initiatives represented—a matter intensified by the fact that several of those initiatives are ongoing at the time of writing. This limitation is not unique to collaborative work. In their systematic review of arts-based international development initiatives, Vicki-Ann Ware and Kim Dunphy found that not one of the twenty-seven studies they examined reported negative or neutral program outcomes, despite the papers being variously authored by insider (emic) researchers, outsider (etic) researchers, and research teams. They postulated that this resulted from the research having "an advocatory intention or function."[62] Referring to scholarship like this (within the discipline of ethnomusicology) as "activist ethnomusicology," David McDonald reflects on the challenge:

> When researchers align themselves with the political projects of their interlocutors [or collaborators], they occupy a precarious, perhaps compromised, intellectual space. These ethical and methodological contradictions can problematize aspects of inquiry, but also generate profound insight otherwise impossible to achieve . . . In many ways, politicized ethnomusicological research is compromised, but also enriched.[63]

This is how I perceive the case study chapters in this book. While they retain criticality, they are undoubtedly moderated, arguably even compromised, by the Story Holders' advocatory and political interests. But these case studies, indeed the book itself, are also enabled and vastly enriched by their contributions. Moreover, to the extent that the following chapters exhibit positive bias, their doing so aligns with my intention to present positive narratives about cultural sustainability and social justice (for the reasons outlined earlier). Thus, I acknowledge their partiality as a limitation, and wholeheartedly embrace the coalitional approach nonetheless.

All that notwithstanding, deep ethical complexities remain when I presume to write about communities, cultures, and social contexts that are not my own—especially those where the privileges, freedoms, opportunities, and rights that I enjoy may not be so easy to come by. I researched and now present these case studies in English, historically a language and a tool of colonial domination and oppression. I present them in an academic platform, a domain that, despite some progress, remains profoundly inequitable.[64] I present them in written form, which (as cultural researchers Miranda Forsyth and Thomas Dick note) "has its own challenge for peoples whose histories exist principally (if not exclusively) as oral and performative artefacts."[65] Recognizing these ironies in his own writings, Portuguese sociologist Boaventura de Sousa Santos argues that "the fertility of a contradiction does not lie in imagining ways of escaping it but rather in ways of working with and through it."[66] Acknowledging the extent to which colonial legacies remain manifest here, then, I offer this book as what de Sousa Santos calls an "enabling contradiction": one that recognizes, even leans towards, the contextual limits of thinking and action. To my mind, this book is an imperfect response—but I hope a worthwhile one nonetheless—to Deonte Harris's appeal for ethnomusicological scholarship that establishes "sustained commitments to struggling alongside, and supporting, the marginalized and oppressed to make freedom, justice, and equality possible for all people, everywhere."[67]

*

Spurred on by the thinking of philosopher and social theorist Nancy Fraser, who contends that "the strategies of approaching justice negatively, through *in*justice, is powerful and productive,"[68] I opened an earlier draft of this introduction differently. I began by laying out how prevailing social structures marginalize, oppress, and discriminate against certain groups of people, and legitimize and privilege certain knowledge systems and ways of being over others; how racism, classism, and sexism are affecting the lives of millions; how Black, Indigenous, and People of Color, women and girls, people with diverse gender identities and sexualities, people with disabilities, and people belonging to various other minoritized social groups continue to struggle for equal rights and opportunities. I wrote about how the COVID-19 pandemic exacerbated global inequalities of health, wealth, and gender; how the spiraling climate emergency portends catastrophe for those who have least contributed and are least equipped to respond; how war and conflict, political persecution, economic hardship, and environmental disasters are forcing millions from their homes in search of security and safety.[69] To seal the rationale for this book, I laid out predictions about impending massive global cultural losses (such as sociolinguists' estimates that about half of the world's 7,000-odd languages are endangered, and that 1,500 of them could disappear by the end of this century).[70] Following Fraser, I reasoned:

> Focusing on the wrong, we need to determine why it is so and how it could be made right. Only through such a process of negative thinking can we activate the concept of justice, redeem it from the realm of abstraction, concretize it, enrich it and make it fruitful for this world.[71]

I concur with Fraser that understanding problems is a necessary precursor to developing effective solutions. Therefore, in this book, I lay out social and cultural problems to the extent necessary to understand possible solutions (the latter represented by the case study initiatives). But "approaching justice negatively," to use Fraser's phrase, carries risks—such as that of fueling pessimism or disillusionment, or of falling prone to what political writer Bonny Brookes calls "the business of outrage" (a common trait of writings about social justice),[72] or of promulgating deficit- rather than strengths-based narratives. On the last of these, David McDonald argues that the "pervasive" ethnomusicological representation of oppressed groups as victims to solicit support for human rights usually only serves to "naturalize the condition": the "romanticization of pain narratives," he writes, "limits our capacity for ethnographic engagement, disempowers Indigenous communities, and further reinforces colonial domination."[73]

I have come to prefer an approach to this book that emphasizes the immense potential of vibrant, viable, and diverse musical practices to move us toward a more secure, sustainable planet with expanding social, economic, and cultural prospects and freedoms.[74] Social justice might often seem like an abstract or merely rhetorical concept, but I invite the reader to consider what the world might be like, in real terms, if social justice were achieved. What would that mean for people's capacity to engage in creative and cultural pursuits? How might it change why and how people participate in cultural practices? If social decisions were made with regard for future generations as well as present ones, what might that mean for the sustainable future of cultural expressions? If this thought experiment seems utopian, it can help to remember that even small advances in social justice bring real-world benefits to individuals and communities. As I argue at more length in the conclusion to this book, imagining a socially just world can inspire and embolden us.

The six case studies in the following chapters provide motivation, showing pathways that carry us, even just a little further, toward that end. The book begins with the story of the Khmer Magic Music Bus (Chapter 1), a group of musicians who travel through the rural Cambodian provinces, sharing traditional Cambodian music with locals through participatory activities and performances. Since the Khmer Rouge genocide of the 1970s, during which an estimated 90 percent of musicians were killed, many Cambodian people have had limited opportunity to engage with the traditional music of their homeland. This is especially true for people living rurally, where resources and infrastructure for learning, teaching, and making music are very limited. Founded by Story Holders Arn Chorn-Pond and Thorn Seyma, the Khmer Magic Music Bus is serving to heal Cambodia's traumatic past, revive its musical practices in the present, and strengthen its prospects for a culturally vibrant future. Illustrating how political and socioeconomic circumstances intertwine with people's capacity to engage in fulfilling cultural lives, this chapter contends that music sustainability is a matter of cultural justice.

Chapter 2 explores the Mission Songs Project, an initiative of Australian First Nations woman and Story Holder Jessie Lloyd. First Nations people of Australia have long been subject to assimilation policies and systemic dispossession of their land; in the late nineteenth and twentieth centuries, many were forcibly relocated from their traditional homelands to missions, where their languages and cultural practices were prohibited. On the missions, the First Nations residents began to co-opt the sanctioned Western musical idioms and instruments for their own purposes, finding new ways to express their cultural and social identities. Through the Mission Songs Project, Jessie Lloyd has rediscovered, recorded, and revived these "mission songs". If the Project is a somber reminder about how cultural and racial oppression can interlock, it is also a surprising example of how new musical creativities sometimes spring from the restrictions borne of social injustice. Through the Mission Songs Project, this chapter explores the mission songs genre as a creative act of resilience, self-determination, cultural expression, and cultural survival that continues to advance cultural and racial justice for Australia's First Peoples.

With a focus on higher education institutions, Chapter 3 examines educational justice in the face of "epistemicide": the ongoing deliberate omission and silencing in these (and other) institutions of certain cultural values and ways of knowing, while attributing truth and validity only to Western ways of producing and transmitting knowledge. Such cultural colonialism works against epistemic and educational justice; in disallowing a place in formal education for "small," local musical and other cultural practices, it inhibits cultural sustainability too. In Brazil, chapter co-author José Jorge de Carvalho founded Meeting of Knowledges, an initiative that welcomes local master-musicians and other cultural practitioners into university settings to teach. Through this initiative, the diverse Indigenous, popular, traditional, and African-derived genres of South America are, for the first time, finding their rightful place in the core curriculum. With the involvement of Meeting of Knowledges master-musician and Story Holder José Bonifácio da Luz (known to his community as Bengala), this chapter articulates the dual benefits for cultural sustainability and educational justice of striving to decolonize music education practices and pedagogies.

Conceptualizing poverty as an issue of social justice, Chapter 4 examines intersections between socioeconomic circumstance and cultural sustainability. With Story Holder musician Saurav Moni, leading exponent of the genre of boat-songs from West Bengal (India) called *bhatiyali*, the chapter considers cultural pathways to building the economic capacities of musicians and their communities, while simultaneously progressing cultural sustainability goals. Through *bhatiyali*, it explores the successes of the Rural Craft and Cultural Hubs—a social enterprise that is improving livelihood prospects for local artists in West Bengal, advancing the sustainable economic development of their communities, and securing viable futures for musical and other cultural practices. The model demonstrates how cultural tourism, cultural sustainability, and economic justice can work in the service of each other, lifting people out of cycles of marginalization and deprivation, and enabling them to lead more culturally and socially fulfilling lives.

When Morocco invaded their homeland in 1975, thousands of Saharawi people fled across the Western Saharan border and set up refugee camps in the Algerian desert, where they have remained ever since. Although their exile jeopardized (to an extent) the continued practice of traditional *haul* music, it has also stimulated among Saharawi people new ways of learning, teaching, making, and thinking about music, even propelling a whole new genre of revolutionary songs, *nidal*. Chapter 5 explores these links between forced displacement, cultural sustainability, and political justice, with a focus on *Portraits of Saharawi Music*—a partnership between Spanish researcher and Story Holder Violeta Ruano Posada, the Saharawi Ministry of Culture (in exile), and the British Library. The project has played an important role in documenting, reinvigorating, and promoting Saharawi music locally and globally; it has also brought wider international attention to the ongoing struggle for political self-determination and independence of the Saharawi people. This chapter is also written in collaboration with Story Holder Mohamed Sleiman Labat, a Saharawi artist who grew up in, and still resides in, the camps.

The final case study, presented in Chapter 6, considers the nexus of climate justice and cultural sustainability for a small Pacific-island community. Facing rising seawaters, increasingly destructive cyclones, and escalating environmental damage to local marine ecosystems, the ni-Vanuatu community of Leweton is on the front line of the climate crisis. Seeking to grow the community's economic and cultural resilience, cultural leader and Story Holder Sandy Sur founded the Leweton Cultural Village, a tourism enterprise that has doubled as a way to maintain and promote local *kastom* (traditional) practices amid rapid change. The key attraction of the Village is *etëtung*, known in English as Vanuatu Women's Water Music, a striking performance practice with deep ties to the local natural environment. As the profile of the Leweton Cultural Village grows, *etëtung* is proving a way for the people of Leweton to participate in local, regional, and international climate discussions. This chapter traces how one small-island community is leveraging its cultural practices, through tourism, to advance cultural sustainability and climate justice goals.

The closing chapter prosecutes the key argument of this book: that cultural sustainability and social justice are deeply intertwined, locally and globally, and that recognizing and better understanding their interrelatedness could expand opportunities for advancing each. This chapter considers the implications of this argument for musicians and other cultural practitioners, for people who belong to oppressed or marginalized groups, for social and cultural advocates, cultural and educational agencies, researchers and policymakers, and for all others committed to advancing equitable social and cultural futures. Drawing on the concept of "future justice" (whereby current generations consider the consequences for future generations of their decisions and actions), the chapter reflects on how the interconnections between cultural sustainability and social justice could help progress important social and cultural agendas, including the United Nations' Sustainable Development Goals. I close with a call for all stakeholders to recognize and fully leverage the potential of diverse, strong, and sustainable cultural practices to secure a more prosperous and socially just world.

Figure 1.0a Arn Chorn-Pond. Photo: Thon Dika.

Figure 1.0b Thorn Seyma. Photo: Thon Dika.

Introducing: Arn Chorn-Pond and Thorn Seyma

Arn Chorn-Pond is the founder of Cambodian Living Arts, a non-government organization whose vision is a thriving Cambodian arts sector. In Arn's harrowing story of surviving the Khmer Rouge regime (a story that came to wide prominence through the acclaimed documentary The Flute Player[1]*), music plays a critical role. Now an internationally renowned human rights activist and peace advocate, music and culture remain core to his humanitarian and peace-building work. Arn has received the Anne Frank Memorial Award, the Kohl Foundation International Peace Prize, the Reebok Human Rights Award, and two honorary doctorates for peace and humanitarian service.*

Thorn Seyma is well known in Cambodia as a singer, cultural advocate, and cultural entrepreneur. She is committed to empowering people who live rurally and regionally—especially women, children, and youth—to engage with Cambodian cultural practices of all kinds. With Arn, Seyma co-founded the Khmer Magic Music Bus, an initiative to return Cambodian music and other performing arts to rural and regional areas of Cambodia following the cultural destruction of the Khmer Rouge era. As artistic manager of the Khmer Magic Music Bus, Seyma is driven by a desire that all Cambodian people may participate in fulfilling cultural lives.

Arn and Seyma vehemently believe in the transformative potential of music, the individual and societal value of cultural participation, and the importance of sustainable cultural futures. When I met with them one evening in downtown Phnom Penh, and they referred to the Khmer Magic Music Bus as a "vehicle," they were not speaking literally. Around the world, they reminded me, musical participation facilitates healing and cultivates hope for a better future. "This is my quest," Arn told me: through music, "to have us dare to dream again, dare to hope."[2]

1
This Music Is Magic Music

With Arn Chorn-Pond and Thorn Seyma

Traveling together in the rural Cambodian province of Oddar Meanchey one steamy day in June 2012, a group of musician friends pulled over to the side of the dusty road for a brief stop. One of them, Mon Hai, idly got out his *khene* (or *ken*), a traditional bamboo mouth organ that had long been part of the cultural heritage of the Khmer people in that province (and other northern provinces). He began to play. As his companions listened and watched on, a few local villagers emerged from their nearby homes, mesmerized by the sound. Then more came. A local media outlet later reported on the occasion:

> The music gradually brought the still surroundings to life. One by one, curious faces popped up behind trees; children tentatively peered from behind their parents' legs; after 15 minutes, 35 people had flocked from different directions to the side of the road to watch [Mon Hai] play. He was transfixed by his instrument, and the crowd was transfixed by him.[3]

Mon later reported feeling "very happy" that so many people came to listen and watch: "I felt that I was giving something to the people," he said.[4] Many of the onlookers had never seen a *khene* before,[5] despite the instrument once being regularly used in their region for a range of social and religious functions, including at funerals, ceremonies, and Buddhist festivals. Some of the older villagers hadn't experienced live Cambodian traditional music-making for years, even decades. For many of the younger ones, this was the first time they had encountered traditional music at all.

In its catastrophically misguided attempt to create an idealized agrarian society, the autocratic and totalitarian Khmer Rouge regime (1975–1979) killed around two million people, over a fifth of the Cambodian population at

Sounding Good. Catherine Grant, Oxford University Press. © Oxford University Press 2025.
DOI: 10.1093/oso/9780197698433.003.0002

that time.[6] Artists were regarded as enemies of the state; an estimated ninety per cent were killed.[7] Musical instruments, performance venues, theaters, libraries, and schools were systematically demolished. By the time the Khmer Rouge regime was deposed in January 1979, the remaining Cambodian population was in dire poverty and health, and the country was in a state of social and cultural devastation. The humanitarian situation remained dismal during the famine and civil war of the 1980s. Reviving musical or other cultural practices was hardly a priority, and the very few remaining artists were forced to look for other ways to eke out a living. By some estimates, around half of all Cambodian musical traditions were lost altogether during the Khmer Rouge regime and its aftermath.[8]

One of the travelers by the side of the road that day, listening to musician Mon Hai share the sounds of the *khene*, was a man called Arn Chorn-Pond. In early 1975, nine-year-old Arn had been leading a quiet life in Battambang in Cambodia's northwest, where his family owned a small theater. When Khmer Rouge soldiers entered the town bearing guns, they separated the young Arn from his family. Sent to a child labor camp along with around 700 other children, Arn was forced to work nineteen-hour days with little food, and witnessed murders daily. When the camp's soldiers decided to run a small music class to teach the children songs of revolutionary propaganda (the only music acceptable to the Khmer Rouge regime), Arn volunteered to participate: perhaps he would be given a little more food, he thought, or receive some other special treatment. Taught by a musician called Yoeun Mek who had been recruited by the soldiers for the purpose, Arn began to learn the *khloy* (Cambodian flute). Arn attributes his life to the fact that he learnt *khloy* fast: three children who learnt alongside him were soon killed, evidently not up to the expectations of the Khmer Rouge soldiers. He estimates that after two years, all but around fifty or sixty of those 700 children had starved to death or been executed.[9]

When the Vietnamese invaded in 1979, Arn was handed a gun and told to fight in defense of the Khmer Rouge. Barely thirteen years old, he managed to flee, malnourished and malaria-stricken, through the jungle to a refugee camp across the Thai border. There, American Lutheran minister and aid worker Peter Pond adopted him and took him to the United States, where Arn spent difficult teenage and early adult years, eventually finding his way as an advocate for peace.[10] He returned to Cambodia in his early twenties. Most of his close family members (including nine of his eleven siblings) had been killed by the Khmer Rouge,[11] but he was able to reconnect with Yoeun Mek, the kind musician who had taught him to play *khloy* in the labor camp. Arn was saddened to discover that the old master was no longer practicing his art—rather, he was "cutting hair and drunk and nobody cared about him."[12] Grasping for the first time the degree of disrepair of his country's cultural traditions and the ongoing challenges facing its artists, Arn decided to set up a non-profit organization devoted to supporting "master-artists"[13] like Yoeun Mek pass on their knowledge and skills. Since its founding in 1998, Cambodian Living Arts has made major contributions to supporting people of all ages learn, teach, play, and enjoy Cambodia's musical and other performance traditions. Among other initiatives, it has facilitated partnerships between masters and students, created cultural enterprise opportunities for Cambodian artists, and provided arts scholarships, workshops, training, and education for emerging artists.[14]

Yet even now, more than four decades since the fall of the Khmer Rouge regime, Cambodia continues to contend with the cultural and social fallout of those years. Ongoing social challenges include widespread poverty, rural-urban disparities, and poor education and health services.[15] Amid rapid socioeconomic, cultural, and environmental changes, these social challenges interweave with, and perpetuate, what has been called Cambodia's "cultural crisis."[16] For the three-quarters of the Cambodian population who live rurally,[17] poverty is higher than in the cities, access to musical instruments and instruction is very limited, and opportunities for cultural participation are few. Several "traditional" music instruments and genres—those pre-Khmer Rouge ones that were historically aurally transmitted from generation to generation—have only a few skilled practitioners who are still actively performing or teaching.[18] Most master-musicians are now in their seventies and eighties, in a country where male life expectancy at birth is sixty-eight years.[19] Within just a decade or so, those few remaining musicians who learnt their art before the devastation of the Khmer Rouge era may well be gone. Moreover, given the insufficiencies of basic services like healthcare and education, the cultural sector is far from a governmental priority, and the Ministry of Culture and Fine Arts has one of the smallest budgets of all ministries.[20] Despite concerted cultural safeguarding and revitalization efforts, and much progress, the future of some pre-Khmer Rouge cultural practices still hangs in the balance. Time is of the essence.

*

While the Khmer Rouge is a historical example of a political regime seeking to regulate, restrict, or outright prohibit the artistic and cultural activities of its population, contemporary examples are unfortunately not difficult to come by. In modern China, the government's long-term systemic persecution of the Uyghur people, a minority ethnic group in the northwestern province of Xinjiang, involves pursuing the wholescale erasure of Uyghur cultural and religious identity through a process of "re-education" that amounts to cultural genocide.[21] Another example is found in Chapter 5 of this book, which describes the political circumstances underpinning the attempted silencing, by a neighboring colonial oppressor, of the cultural practices and identities of Western Sahara's indigenous people. These cases run along ethnic lines, but various other minoritized groups experience violations of artistic and cultural freedoms too, including women, people of certain faiths and religions, and people of "othered" genders and sexualities. In 2020, for instance, the independent international organization Freemuse (which identifies, monitors, and exposes violations of artistic freedom) identified "at least 77 countries" that silence LGBTIQ+ artists by exploiting laws and regulations that criminalize homosexuality.[22]

The concept of artistic freedom differs across countries and cultural contexts, as does the way it is valued and experienced. From a Western standpoint, matters of artistic freedom may appear quite distinct from matters of cultural freedom, but many First Peoples and other cultural groups around the world do not make the same distinction between arts and culture that is common in the West. For these peoples, artistic freedom and cultural freedom are not only intertwined, but may be indistinguishable.[23] The International Federation of Arts Councils and Culture Agencies describes artistic freedom embracingly, as the ability to express oneself freely without fear of persecution; the ability to access artistic and cultural resources and platforms that do not discriminate based on gender, sexuality, ability, age, race, culture, belief, citizenship, or other grounds; and the ability to see oneself reflected in society and in public life.[24] Similarly, UNESCO refers to artistic freedom as all people being able to imagine, create, enjoy, and engage in diverse cultural expressions without governmental censorship, political interference, or pressure from other quarters.[25]

It is not hard to grasp why tyrannical regimes have a vested interest in constraining artistic freedom: if oppressed peoples are permitted to express themselves freely, they might (and often do) strengthen their collective cultural and social identities in ways that counteract the ideologies of those with power. Permitting freedom of musical expression, for example—or unsuccessfully attempting to inhibit it—risks giving rise to musical practices that critique or contest those ideologies, or that rally widespread support for countervailing social movements. (So it was, and remains, in the case of the Saharawi people of Western Sahara, as described in Chapter 5.) It is hardly surprising, then, that artists are so often persecuted by authoritarian regimes, as they were in Khmer Rouge-era Cambodia, and are now in Xinjiang province (China), Western Sahara, Ukraine under Russian invasion, Afghanistan under Taliban control, and many other sites around the globe.

Worryingly, the trajectory of artistic freedom seems to be tracking in the wrong direction. In 2019, the Office of the High Commissioner for Human Rights reported an increase in known violations of artistic freedom over the preceding years,[26] and in 2022, Freemuse warned that the global state of artistic freedom had reached its lowest point in a decade, and was continuing to deteriorate.[27] Despotic regimes, racism, sexism, homophobia, the interests of power and commerce, and the state-sponsored silencing of political dissent all appear to be increasingly constraining freedom of artistic expression. In its flagship report from 2022, Freemuse identified over 1,200 violations of artistic freedom in the previous twelve months across more than a hundred countries (and online); in addition to the imprisonment, detention, prosecution, persecution, sanctioning, or censoring of hundreds, thirty-eight artists had been killed. Consistent with previous years, Freemuse identified musicians as the group of artists whose freedoms were most violated.[28]

Artistic freedom is recognized and protected under international law. Several international declarations and conventions, including the United Nations' foundational *Universal Declaration of Human Rights* of 1948, stipulate that individuals and groups should be able to access, participate in, and contribute to artistic and cultural practices of their choosing, without discrimination, censorship, or intimidation.[29] The case of the Khmer Rouge era in Cambodia illustrates how intimately artistic freedom can intersect with wider matters of human rights. It also makes clear how certain political conditions are necessary for artistic freedom. But even once the Khmer Rouge had fallen and political conditions once again allowed for freedom of artistic expression, the social and economic challenges facing the Cambodian people continued to inhibit their capacity to engage in cultural and artistic expression. Certain social and economic conditions, not only political ones, are necessary for artistic freedom.

In this sense, artistic freedom can be understood in terms of cultural rights—that is, the rights of individuals and groups of people "to develop and express their humanity, their world view and the meanings they give to their existence and their development" through their values, knowledges, belief systems, languages, arts, institutions, and ways of life.[30] Although the United Nations' mandate on cultural rights does not extend to cultural sustainability per se, it does aim to promote the conditions that allow "all people without discrimination to access, participate and contribute to all aspects of cultural life in a continuously developing manner,"[31] as well as those that protect people's access to the heritage and resources that enable artistic and cultural freedoms. As such, matters of artistic freedom and cultural sustainability both interlock with matters of cultural rights.[32] Like artistic freedom specifically and human rights more broadly, cultural rights are protected by various international instruments, including (among others) the *Universal Declaration of Human Rights*,[33] the *International Covenant on Social, Economic and Cultural Rights*,[34] the *UNESCO Universal Declaration on Cultural Diversity*,[35] and the *United Nations Declaration on the Rights of Indigenous Peoples*.[36]

A few years ago, in a research collaboration with Cambodian Living Arts, I spoke with Cambodian musicians in their late teens and twenties about their motivations for learning Cambodian traditional music and the challenges they faced in doing so.[37] Consistently, these young people told me that they believed these traditions were culturally precious, but at serious risk of disappearing. While they recognized the importance and urgency of learning from the older generation of musicians, one after another described socioeconomic obstacles to doing so. One could not afford the *moto* fare to his teacher's house, let alone the music lessons. Another worked in the rice paddies after school to support her family, leaving no time for leisure activities like music. A third had won a scholarship for music tuition in the capital city, but the cost of urban rent meant that a musical instrument to practice on was unaffordable. News of the serious illness of an eighty-three-year-old musician in the provinces, the last remaining master of his instrument and its repertoire, left me wondering whether socioeconomic pressures might ultimately be the determining factor in the future of some of these cultural practices.[38] Artistic freedom is not only a cultural rights issue, that is, but also one of social justice: it relates to the fair opportunity for all people to engage in vibrant and meaningful cultural lives according to their preferences, and to reap the various personal and social benefits that result.

When artistic freedom is restricted across a population, the vitality and viability of cultural practices can come under threat. Musicians who experience external restrictions on their freedom of expression may not regain their former musical activity for long after the repressive conditions have passed—as demonstrated by the circumstances of Cambodian *khloy* teacher Yoeun Mek in the 1990s, whom Arn Chorn-Pond found no longer making music, and living in a state of poor social, economic, and physical wellbeing. At a societal level, the cultural damage can last years or decades after the repression itself has ended. The violation of artistic freedom (and nearly all other human rights) during the Khmer Rouge regime continues to hinder cultural vitality and viability in Cambodia today, constraining people's capacity and resources to freely participate in cultural practices, and jeopardizing the sustainable futures of those practices. Despite the relative successes of cultural revitalization efforts in general terms, few Cambodian traditional music genres have regained anything like their former vibrancy.

Afghanistan is another setting that makes egregiously apparent the direct correlation between artistic freedom, cultural rights, and cultural sustainability on the one hand, and between artistic repression, cultural rights violations, and cultural endangerment on the other. During its control of most of that country between 1996 and 2001, the Taliban severely suppressed freedom of artistic and cultural expression, in effect destroying cultural life. Following the fundamentalist militant group's fall from power in 2001, various vigorous grassroots, regional, and international efforts sprang up to attempt to revive Afghanistan's ailing cultural practices. Among the most internationally profiled of these was the Afghanistan National Institute of Music (ANIM), the first and only music school in the country, established in Kabul in 2010 with assistance from the World Bank. Founder and director Ahmad Sarmast established ANIM with two intentions: to safeguard and revitalize Afghan music traditions following the years of Taliban rule; and to provide a general education to the most disadvantaged members of society, regardless of gender, ethnicity, or social circumstances.[39]

Over the following decade, ANIM made considerable progress in these dual aspirations towards social justice and cultural sustainability. Within a few years, it had increased the proportion of its students who were female, and the proportion of those from disadvantaged backgrounds, to more than half of its approximately 300 students.[40] Seventeen-year-old ANIM student Negin Khpalwak conducted an all-female ensemble in performance in Kabul (and was thus hailed, in 2015, as the country's first female conductor);[41] two years later, an ensemble of ANIM-trained female musicians performed under her leadership at the World Economic Forum in Davos, Switzerland.[42] By the end of its first decade, ANIM had taught thousands of young Afghan people—and many other people around the world—about the musical repertoires, instruments, and traditions of Afghanistan, thereby slowly repairing some of the cultural losses of the Taliban era.

In August 2021, after nearly twenty years of insurgency, the Taliban seized back control of Afghanistan. One of many artists who feared for their lives, Khpalwak hastily gathered up the press clippings and photographs from her performances, burnt them, and fled the country (safely settling in the United States).[43] Just as Khpalwak had suspected, the Taliban began once again to severely curtail the human rights of its population—the right to decent work and education, the right to freedom of movement, the right to artistic freedom. Except for sanctioned religious vocal music, it banned music in public spaces,[44] and in some parts of the country prohibited radio stations from playing music.[45] ANIM shuttered its doors. With this violent interruption to cultural lives, cultural practices, and the intergenerational transmission of cultural knowledge, the previous two decades of cultural revitalization efforts seem likely to be undone. If the case of Cambodia is indicative, the cultural disruption may well be felt for generations to come, in both cultural and social ways (a matter I return to in the closing chapter of this book, which explores the theme of future justice).

In its *Convention on the Protection and Promotion of the Diversity of Cultural Expressions*, UNESCO states that the vitality, viability, and diversity of cultural practices can be maintained "only if human rights and fundamental freedoms, such as freedom of expression, . . . are guaranteed."[46] The history of Afghanistan over the last quarter-century makes this abundantly and tragically clear—from the violations of artistic freedom and other human rights under the Taliban, to twenty years of efforts to repair the calamitous social and cultural consequences, and back again.

*

Observing the villagers listen to the *khene* in amazement that June day in 2012, Arn Chorn-Pond and his traveling companions—who included Cambodian singer Seyma Thorn—had an idea: why not bring Cambodian traditional music to people in rural areas across the country, for whom music is largely absent from their lives?[47] From that seed grew the Khmer Magic Music Bus, which Arn and Seyma established in 2013 with the support of a partnership from the USA (see ▶ video Example 1.1 and website Example 1.2). From the start, their aim has been "to carpet Cambodia with music by helping Cambodian master musicians and their students return traditional music performance and education to the people of rural Cambodia, one village at a time."[48]

Most of Cambodia's few remaining elderly master-musicians now live in urban and peri-urban areas, including the capital city, Phnom Penh. There, they have greater opportunities to perform and teach compared with rural locations, and can more easily access healthcare and other services; they may also be practically supported by urban cultural networks or organizations, such as Cambodian Living Arts. The Khmer Magic Music Bus enables these masters and their urban-dwelling students to share their musical knowledge and skills with people living rurally. The twenty-five-seater bus takes the musicians to provincial villages across Cambodia, where opportunities for musical participation are limited. If the village residents are willing, some communal outdoors space is found—perhaps in a central area of the village, or in the shade underneath someone's house—where the musicians play, sing, and dance for and with the locals. Often, these are small, informal affairs involving just a handful of traveling artists (who are employed casually by the Khmer Magic Music Bus). Traditional and Western instruments (like guitars) may both make an appearance, and the villagers and visitors will take the opportunity to exchange stories and knowledge about musicians and musical practices from that province and beyond (see Figure 1.1). On other occasions, with prior arrangement, the full busload of visitors might stage a performance, involving not only music and dance, but perhaps also shadow puppetry, theater, games, or other traditional cultural practices (see ▶ video Example 1.3). At other times, the visiting musicians might present a workshop about traditional Cambodian music and musical instruments at a local school, sometimes to hundreds of children (Figure 1.2; see also ▶ web Examples 1.4 and 1.5).

On all these excursions, the musicians from the Khmer Magic Music Bus encourage the villagers to try out the musical instruments they brought with them on the bus, especially the Cambodian traditional instruments that the younger people may never yet have encountered. In this way, the local people are sometimes surprised to discover a musician, or several, among their own

Figure 1.1 Khmer Magic Music Bus musicians perform songs for residents of Bramath Dey village, Kampong Thom province, June 28, 2019, with the Bus in the background. Singer Thorn Seyma (left) with Young Yorn (singer) and guitar players Yen Boren and Thuch Savang. Note the Cambodian traditional instruments (*skor* drum and *chapei dong weng* lute) in the background. Photo: Thon Dika.

Figure 1.2 Khmer Magic Music Bus artist Pich Sarath presents the traditional Cambodian instrument *chapei dong weng* to local children, Tang Kok primary school, Tang Kok village, Kampong Cham province, January 19, 2019. Photo: Thon Dika.

number. By actively encouraging local participation, the project has identified a handful of otherwise unknown master-musicians, as well as some small enclaves of musicians from ethnic minorities of Cambodia.[49] The Khmer Magic Music Bus sometimes invites one or more of these local musicians to join a future tour of the bus, offering them an artist fee. In addition to respecting, recognizing, and celebrating the cultural knowledge and skills of these artists and their communities, this practice has several further benefits: it raises the profile of musicians and musical traditions in their local villages and areas; it expands the opportunities for musical exchange between Cambodia's rural provinces, which are otherwise very few; and by demonstrating intrinsic and extrinsic benefits to artistic practice (the latter including public recognition, travel, and modest revenue), it incentivizes younger people to take an active interest in traditional cultural practices.

As this approach indicates, the Khmer Magic Music Bus strives to learn about local musical expressions (and musicians) as much as to teach and share them. It is intergenerational, involving children and adults of all ages, while duly acknowledging and celebrating the skills of older master-musicians. It is grassroots rather than top-down, facilitating the exchange and spread of knowledge and skills about Cambodian music from village to rural village. It is participatory, encouraging musicians and non-musicians in rural areas to join, not only to witness, its musical activities. Arn and Seyma see the Bus as a way to foster Cambodian cultural identity and values, too.[50] The project's name reflects their belief that Cambodia's traditional music can transform. Arn calls it "magic music" because "it heals everything," he says, "including hate."[51]

In 2017, the Khmer Magic Music Bus became a program of Cambodian Living Arts (see ▶ video Example 1.6). This has facilitated access to infrastructure, seed funding, and administrative resources that have enabled the Bus to implement small-scale measures that support the sustainability of specific rural cultural practices.[52] In 2019, the Bus traveled to a small village in Chhay Areng valley in the Cardamom Mountains, in Cambodia's remote southwestern Koh Kong province. There, master Doung Nhoek, then in his mid-eighties, is believed to be the only living person holding the knowledge and skills to make and play the *ploy*,[53] a traditional wind instrument (comprising a dried calabash gourd and a handful of bamboo pipes of differing length). Historically, the *ploy* played an important role in wedding and ritual ceremonies of the Chorng ethnic minority group.[54] For the Chorng people, the cultural losses resulting from the Khmer Rouge era have lately risked being exacerbated by pressures from development projects in the area, which threaten to disrupt the local environment and therefore also their cultural practices.[55] Recognizing the precarious situation of *ploy* and other Chorng musical practices, the Khmer Magic Music Bus visited master Doung in his village, finding, however, that the latter insisted he could no longer play the instrument.[56] Yet with encouragement (and financial support provided by the Bus), Doung began to play the *ploy* again, and soon established a local music class in which he taught three local youth how to play.[57] Not long after, one of these students participated in a tour of the Khmer Magic Music Bus to the adjoining province of Kampot—in all likelihood, the first time that the sounds of the *ploy* had been heard outside its own province.[58]

In post-conflict settings around the world, initiatives that seek to restore opportunities for people's cultural participation are serving social ends, as well as cultural maintenance ones. One such initiative with striking (albeit coincidental) similarities to the Khmer Magic Music Bus is the Music Bus, the first long-term project of Musicians Without Borders. A non-profit organization based in the Netherlands, Musicians Without Borders collaborates with local musicians and organizations to "bring music to people and places affected by war, armed conflict, and displacement."[59] From 2003 to 2011, its Music Bus program (and its related Children's Music Theater) carried local folk music, dance, and theater to children in the town of Srebrenica and its surrounds, including to refugee camps where children from Srebrenica and their families had been displaced. Some years earlier, during the Bosnian War

(1992–1995) in Bosnia and Herzegovina, Srebrenica had been the site of the massacre of several thousand Bosniak (Bosnian Muslim) men and boys, an event that international courts of law subsequently designated as genocidal. At the time the Music Bus began its work in Srebrenica, ethnic divisions and tensions remained palpable, with the Serb people mostly living in town, and the Muslim people in refugee camps. Engaging children from both sides of the divide, and prioritizing inclusive and participatory music-making, the Music Bus offered the local children opportunities to engage (or re-engage) with music from their region.[60] It also provided cultural leadership training, equipping youth with the skills to carry forward the work of the project even after its formal end. Through long-term engagement and working closely and collaboratively with local musicians, the Music Bus helped restore music access and participation to the children of Srebrenica, thereby also contributing to reviving the music of the region. Musicians Without Borders has since implemented over a dozen music programs in conflict-affected countries around the world.

Peacebuilding scholar Cynthia Cohen proposes that music is a particularly powerful peacebuilding resource in post-conflict settings—not because of its "universal appeal," but because its place in cultural traditions and historical events means it holds distinctive meanings for individuals and communities.[61] If a musical or other cultural practice is "small" (practiced by relatively few people) and place-specific, it may be especially meaningful to its practitioners and community, whether as a distinctive marker of identity or for other reasons (like carrying uniquely local knowledge). However, these same characteristics of place-specificity and "smallness" can render cultural practices vulnerable to war and conflict, violations of artistic freedom, or indeed anything else that might jeopardize cultural vitality and viability. In the West African nation of Sierra Leone, cultural practice and transmission were severely disrupted during the civil war from 1991 to 2002, which internally and externally displaced 2.5 million people and left more than 50,000 dead.[62] The music and dance practices most affected were those small, local traditions primarily practiced in rural areas of the country. Throughout the difficult recovery, cultural revival efforts took on a socially as well as culturally restorative role. Many local musical practices whose futures had been jeopardized were harnessed within their communities for social ends: to support personal emotional healing, to educate people about important health matters, to mobilize and engage people in health promotion, and to bring people together in solidarity and community.[63] Re-engaging with their cultural practices helped these communities come to terms with the atrocities of the past and set a new direction for the future.[64]

From Sierra Leone to Srebrenica, from Cambodia to Afghanistan, the post-conflict settings mentioned so far in this chapter illustrate how cultural revitalization initiatives (or more precisely, initiatives with cultural revitalization outcomes) can advance transitional justice. Transitional justice refers to the range of processes that aim to help a society come to terms with the complex legacies of serious conflicts, repressions, and human rights violations; it functions to ensure accountability, address grievances, achieve reconciliation, and ultimately move towards a more peaceful and just future.[65] The past decade or two has brought increasing recognition that cultural practices can help connect, empower, and ultimately transform post-conflict societies,[66] though some scholars believe that cultural practices remain under-utilized in efforts toward transitional justice. Ethnomusicologist Angela Impey explores the case of South Sudan, which has experienced civil war for most of the last seven decades. For the pastoralist Dinka people who comprise over a third of the population and who live mostly rurally, Dinka-language songs hold a "critical role in the citizenly dialogue about peace, forgiveness, and reconciliation."[67] Despite being somewhat compromised by population dispersal and other effects of war, some Dinka song genres—such as ox songs—continue as relatively strong local traditions.[68] In their capacity as public hearings, ox songs have offered a culturally legitimate, local public space that allows Dinka people to tell their stories about the conflicts, express a range of positions, and listen to and seek to understand each other. Impey argues that in South Sudan and potentially other contexts too, performance practices could be better valued and utilized (by government and other stakeholders) as a means for truth-telling, justice, and reparation, and to inform policy decisions about how to address social concerns.[69] Especially in contexts where local cultural practices have been adversely affected by war or conflict, drawing on cultural practices in this way could also support their sustainability.

In the Introduction to this book, I defined cultural sustainability as people being able to make their own free choices about which cultural practices they engage with, and how. By this characterization, artistic freedom is a necessary precondition for cultural sustainability, because when people are not able to make those free choices—that is, when they lack artistic freedom—cultural sustainability suffers by definition. (Consider the case of Cambodia under the Khmer Rouge.) However, for people to be able to freely express themselves through cultural practices of their own choosing—that is, for them to experience artistic freedom—those cultural practices must be accessible and available to them. In other words, those cultural practices must have a level of vitality that allows people to engage with them; moreover, their broader social, cultural, economic, political, and religious settings must allow for people to access and participate in them too. (Consider Cambodia in the Khmer Rouge aftermath, when the lack of artistic freedom was less a function of political repression than it was of massive prior cultural losses, psychosocial trauma, and socioeconomic impediments to cultural participation.) When cultures are strong and sustainable, people can enjoy artistic freedom, exercise their cultural rights, and experience cultural justice. Thus, cultural sustainability is not only *interconnected* with matters of social justice; it *is* a matter of social justice.

*

At the time of writing (mid-2023), Mon Hai from Oddar Meanchey province, now sixty-seven years old, is considered the last living *khene* master in Cambodia. Over the last few years, the Khmer Magic Music Bus has connected Mon with young people from his local area who have expressed interest in learning the instrument. With the support of Cambodian Living Arts, the Bus began to provide Mon with a salary to enable him to focus on passing on his musical knowledge and skills. In this way, four young students—a boy and three girls aged between ten and fifteen years old—began learning *khene* and have reached a level of proficiency on the instrument. A fifth student, a man in his early thirties from the southern province of Tboung Khmum, has recently joined Mon's class too. In 2022, the Khmer Magic Music Bus and Mon Hai negotiated an agreement with the culture and education departments of the Oddar Meanchey provincial government that the *khene* be taught as part of the curriculum at the primary school in Mon's village, Krasaing.[70] The program has recently begun, and now the Khmer Magic Music Bus is planning to support Mon to revitalize the local practice of *khene*-making.[71] The future for the instrument and cultural practice looks promising once more.

Just as violations of artistic freedom can lead to cultural loss, expanding artistic freedom can advance cultural sustainability—and often does, if the few examples in this chapter are any indication. The pursuit of artistic freedom, cultural rights, and cultural justice doubles as the pursuit of cultural sustainability: in a sense, these endeavors are one and the same. The Khmer Magic Music Bus demonstrates in practical terms how this can work. By aiming to restore traditional Cambodian music genres to a state of vitality, the Khmer Magic Music Bus counters the ongoing cultural, social, economic, psychological, and emotional legacies of historical human rights violations. It is reconnecting Cambodian people with their cultural heritage and cultural identities. By sharing music within and between all twenty-five provinces, as well as by involving musicians from ethnic minorities, the Bus celebrates and promotes Cambodia's social and cultural diversity. By involving master-musicians, their students, and villagers of all ages, it encourages intergenerational dialogue and cultural transmission. It expands cultural opportunities for masters and their students who live in urban areas, while also fostering cultural participation in rural communities. It provides a modest income for its regular artists, as well as for those musicians from poorer rural areas who join the Bus on occasional tours. By enabling and expanding opportunities for cultural participation, it helps improve the quality of life for people living in rural areas. In all these ways, the Khmer Magic Music Bus is not only making positive social inroads in Cambodia but also advancing the prospects for vibrant and sustainable musical practices and musical lives.

Figure 2.0 Jessie Lloyd. Photo: https://jessielloyd.com/epk/ (archived).

Introducing: Jessie Lloyd

Jessie Lloyd is an Australian First Nations performer, producer, and creative entrepreneur of both Aboriginal and Torres Strait Islander heritage. She grew up in north Queensland among a musical family. Her grandfather Albie Geia was conductor of the Palm Island Brass Band, and her father, senior songman Joe Geia, is a pioneer of contemporary Australian First Nations music. Since releasing her debut album Other Side of the Room *(2014), Jessie has led a range of acclaimed creative projects and collaborations as singer, guitarist, bassist, and ukulele player. Her projects often offer historical and social insights as well as musical and cultural ones. One example is the Mission Songs Project, a research and performance endeavor to revive twentieth-century First Nations songs sung on the missions and state-run settlements where Aboriginal and Torres Strait Islander people were forcibly relocated. Reaching an audience of both Indigenous and non-Indigenous Australians, the project has received national attention and critical acclaim, prompting challenging discussions and new shared understandings of Australian cultural and social histories.*

Jessie is committed to promoting and progressing First Nations music in Australia. She is former CEO of both Songlines Aboriginal Music (Melbourne, Victoria) and South West Aboriginal Entertainment (Perth, Western Australia), organizations that advocate for greater recognition of contemporary Aboriginal performing arts and artists. Recently, she created a music series for National Indigenous Television (NITV), including ten episodes about the Mission Songs Project. Jessie believes in the capacity for First Nations music to shape more constructive relations between Indigenous and non-Indigenous peoples in Australia, and to create positive social change. For First Nations people, Jessie says, "Music is a powerful tool to transport us back to where we come from and who we are. That's what I'm passionate about."[1]

2
Oh Give Me a Land

With Jessie Lloyd

When police beat down the door to Albie Geia's home with a telegraph pole early one June morning in 1957, Palm Island Aboriginal Settlement had already secured a reputation for being "the ultimate punitive destination for [I]ndigenous people in Queensland."[2] Under the command of Superintendent Roy Bartlam of the Department of Native Affairs of Queensland (Australia), the island settlement was characterized by systemic segregation, police brutality and intimidation, and military-style discipline. Bartlam's leadership from 1953 to 1965 was considered among the most oppressive in the settlement's more than five decades of operation. The First Nations residents were "forced to salute all whites whom they passed by, to work without pay, to queue for rations of flour, tea, sugar and the offcuts of meat and to parcel out the decent portions for the enjoyment of white staff."[3]

The Palm Island settlement had been established in 1918 under the *Aboriginal Protection and Restriction of the Sale of Opium Act* of 1897. The "Protection Act" granted the Queensland state government the power "to cause Aboriginals within any district to be removed to and kept within the limits of any reserve situated in the same or any other district."[4] Between 1918 and its eventual closure in the 1970s, nearly four thousand First Nations children and adults were removed to Palm Island settlement under the Act.[5] The Protection Act was one among a raft of government laws, policies, and practices around Australia, spanning most of the nineteenth and twentieth centuries, that authorized the forcible removal of Aboriginal and Torres Strait Islander children and adults from their homelands. Children were especially targeted: under these practices, somewhere between one in three and one in ten First Nations children—the "Stolen Generations"—were separated from their families and communities, purportedly for their better care and education.[6] Tens of thousands of First Nations people were relocated to reserved

Sounding Good. Catherine Grant, Oxford University Press. © Oxford University Press 2025.
DOI: 10.1093/oso/9780197698433.003.0003

lands ("reserves") under government control (see Figure 2.1), where the practice of their languages, cultures, and spiritual beliefs were usually prohibited.[7] Some of these settlements and reserves, including Palm Island, also operated as missions, where First Nations residents were taught the Christian faith.

A few days before armed police made their pre-dawn raid that June morning, Palm Island resident Albie Geia had led a small group of other First

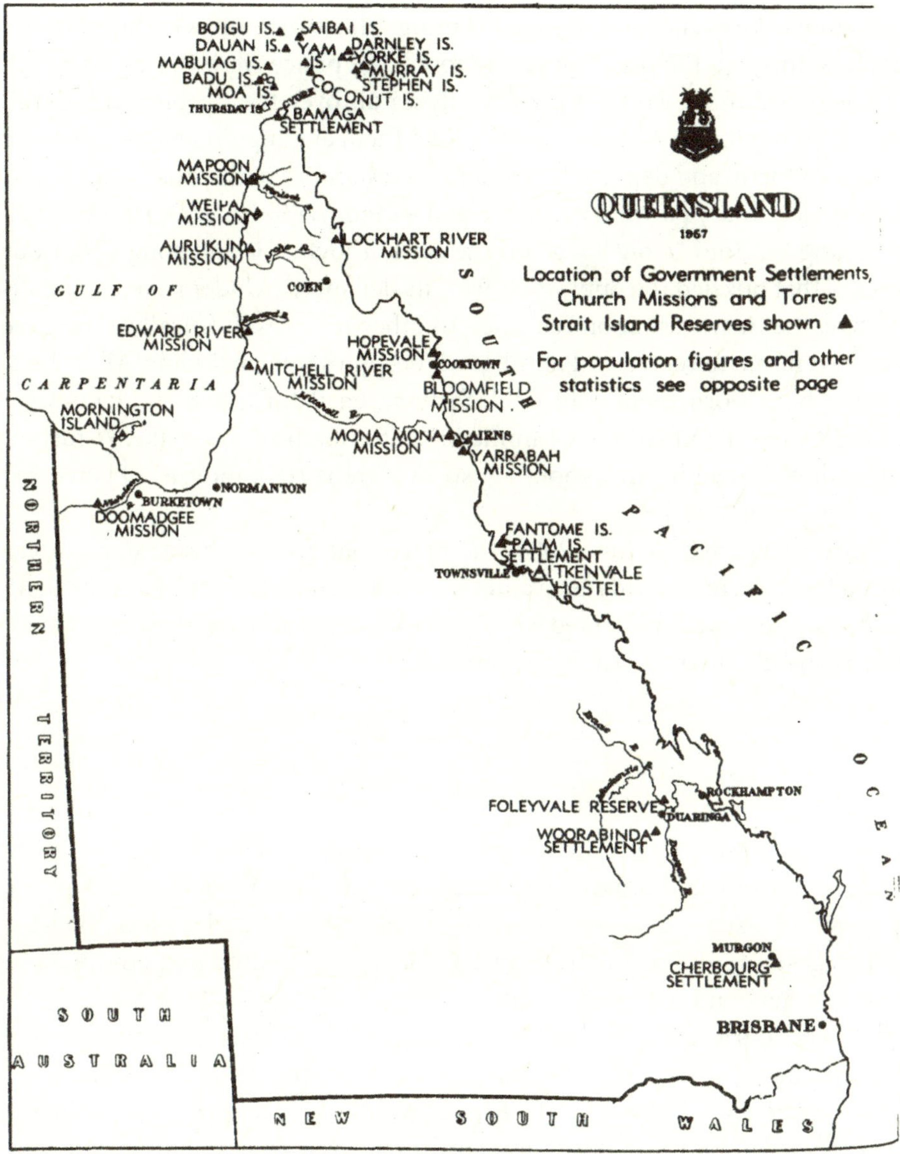

Figure 2.1 Location of government settlements, church missions, and Torres Strait Island reserves in Queensland, 1957. Queensland Government (1958).

Nations men—Sonny Sibley, Freddie Clay, George Watson, Billy Congoo, Eric Lymburner, and Willie Thaiday—in a strike protesting the decades of brutal conditions on the reserve.[8] Joined by other Bwgcolman people (First Nations people resettled on Palm Island), they had protested against the poor housing, meagre rations, authoritarian rule, poor treatment of women, and slave-like work conditions. Geia's granddaughter Jessie Lloyd, Story Holder for this chapter, says that the Elders of her community (who were children at the time) remember the events of that June morning. Those memories include "an axe coming through the door" of Geia's home: the police were "trying to smash it down and these wood chips were flying all over the sleeping children."[9] After raiding the men's homes, police held them at gunpoint, handcuffed and shackled them, and deported them and their families to the Australian mainland on a military patrol boat.[10] One of the men, Willie Thaiday, later recalled breaking out into "a big song" on the boat, a joyful "island song about our home" that puzzled the oppressors with its defiance.[11] Under government directive, the men were soon relocated to other reserves. Ironically, they were ordered never to return to Palm Island, despite some, including Albie Geia, having been born there.[12] In total, forty-seven Palm Island residents were exiled to the mainland in the immediate aftermath of the strike. A further fifty followed over the next month or so, in a "frenzy of removals" of perceived "troublemakers."[13]

Fifty years later, in June 2007, the Queensland state government apologized for the arrests. Alma Geia and Pansy Watson, widows of two of the Palm Island strikers, were presented with "strike medallions" in recognition of their late husbands' involvement in the protests.[14]

*

Through the centuries and around the world, settler colonizers have employed various tactics of domination, forcing people off their lands, removing children from the "barbaric" influences of their families and communities, imposing Western values and Christian belief systems, and prohibiting local languages and cultural practices. Such tactics intentionally disrupt the practice and intergenerational transmission of culture. In Canada, First Nations cultural practices were decimated as a result of child removal policies, residential schools, forced assimilation policies, and other acts of colonial violence.[15] For the Sámi people (who live in the Sápmi region of Norway, Sweden, Finland, and the Russian Kola peninsula), a long history of state assimilation, land dispossession, and Christianization brought about the near disappearance of many cultural practices, including the culturally significant vocal tradition *joik* (which has since undergone a revival).[16] In Australia, around 98% of pre-colonial Aboriginal and Torres Strait Islander performance practices are estimated to have disappeared since colonization—and according to the local committee of the International Council for Traditional Music and Dance, those that remain are "in crisis" due to the ongoing impacts of colonization.[17] A multitude of further examples exist around the world. In brief, even if colonization is not among UNESCO's forty-six identified "threats" to intangible cultural heritage, it has indisputably precipitated many of them, including *loss of ancestral language, loss of cultural spaces, loss of knowledge, reduced practice, reduced repertoire, few practitioners, halted transmission, intolerance, misappropriation*, and *repressive policies*.[18]

On the Palm Island settlement, the authorities sanctioned only certain kinds of cultural activity. Although "traditional" music, dance, and ceremonial practices were prohibited, the First Nations residents were permitted to became familiar with Western popular songs of the time, through jukeboxes and the wireless. They could also join in the music-making at Sunday church services, where Western-idiom, English-language Christian hymns were sung, often accompanied by Western instruments brought by missionaries.[19] After a church service had finished, the residents would often take the opportunity to continue making music, creating, adapting, playing, and singing their own secular songs—obligatorily in English—that told stories of daily life on the mission. Given similar circumstances on other government reserves and Christian missions, songs like these sprang up around the country, and have come to be known as "mission songs." Over time, as Aboriginal and Torres Strait Islander people moved—or were moved—between the reserves and missions and outside of them, they took songs with them. In this way, mission songs were shared and spread, along with the stories and knowledge they carried about the distinct cultural and social identities of the various mission communities. As a living cultural practice, mission songs continued for as long as the missions did, well into the twentieth century. By around the 1970s, most missions, reserves, and settlements had closed, their residents often reclaiming them as First Nations communities.[20]

Mission songs offer a window into the social, cultural, and emotional lives of those who lived on the missions and reserves. They tell of manual labor, nostalgia for home, separation from loved ones, and dreams of freedom. The Palm Island mission song "Down in the Kitchen," which Alma Geia adapted from the American folk tune "Down in the Valley," refers to the rations of damper and weak tea given to the children living in the reserve dormitories. Another song, "Own Native Land," which Alma's husband Albie Geia wrote shortly after leading the 1957 Palm Island strike, tells of Geia's longing for Country as he knew it (see ▶ video Example 2.1):

Oh give me a land where I may roam
Where no other would build and call it their home
Where men of one colour together would live . . .
I never knew that I would be, one day, a foreigner's slave.

A third song, "The Irex," is named for the boat that transported people and supplies to and from the Palm Island settlement (see ▶ website Example 2.2). Composed by an unknown First Nations resident around the 1920s or 1930s,[21] the song refers to the boat carrying First Nations people back to the mainland—something that the authorities often exacted, ironically, as a punishment[22]—and the good wishes of those left behind on the settlement. These songs epitomize the genre in referring to the daily tribulations, hopes, and sometimes also the joys of mission life.[23]

Although some mission songs comment on matters of material fairness (like "Down in the Kitchen," which refers to meagre food rations), no evidence suggests that the songs significantly advanced distributive justice in any real sense for the First Nations residents of Palm Island settlement, or other reserves or missions around the country. As the decades passed, the White authorities on these settlements continued to purposefully restrict or withhold material resources (like satisfactory food and housing) and human rights (like linguistic, cultural, spiritual, economic, social, and political self-determination) from First Nations people. Political philosopher and social justice activist Nancy Fraser has argued, however, that when a social group faces a struggle for cultural recognition, even such important concerns about distributive fairness often assume secondary importance, for the oppressed group, to matters of cultural identity and cultural agency.[24] For Australian First Nations people, the mission songs were a way to maintain cultural identity and agency, even when denied material goods, resources, opportunities, and freedoms—including the right to practice and transmit their own cultural expressions as they had done for tens of thousands of years. Co-opting the sanctioned Western musical idioms and instruments for their own purposes, they found new ways to express their cultural and social lives.

Amid the systemically racist policies and practices of the time, the mission songs exude resourcefulness, resilience, and general optimism—rather like the "singing like anything" of the seven men being deported from Palm Island after the 1957 strike. Though remarkable, these traits are not unique to the mission songs. Around the world, from blues, reggae, Brazilian samba, and hip-hop to various protest song genres, spirited musical practices have sprung from, and been sustained by, conditions of social injustice. In New Caledonia in the 1980s, *kaneka* music arose as a way for young Indigenous Kanak people to express their cultural identity and resist the forced labor, displacement, and cultural suppression of French colonial rule.[25] In the Maghreb region of northwest Africa, revolutionary *nidal* songs arose from the Saharawi people's experience of political oppression and forced displacement (see Chapter 5). In addition to the mission songs, a further example from Australia is *salvesen* ("salvation"), a song and dance genre that emerged from the grueling circumstances of South Sea Islanders' indentured labor on Queensland farms and sugar cane plantations for around four decades from the 1860s. Drawing on the Pacific Island traditions of its practitioners as well as African American spirituals and gospel hymns of the time (which were learnt at plantation night schools), *salvesen* embodies cultural strength and resilience; ethnomusicologist Michael Webb call it a testimony to the South Sea Islanders' capacity to turn sorrow into a lasting expression of joy.[26] Music genres like these illustrate that social injustices are not always damaging to cultural vitality and cultural survival. Sometimes, in some ways, they give rise to them and sustain them.

*

When Jessie Lloyd, granddaughter of Palm Island strike leader Albie Geia, first heard the women Elders of her Palm Island community singing "The Irex," she became curious. In time, she embarked on a journey across Australia, inviting older First Nations people to share what they recalled of the mission songs. In her approach, she prioritized First Nations values, from storytelling and creativity to relationships and community, thereby countering the settler colonial oppression that many people she spoke with had experienced daily on the missions (and continue to experience as First Australians today). Her travels took her to several communities where the mission songs originated, many of which (like Palm Island) retain a strong sense of their histories.[27] The older people gladly shared their memories of this once-thriving cultural practice—not only with Jessie, but often with each other too. As they recalled the lyrics and melodies of the old songs, memories of mission life resurfaced, as did knowledge about Elders, families, and mission communities. In this way, younger generations of these communities sometimes came to hear these songs and stories for the first time. Jessie's inviting people to recall and share "sonic histories"[28] can be understood as a form of cultural reclamation: it returned these songs and their stories to their communities of origin, sometimes decades after they had last been sung. As Jessie gathered several dozen songs across the country, and supplemented this living knowledge with archival research, she began to develop a sense of the social histories of the mission communities, through the songs. For the first time, these social histories were being told through a First Nations voice, providing new perspectives on storylines of the past.

This endeavor became the Mission Songs Project, officially launched in 2015 (see ▶ website Examples 2.3 and 2.4). Joined by other Australian First Nations musicians, Jessie has since performed these songs around Australia and abroad (see Figure 2.2). In 2017, she released the album *The Songs Back Home*, with her vocals backed by ukulele, piano accordion, and pedal-steel guitar.[29] The album comprises ten mission songs, mostly from the early twentieth century, which Jessie encountered through her travels. Each track was recorded in a single take, the four vocalists sharing a single microphone, in an effort "to create the feel of sitting in the backyard . . . somebody grabs a guitar and everybody starts singing."[30] The album booklet includes the song lyrics and guitar chords, and a choir songbook is available too, with the intent to encourage teaching and learning of the songs, including by non-Indigenous children and adults. Hoping to capture the interest of musicians, teachers, researchers, historians, and the public, she also created a ten-episode video series about the songs, which was released in 2020 by the Australian Broadcasting Corporation.[31] "My aim is to start making these songs Australian classics," Jessie explains.[32]

In reviving memories of a nearly forgotten cultural practice, the Mission Songs Project provides a window into a largely overlooked aspect of Australia's past. Few non-Indigenous Australians would have more than surface-level knowledge of the mission era, let alone how mission life may have been experienced by First Australians.[33] (As early as 1935, Australian novelist and travel writer Dora Birtles was referring to apathy of the wider Australian public regarding the situation on Palm Island: "Great Palm Island is something most Australians do not know about, or, if they know, they do not like to think about.")[34] In this context, the Project makes the lived experiences of First Nations people more visible, informing and educating non-Indigenous Australians and offering them a way to expand their understanding of Australia's cultural and social histories. Even in itself, this greater visibility arguably advances racial equality and racial justice. Of the northern European context, ethnomusicologist Thomas Hilder has described how the contemporary revival of the *joik* and other musical practices has been a means for the Sámi people to resist the ongoing injustices and impacts of colonization—not only via Sámi musicians using music to educate and inform people about matters of social justice and human rights, or adopting overt political stances

Figure 2.2 Jessie Lloyd performs as part of the Mission Songs Project (National Folk Festival, Canberra, 2017). Still image from "Yil Lull" video at https://jessielloyd.com/epk/ (archived).

in their music (though these have certainly been important strategies), but also simply via the fact that Sámi music promotes the visibility of Indigenous people, culture, and world views in the societies where they live.[35]

In a national survey conducted in 2021, fewer than half (47%) of Australians surveyed believed that racism is a problem in Australia; yet in 2020, more than half (52%) of First Australians reported experiencing an incident of racial prejudice within the preceding six months.[36] As in other settler colonial societies, race and racism are difficult and divisive topics in Australia. The notion of racial justice—the "systematic fair treatment of people of all races that results in equitable opportunities and outcomes for everyone"[37]—can be uncomfortable for privileged (White) sectors of society, because improving outcomes for marginalized social groups must diminish the relative power of those groups who currently hold it.[38] Non-profit racial justice organization Race Forward describes how many people in the United States, even those who hope for a more racially just society, are averse to discussing matters of race. Its observations largely apply to Australia too:

> These varied aversions to talking about race demonstrate that our national conversation on race is stuck. One segment of the country wants to talk about race as little as possible—restricting the definition of racism to a very limited set of overt intentional acts or thoughts held by individuals. And another segment of the country is frustrated by the infrequent and stifled nature of how racism is defined

> and discussed. Both are eager to produce and advance positive images and stories about people of color and our communities in order to supplant the negative, ostensibly "race-neutral" or "race-silent" frames and stories that often dominate the general public's mind and decision-making.[39]

Further to their role in promoting visibility, cultural practices—and initiatives to sustain them, like the Mission Songs Project—can productively advance racial discourses in three key ways. One is by offering pathways for people to learn about, and reflect on, historical and contemporary racism. When conversations about race are "stuck," cultural practices can act as lubricants, conveying difficult messages to audiences in ways that often resonate more easily than polemics (and reaching those who may not engage with conventional news or policy outlets). The mission songs' English-language lyrics and Western musical idiom makes them accessible to a wide Australian public. Their creative format provides an alternative to more explicit modes of teaching about racism, which risk distancing those not receptive to the uncomfortable message. Thus, while "The Irex" (for example) alludes to the forcible removal of Bwgcolman people from Palm Island reserve, the song is not overtly about racist government policies, or the racialized injustices First Peoples experienced at the hands of White mission authorities and other colonial settlers. Rather, it foremost expresses a gentle sentiment that nearly all humans would recognize and empathize with: namely, in Jessie's words, "I wish you well and I hope to see you again."[40]

For this reason, Jessie believes that the mission songs hold more than historical and educational value to contemporary Australia, more even than the capacity to bring to greater visibility the lived experiences and shared histories of First Australians: they can also motivate intercultural dialogue and reconciliation, and form "a bridge between black and white Australia."[41] Several of the processes of reconciliation identified by scholar of peacebuilding Cynthia Cohen are engaged through the Mission Songs Project, including "appreciating each other's humanity and respecting each other's culture; telling our own and listening to each other's stories, and developing more complex narratives and nuanced understandings of identity; [and] acknowledging harms, telling truths, and mourning losses."[42] The Mission Songs Project invites White Australians not to turn away from the racial injustices of the past and the present, but to listen deeply, bearing conscious witness to the historical and contemporary impact of systemically racist policies and practices.

The second, related, way in which the Mission Songs Project advances the racial discourse in Australia is by foregrounding narratives than humanize

First Peoples. The project shows how cultural practices can disrupt dominant mainstream narratives that present Indigenous, Black, and People of Color either as ill-fated victims or as perpetrators of their own troubles, supplanting them with more racially just narratives.[43] Through its live performances, recordings, and educational resources, the project invites non-Indigenous Australians to step away from harmful stereotypes, and to learn about an era in recent Australian history through First Nations lives and experiences. In the short ABC television series, for example, Jessie introduces and reflects on several mission songs in turn, sometimes offering insights into her own family and community, sometimes introducing Elders of other communities who, with gentle good humor, share their memories of mission times. Native American Lakota scholar Hilary Weaver reminds us that in settler colonial societies, (re)building healthy relationships between Indigenous and non-Indigenous people is a vital restorative act,[44] whose necessary basis is the recognition of one another's shared humanity. Through its humanizing narratives, the Mission Songs Project is contributing, however modestly, to reconfiguring racial stereotypes and generating productive racial discourses in Australia—discourses that center First Peoples as the agents in their own lives and stories.

Third, the Mission Songs Project prompts consideration of institutional and structural racism in Australia: that is, racial bias in the form of unfair policies and discriminatory practices among institutions and across society that routinely advantages White and disadvantages First Nations people (and Black people and People of Color). Institutional and structural racism constrain a prosperous, just, and equitable society just as racism directed against, or perpetrated by, individuals does, but these structural forms of racism are comparatively less profiled in mainstream media, public discourse, and political circles.[45] From the deportations on the Irex to the government rations, the stories told in the mission songs connect the lived experiences of mission residents to the racially unjust systems of the time, including the institutional structures of White authority and the assimilation policies in place across the country. By sharing these songs and their associated stories with a wide contemporary audience, the Mission Songs Project invites White Australians to reflect on the ongoing legacies of this historical racism. These legacies include gross disparities in educational opportunities, employment, health, housing, criminal justice, voting access, and life expectancy for Indigenous compared with non-Indigenous people.[46] In this way, the Project invites reflection on the many ways racism remains manifest in Australian social and political institutions: the criminal justice system, healthcare, government, mainstream media, educational institutions, and more.

Thus, in revitalizing a nearly-forgotten cultural practice, the Mission Songs Project contributes to racial justice: by raising the visibility of First Nations peoples and cultures in contemporary Australia, by promoting humanizing and accessible narratives about First Australians, by drawing attention to the role of systemic and institutional racism in the lived experiences of First Australians, by educating White Australians on how systemic racism affected the lives of First Australians in the past, and by provoking reflection and dialogue on the ongoing manifestations and cumulative effects of systemic racism for First Australians today.

*

Over the past couple of decades, an intensifying ethnomusicological interest in matters of cultural sustainability has occurred in tandem with scholars' growing attention to the ethics of research relating to marginalized or oppressed groups, including First Peoples.[47] In Australia in 2002, the Australian Institute of Aboriginal and Torres Strait Islander Studies (AIATSIS) published its first edition of the *Guidelines for Ethical Research in Australian Indigenous Studies*, laying out the ethical principles that should guide all research involving First Nations peoples.[48] The Guidelines emphasized to non-Indigenous people the ethical imperative to consult on an ongoing basis with First Nations peoples during research that involves them. They also underscored the principles of First Nations self-determination in such research, and of that research directly benefitting First Nations peoples in some way. In the couple of decades since then, collaborative and applied approaches to supporting cultural sustainability have been prominent among non-Indigenous researchers (and cultural advocates and agencies) in Australia. Similar shifts have occurred in other contexts around the world, as concepts of ethical research practice developed, and as it became more accepted for researchers to want to influence the cultural, social, and political realities of the communities or settings in which they worked.

The shift toward collaborative approaches has clearly represented a marked improvement, in ethical terms, from many "outsider" approaches to cultural sustainability research that were common in the twentieth century (and earlier). Yet it generates its own set of ethical challenges, as mentioned in the Introduction to this book. Collaborative research can be an impost on the time, energies, and resources of individuals and their communities. Its ubiquity as a methodological approach risks it becoming entrenched in the expectations of institutions, funding bodies, or other agencies with oversight on research endeavors. According to Ngarinyin and Nyigina (Australian First Nations) scholar Rona Googninda Charles and non-Indigenous Australian scholar Sally Treloyn, the collaborative turn has sometimes resulted in Australian First Peoples being "compelled to engage and collaborate with outsider-researchers and archives if they wish to retrieve their songs and cultural practices."[49] When cultural sustainability initiatives are fully First Nations-led—like the Mission Songs Project, conceived, designed, and implemented by a First Nations woman with First Nations collaborating artists and advisors and directly involving First Nations people and communities—such challenges are minimized or altogether avoided.

Over these last two or three decades, Australian government bodies and cultural agencies have become increasingly attentive to the devastating and ongoing impacts of colonization on First Nations cultural practices, and to the urgency for measures to support those practices. In 2002, the same year as the AIATSIS released its Guidelines on ethical research, the Garma Statement on Indigenous Music and Performance proclaimed:

> Performance traditions are the foundation of social and personal wellbeing, and with the ever-increasing loss of these traditions, the toll grows every year. The preservation of performance traditions is therefore one of the highest priorities for [Australian] Indigenous people.[50]

Since then, various government and non-government cultural documentation, maintenance, and revitalization initiatives have been instated (or reinstated) in support of this goal. Creative Australia—the federal government's principal arts funding and advisory body—runs grant schemes, awards, and fellowships intended to promote First Nations arts and cultural practices. Another government initiative, the multi-million-dollar federal Indigenous Languages and Arts program, aims to support First Nations people "to express, preserve and maintain their cultures through languages and arts activities."[51] The National Recording Project for Indigenous Performance in Australia (NRPIPA) is a third example, a long-term non-government documentation and archiving initiative emanating from the Garma Statement. Integrally involving First Nations researchers and communities, NRPIPA was established to "systematically record and document the unique and endangered performance traditions of Indigenous Australia."[52] Further examples exist.

While Australian cultural maintenance and revitalization programs nowadays generally cater for the full diversity of First Nations cultural expression, those cultural practices that emerged in the colonial era have attracted relatively little external support, compared with either "traditional" (pre-colonial) practices or those deemed "contemporary."[53]

First Nations cultural practices from any historical period—including the colonial—may hold cultural significance for their practitioners and communities, and benefit from cultural support. Sung in English in a Western musical idiom with Western instruments, the colonial-era mission songs are not, however, the kind of First Nations cultural practice that governments, cultural agencies, or non-Indigenous researchers have typically prioritized for attention or support—despite those songs having essentially fallen away as a living cultural practice (prior to the Mission Songs Project), with very limited documentation available and many not having been sung for decades.

When cultural sustainability decisions are made or managed by outsiders, one risk (among many) is that those decisions fall prey to what ethnomusicologists Beverley Diamond and Salwa El-Shawan Castelo-Branco call the "problematic representation" of racial "others" as "static and anti-modern."[54] In its ethical principles on cultural safeguarding, UNESCO advises that the value of a cultural practice should be judged by its own practitioners and community, rather than being subject to external judgements of worth.[55] The Mission Songs Project is an example of a cultural sustainability initiative that challenges problematic colonial presumptions about the scope and type of First Nations cultural practices that are worthy of research, documentation, and support. In revitalizing a cultural practice of the kind not often associated (in the White imagination) with First Nations culture, the Project resists narrowly conceived colonial ideas about what (and how) to safeguard culture. When scholars like Tim Frandy and Timothy Cooley refer to *cultural sustainabilities* (in the plural),[56] they are referring at least partly to this: to expanding Western notions about cultural sustainability to embrace the multiplicity and wisdom of First Nations ways of thinking about, knowing, practicing, and maintaining culture.

Around the world, First Nations peoples are resisting colonial notions of cultural sustainability, and in this way, embodying First Nations self-determination and cultural agency. In Vanuatu, the people of Tafea Province are conceiving of mission sites as Indigenous heritage that preserves Indigenous memories, and that are therefore worth preserving and protecting.[57] This conceptualization can be surprising to outsiders (like tourists and researchers), who tend to perceive mission sites as the heritage of outsiders—and often colonialist heritage at that. According to anthropologists James Flexner and Matthew Spriggs, this case from Vanuatu represents "a useful challenge to essentialist models" of cultural heritage that assume a divide between Indigenous and colonial heritage. In Vanuatu, as in Australia, First Nations and colonial heritage are "not separate categories, but two sides of the same coin"[58]—and this remains true whether for tangible heritage (like artifacts and archaeological remains) or intangible heritage (like music, dance, belief systems, and worldviews).

In short, postcolonial, Western-influenced First Nations cultural practices like the mission songs in Australia are not cultural aberrations: they are a valuable part of the rich and ever-evolving tapestry of tens of thousands of years of First Nations cultural expression.

*

On November 19, 2004, Aboriginal Palm Island resident known, after his death, as Mulrunji,[59] was found dead in a cell at the Palm Island police station, having been arrested by a White police officer only an hour earlier for allegedly causing a public nuisance. When Senior Sergeant Chris Hurley first encountered Mulrunji that day, the latter was walking along the street, singing his favorite song, "Who Let the Dogs Out?"[60] A week later, an autopsy report identified that massive internal injuries caused his death, including four broken ribs, a ruptured spleen, and a liver almost severed in two. In 2007, Hurley was tried for manslaughter, and acquitted. Mulrunji is one of over 470 Aboriginal and Torres Strait Islander people to have died in custody since 1991, when a royal commission into Aboriginal deaths in custody took place.[61]

When the people of Palm Island first learnt the outcome of Mulrunji's autopsy in 2004, a riot ensued, during which the local police station and other police buildings were burnt down. In an apparent attempt to restore order, the state government flew in dozens of riot squad members.[62] According to a later media report, in the immediate aftermath of the riots, early-morning raids reminiscent of the 1957 Palm Island strike fallout were executed, in which "balaclava-clad officers marched through the small community of fewer than 2,000 residents and pointed large guns at children's heads."[63] In the raids, armed police broke into the homes of eighteen families, charging several people.[64]

It took twelve years, till 2016, before a federal court judge deemed that the police response to the riots had been disproportionate and excessive.[65] The Australian Human Rights Commission referred to the case as "one of the most significant racial discrimination cases in Australia's history."[66] The judge stated in summary:

> I have found they (police officers) conducted themselves . . . with a sense of impunity, impervious to the reactions of Palm Islanders. . . . I have found

that police acted in these ways because they were dealing with an Aboriginal community.[67]

Upon this verdict, the State of Queensland, Queensland Police Union, and Commissioner of Police continued to deny all allegations of racial discrimination.[68] As part of a subsequent class action settlement on the matter, the Queensland Government finally agreed to issue a formal apology over the riots, though the state's police union continued to deny any racism on their part.[69] The government apology, published in local newspapers on June 28, 2018, read in part:

> As a Government, we acknowledge that this experience (between 19 and 29 November 2004) has impacted significantly on your lives. As a Government, we have learned from your significant pain and suffering, and have taken significant steps to ensure that none of our citizens will again suffer discrimination at the hands of their government.[70]

It had been precisely a hundred years since the founding of the Palm Island government settlement under the Protection Act, and eleven since the government's 2007 apology to Alma Geia, Pansy Watson, and other Palm Islanders for the violent arrests and deportations made fifty years earlier, following the 1957 strike. At the time of writing, no one has yet been held accountable for the death of Mulrunji.

Amid persistent and pervasive systemic racism, it may seem difficult to envisage a meaningful role for cultural expressions in the pursuit of justice, or to believe that cultural strength, sustainability, or reclamation could be matters of priority for those who are the subjects of racial violence. But addressing racism demands a multitude of responses. As the Mission Songs Project illustrates, cultural practices and initiatives to support them can contribute to racial equality and racial justice in distinctive and important ways: disrupting negative stereotypes and racial discourses, advancing humanizing narratives, informing and educating, inviting respectful dialogue—all while strengthening the cultural identities, cultural practices, and visibility of those oppressed. I close this chapter with the words of Bundjalung Widjabul woman Rhoda Roberts, who weaves together these threads of cultural strength, cultural sustainability, and racial justice:

> Dispossession and assimilation policies continue to affect Australia's First Peoples, undermining community, leadership, and cultural strength. There is a crisis across

Aboriginal communities resulting from our brutal history, inter-generational trauma, and ongoing racism, when combined with the everyday issues affecting families such as poverty, unemployment, and overcrowding. A certain social isolation and marginalization within the dominant society becomes a reality. We constantly hear the negative: we are said to be the problem, the Aboriginal disadvantage. But actually the reality is that we have the advantage: our culture, the oldest living and adapting culture on the planet. It is the advantage.[71]

Figure 3.0a Bengala. Photo: Pedro Aspahan, 2022.

Introducing: José Bonifácio da Luz ("Bengala")

José Bonifácio da Luz, known by his ritual name Bengala, is a senior of his African-descendent Maroon[1] community of Arturos, a group of around 600 people who live on the outskirts of Belo Horizonte, one of Brazil's biggest cities. Bengala is a third-generation practitioner and master of Congado,[2] a devotional-ceremonial performance ritual involving singing, dancing, percussion, and procession that is practiced by Afro-Brazilian communities across Brazil. As a child, Bengala learnt Congado by listening and observing, a method of transmission he calls "paying attention." He refers to Congado as "a ritual with a beginning but no end" comprising socio-musical "moments": "Where you are, where you are going, what you are doing, who you are with—all these things affect the musical decisions. The music depends on the present moment."[3] Congado is one among a cycle of African-derived sacred and secular cultural practices, rituals, and festivities that has been practiced and intergenerationally transmitted by Bengala's community since 1885, when the community of Arturos was founded.[4]

Bengala was one of the first Masters to teach through the Meeting of Knowledges program at the University of Brasília, and now teaches Congado as part of that program at the Universidade Federal de Minas Gerais (UFMG) in his home city of Belo Horizonte. In 2022, UFMG bestowed on him the title of Doutor em Música por Notório Saber ("Doctor of Music by Acknowledged Higher Knowledge") for his cultural knowledge, skills, and contributions. Bengala believes that profiling diverse knowledges in music education is about more than educational and social outcomes: it is also a way to celebrate, promote, and ensure a strong future for local cultural practices. "My participation in Meeting of Knowledges has led to people accepting and responding positively to my cultural heritage and my community," he explains, "and there are no words to describe how that makes me feel."[5]

Figure 3.0b José Jorge de Carvalho. Used with permission.

Introducing: José Jorge de Carvalho

Brazilian anthropologist, ethnomusicologist, professor, and co-author of this chapter, José Jorge de Carvalho, is committed to inclusive policies and practices in higher education. In 2003, Jorge spearheaded a new affirmative action policy at his university, the University of Brasília, including a racial quota system that resulted in significantly higher enrolments of Black and Indigenous students. Recognizing the concomitant need for the curriculum to cater for a more diverse student cohort, Jorge collaborated with Black, Indigenous, Maroon, and Afro-Brazilian senior culture-bearers across Brazil to establish Meeting of Knowledges, the program that is the focus of this chapter. Since its founding over a decade ago, Meeting of Knowledges has expanded nationally and internationally (as this chapter describes), promulgating what Jorge describes as a "pedagogy of conviviality" that recognizes and celebrates the diverse peoples and cultures of Brazil.[6]

According to Jorge, integrating diverse cultural knowledges into higher music education is an educational and ethical imperative. Its relationship to social justice lies in recognizing "the full humanity" of all groups of people that constitute a society. "A monomusical school that teaches only Western music in plurimusical countries is affirming, through silence, . . . the superiority of Western music over the other musical systems of those countries," he says. "I believe it is possible to imagine a new school of music."[7]

3

Masters in the Academy

With José Jorge de Carvalho and José Bonifácio da Luz ("Bengala")

Enrolled in a higher music institution somewhere in the United Kingdom, or perhaps New Zealand or Canada, is an earnest and dedicated student—let's call her Marina. Marina was born in a regional town somewhere in the Global South and grew up speaking her Indigenous language and Spanish, the official language of her country. As a youngster, Marina and her family enjoyed listening to local and regional popular songs on the radio. Observing Marina's musical interest, her uncle taught her to sing and play a few tunes on a local folk instrument. When she reached her early teens, Marina's family emigrated to the West, where her new high school offered a multicultural music program for children of migrants, subsidizing the cost of instruments and lessons. Marina joined the program and did well. As she drew near to completing high school, she was excited at the prospect of enrolling in a university music degree. She auditioned at the local university music department on her folk instrument and was delighted to be accepted.

As it turned out, though, the university had no staff members of Marina's ethnicity, or who knew how to play her instrument. Marina could source private lessons from a member of her community, she was told, and the university would grant credit towards her degree—but those external lessons would be at Marina's expense. Already working twenty hours a week to support herself and her family, and fearing that working more to cover the cost of private lessons would adversely affect her studies, Marina chose piano as her primary instrument instead, even though she had never learnt it formally. At university, Marina was also asked to choose a major study: Western classical music, jazz, or popular music. None of these quite suited, but she chose the latter, only to soon discover that it referred exclusively to Western popular music. Marina felt behind from the start: the other students seemed to know a lot of the profiled artists and repertoire, and many had already had formal training in their

Sounding Good. Catherine Grant, Oxford University Press. © Oxford University Press 2025.
DOI: 10.1093/oso/9780197698433.003.0004

chosen instrument. Hoping to develop her knowledge about Indigenous and folk cultures, she enrolled in the elective "World Music"—but encountered there no reference to her own culture, had limited scope to pursue her particular interests, and was not invited to share her own musical knowledge or skills with the class. She explored opportunities to play and perform her folk instrument with other students, but aside from the institution's Balinese gamelan, all its ensembles were jazz or Western ones. Even informally, other students found it difficult to jam with Marina, the different scale and tuning systems and repertoires proving an insurmountable hurdle. With little opportunity to make music with other students, Marina found it hard to make friends. Despite her best efforts, her first-year grades were mediocre, and she began to doubt her capacity and will to study music at university after all.

*

In the 1970s, political philosopher John Rawls advanced the notion of a "Veil of Ignorance," an imaginary veil that would prevent us from knowing anything about our position within a given society—not our ethnicity, gender, social status, identities, abilities, interests, or any personal circumstances.[8] Rawls bid us to imagine constructing a society from scratch from behind a Veil of Ignorance, whereby the decision-makers would not know which social position they would ultimately occupy. The likely outcome (argued Rawls) would be a social contract and social institutions founded on principles of social justice, where every individual had a fair chance of prospering.

What if a Veil of Ignorance were applied to higher music institutions? If we knew nothing about ourselves and didn't know which music institution we would end up in, what sort of institution might we create? Presumably not the one Marina found herself in, which validated and promoted certain music genres and cultures over others, signaling that not everyone's music is valued or even recognized. Backed by institutional and social power, the policies and practices of Marina's institution silence certain individuals and groups, even when implemented by well-meaning authorities oblivious to the detrimental effects on the educational experiences, learning, and lives of certain students. Within and beyond the institution, such policies and practices serve to reinforce and intensify social and cultural inequalities.

Although Marina and her institution are fictional, the inequitable model of higher music education presented in her story will be recognizable to those working in the sector. Around the world, many higher music institutions were founded in the colonial tradition during times of colonial rule, fashioned after the European universities of the time. Propounding what are now widely recognized as inherently racist and patriarchal ways to classify, organize, and transmit knowledge, these institutions taught the Western musical canon in Western ways, prioritizing "the music itself"[9] and deriving standards of excellence from the Western classical tradition. Indigenous, popular, folk, and traditional local cultural practices and knowledge systems were usually completely excluded, as were those of women and minoritized "Others."

Despite the escalating urgency felt by many contemporary higher music educators and their institutions to address these injustices, the colonial legacy persists. In South Africa, Westernized universities only minimally represent African cultural practices, their curricula remaining "foreign and colonised" and disconnected from local realities and the lived experience of most Black South Africans.[10] In Australia, despite a recent florescence of contemporary music research that engages Australian First Nations people and knowledges, such research "has seemingly scarcely influenced the core business of Australia's music institutions and most domestic music studies, which remain predominantly grounded in Europe's classical traditions and continue to position Indigenous people and music on the fringe."[11] Western music genres and pedagogies continue to be centered in higher music curricula not only in "WEIRD" (Western, Educated, Industrialized, Rich, and Democratic) countries like Australia, Canada, or the United States, but also in Westernized universities in the Global South, from Cambodia, to Ghana, to Brazil.[12] Brazilian cultural theorist Augusto Boal would call this cultural colonialism in action: marginalizing and devaluing the values of some cultures over those of others, in ways that lead the oppressed to internalize the belief that the cultural values of the oppressors are superior and valid for all places.[13]

The contemporary Westernized university's intensifying espousal of neoliberal and capitalist principles—assessment, individualism, competition, economic growth, marketability, standardization, international institutional rankings, and a fixation with graduate "job-readiness"—only aggravates the cultural colonialism that Boal laments.[14] Subtly or more overtly, this neoliberal ethos suggests to students and the general public that the key function of an education is to produce economically productive individuals. Educationally, this alienates prospective and current students whose priorities and values lie in areas other than economic productivity—for example, in cultural and environmental stewardship. It also radically depletes the capacity of the university to effectively perform what should arguably be one of its key functions as a social institution: supporting students to become rational, creative, socially conscientious individuals who are intellectually and morally capable of and committed to advancing social justice and human rights, supporting artistic and cultural expression, caring for the environment, and generally leading social transformation for a sustainable future.[15]

For as long as higher education attributes truth and validity only to Western knowledge and ways of producing knowledge, and for as long as it continues to venerate neoliberalism, it remains epistemically unjust; that is, it fails to sufficiently recognize the diverse values, knowledges, and systems of knowledge transmission by which people around the world live their lives and bring meaning to their existence.[16] Entwined with colonialism, capitalism, and patriarchy, epistemic injustice is a largely overlooked dimension of social justice—yet in a sense, it undergirds all others, because ultimately, it leads to "epistemicide": the orchestrated loss of knowledge systems around the world.[17] Here, then—at the crossroads of systemic inequities, cultural colonialism, and epistemic injustice—music education and social justice begin to converge with matters of cultural sustainability.

In the early 1970s, American folklorist and ethnographer Alan Lomax published an "appeal for cultural equity," prompted by what he regarded as the "greying out" of global cultural diversity and the rapid and widespread extinction of local musical and other cultural expressions. Cultural endangerment, loss, and homogenization were not only leaving the world culturally and intellectually impoverished, Lomax argued, but also diminishing people's capacity to enjoy rich and fulfilling cultural and social lives.[18] In part, Lomax laid the blame for this "greying out" at the feet of the mass media and entertainment industries, for profiling only a few standardized, commercialized musical practices—but he also found fault with the "brutal educational approach" that exalted Western music above all others.[19] Pleading for an educational system that would hold the musical expressions of all peoples in equal value, he argued that the future of global cultural diversity "all depends on whether the center can overcome its own cultural myopia and give unwritten, non-verbal traditions the status and the space they deserve."[20]

Through much of the second half of the twentieth century, and thus also at the time of Lomax's appeal for cultural equity, many higher music institutions were expanding their curricula from Western and cognate genres (classical, popular, jazz, and select folk genres) to include "world music" traditions. This expansion introduced greater cultural diversity to higher music education and served a valuable educational purpose. However, the musical practices in question were typically elite, well-documented, well-theorized, notated ones from geographically distant countries, rather than those geographically and socially proximate to the students' lives. By the twenty-first century, these few "world music" genres had become (and largely remain) pervasive in Westernized higher music institutions: of the tens or even hundreds of thousands of musical practices in the world,[21] only perhaps a dozen strong traditions became established as areas of major study (among them, the classical traditions of India and the Middle East, and some major Asian traditions, including Balinese gamelan, Japanese gagaku, and Chinese pip'a).

Teaching a select few major traditions is no longer a sufficient or satisfactory way for Westernized higher education institutions to attempt to advance cultural equity, cultural diversity, cultural sustainability, or anti-racist and decolonial endeavors. Some institutions tokenistically point to curriculum offerings in these traditions as their response to matters of inclusivity and diversity, while small, localized cultural practices—those least likely to be well documented or resourced, and most likely to be facing challenges to their sustainability—continue to be overlooked. Similarly, other well-intentioned institutional initiatives sometimes inadvertently reinforce the very systemic inequalities and racist ideologies they attempt to dismantle.[22] For example, when departmental boundaries sever the study of Indigenous or other localized musical practices from their social, cultural, linguistic, ritual, religious, philosophical, performative, or other aspects from which they are indivisible, the inevitable result is an impoverished representation of these practices in the curriculum. The same happens when institutions formalize the teaching of these musical practices into Western pedagogical molds—a hegemonic practice that, over time, can jeopardize their transmission even outside of the institution.[23] Also harmful are those curricular structures where the music of a dominant culture (most commonly, Western classical music) is set as a neutral center around which various "other" musics are peripherally arranged—for example, with those "other" musics taught as minor rather than major studies, as elective rather than core subjects, or by individuals who are not culture-bearers of the practices in question.[24] In these cases, cultural colonialism wins out. As students graduate and forge pathways as professional artists, teachers, and scholars, their education influences how they perceive, value, and engage with such musics, and they risk devaluing these music practices (unconsciously or consciously), just as their educational institutions have done. This perpetuates the cycle of these music practices being minimally or oppressively represented in classrooms, community settings, the media, and the music industry—in turn potentially jeopardizing the economic, social, and cultural wellbeing of the practitioners and the strength and sustainability of the practices themselves.

Evidently, achieving cultural equity, cultural sustainability, and educational and epistemic justice demands a different approach. Many educators and scholars recognize the ethical and educational "urgency . . . to transform the unmarked, white supremacist, and settler colonial structures that guide our music education systems".[25] In many institutions, concerted efforts are underway to dislodge the Eurocentric epistemic paradigm and replace it with a more equitable, diverse, representative, and inclusive model of higher music education.[26] The following section, written by chapter co-author José Jorge de Carvalho, describes one such effort.

*

In the early 2000s, at the University of Brasília, I (Jorge) had become frustrated by the predominantly White and segregated policies and practices of that and other universities across South America. I advocated for my university to introduce a racial quota system to redress the underrepresentation in the student body of Black and Indigenous people, who together comprised around half of Brazil's population. In the decade following its implementation in 2003, this affirmative action policy led to significantly increased enrolments by Black and Indigenous students at the University of Brasília.[27] *Witnessing its success, other universities across Brazil adopted the quota system too.*

As the roll-out progressed, these universities were faced with a new challenge: that of transforming the Eurocentric curriculum that characterized nearly all public and private Latin American universities into one that catered for the growing racial and ethnic diversity of their student body. Elsewhere, I have referred to this as the imperative for "double inclusion" in higher education: that is, epistemic inclusion in addition to ethnic and racial inclusion.[28] *Since the establishment of higher education institutions in Brazil toward the end of the nineteenth century, their curricula had remained nearly wholly mono-epistemic and mono-cultural. But as I saw it, a homogeneous and uniform musical curriculum made sense only within the colonized Eurocentric model. Now the educational imperative was to overturn the old exclusionary policies and practices and arrive at a curriculum that better reflected the multitude of musics, cultures, histories, epistemologies, ethnicities, languages, and worldviews represented in the student body, and across Brazil at large. In my view, the curriculum of every higher music education institution the world over should strive, as an institutional policy, to reflect the whole musical profile of the region where it is located.*

Supported by the University of Brasília and the national ministries of Culture and Education (which oversee the higher education curriculum of Brazil), I began to consult with local Indigenous, Black, Maroon, and Afro-Brazilian communities about what might be done. The "Masters" I spoke with—senior culture-bearers holding the deep musical, cultural, environmental, historical, artistic, medicinal, ceremonial, sociological, and architectural knowledge of their communities[29]*—requested that they come to teach at the university. In this* *way, in 2010, Meeting of Knowledges ("Encontro De Saberes" in Portuguese) was founded. (Soon after, Bengala became involved in the program as a Master; see ▶ website Examples 3.1 and 3.2.)*

The theory and methods of Meeting of Knowledges are described in detail in several publications[30] *(and in ▶ video Example 3.3). In brief, the program involves the development and delivery of university courses, offered across departmental and disciplinary boundaries, that teach students about the music, cultures, and knowledges of local Indigenous and African-derived communities. These courses are afforded equal institutional standing as those Eurocentric courses that historically constituted the core curriculum. Each course comprises a series of two- to four-week modules, each module taught by a different Master. The Masters are remunerated as "visiting professors," while a tenured academic takes the role of "partner-lecturer" and engages in dialogue with the Masters through the course. Some Masters choose to invite one or more apprentices from their communities to join them in teaching. In designing and delivering their modules, the Masters are free to determine not only the content they teach, but also how they teach it. In this way, the program allows the Masters the opportunity— both political and aesthetic—to teach their musical and cultural practices on their own terms, in an integrated and holistic way. This approach means that the nature and outcomes of Meeting of Knowledges vary from one university to another, as the Masters tailor the curriculum to represent and reflect their own cultures and communities.*[31] *(See ▶ video Example 3.4, which shows Bengala teaching Meeting of Knowledges university students a song from his community of Arturos).*

I estimate that Meeting of Knowledges has brought to Brazilian higher music education a greater number of music genres than the sum of all those taught in the preceding 150 years, when the first institution of higher music education was established in this country. As of mid-2023, Meeting of Knowledges has spread to twenty universities across Brazil,[32] *with a further five or six planning to establish the program in the next twelve months; around 230 Masters from well over a dozen language groups have been involved, as well as around 120 partner-lecturers.*[33] *Recently, the model has been taken up by universities in Colombia, Ecuador, and Austria, tailored for each local context. At the University for Music and the Performing Arts in Vienna, for example, the program invites and enables newly-arrived immigrants, refugees, and members of excluded minorities to teach—propelling a curriculum that caters for, and drives, an increasingly diverse student population.*[34] *The potential for Meeting of Knowledges to be adapted for implementation in European and other universities around the world is also being explored.*[35]

Meeting of Knowledges holds educational benefits for students of all sociocultural backgrounds. Those from underrepresented and minoritized groups finally see (or can at least envisage) their own cultural histories, cultural practices, and knowledge systems being taught and learnt in an institutional context. This signals to these students that their cultures and knowledges are institutionally recognized and valued. It enables these students to explore their own musical and cultural identities and affinities in the course of their education, and to contribute their cultural knowledge to the educational conversation. In turn, this supports the participation, retention, and success of these students.[36] According to Bengala, until fairly recently, the younger people from his Maroon community were "timid" at the thought of applying for or attending university, but the mere knowledge that a senior from their own community had taught at university has given them courage.[37] The classroom, which had previously seemed foreign, had begun to look and sound familiar to them.

Concurrently, Meeting of Knowledges stimulates students from dominant social groups to critically reflect on their positionality and socialization into the web of unequal power relations in higher education. Through the program, these students may recognize, for instance, that their musical affinities have been shaped by narrow experiences of music or music education. Meeting of Knowledges is not about replacing Western music in the education or lives of these students, but rather about expanding their musical worlds. According to Jorge, one colonizing effect of teaching only Western music is that a primary affective bond is fostered exclusively with such music. Meeting of Knowledges allows students to develop new affective bonds with non-Western musical genres, building on the identification they already have with Western music.[38]

Meeting of Knowledges also begins to equalize hegemonic power relations in Westernized universities, where White academics have long presented as authorities on cultures to which they do not belong, dominating teaching and research about the music, cultures, and knowledges of "Others."[39] In these universities, understanding "Others" has typically entailed knowing about them through Western means, and in ways that never fully acknowledge them as thinking, knowledge-producing people.[40] In a widely circulated "Open Letter on Racism in Music Studies—Especially Ethnomusicology and Music Education," Black Caribbean American scholar, musician, and educator Danielle Brown argued that the ongoing domination of White voices in the educational conversation about Black, Indigenous, and People of Color "only leads to ideologies that support white supremacy and contribute to inequalities for BIPOC," and that Black, Indigenous, and People of Color "must be at the forefront of telling their stories until some sort of equity is reached."[41] Meeting of Knowledges provides one model to this end: in the program, those same people who teach their cultural practices in university classrooms are those who practice them in their everyday lives and in their communities. Curating their own stories, the Masters are free to pass on their knowledge in ways that align with the values and practices of their own cultures and communities. Rather than adopting Western pedagogical strategies that tend to promote disembodied, decontextualized, intellectual authority,[42] the Masters in Meeting of Knowledges nearly always choose embodied, holistic, contextualized, relational, creative, situated ways of learning and teaching, including musicking, dancing, art-making, games, storytelling, experiential learning, collaborative learning, and performance participation (see Figure 3.1).[43]

In welcoming the Masters as academic partners, and in accepting their diverse cultural, epistemic, and pedagogical practices and approaches, Meeting of Knowledges disrupts certain "rules" of academia, including

Figure 3.1 Bengala (center left) leads a representation of the *João do Mato* ceremony, a performance ritual of the Arturos community, with students of the Traditional Knowledges Program at Federal University of Minas Gerais (that university's iteration of Meeting of Knowledges; see www.saberestradicionais.org). This teaching experience appears in the film *Lá nas matas tem* (*Something in the woods*, 60', 2022, directed by César Guimarães and Pedro Aspahan, *Saberes Tradicionais*). Photo: Pedro Aspahan, 2022.

about who teaches what, and about what kind of knowledge holds authority. This is "counterstorytelling:" a means of attenuating the epistemic violence that has characterized Westernized music education for the duration of its modern history, of honoring experiential and embodied knowledge, and of advancing anti-racism, anti-oppression, and decolonization.[44] In presenting and exploring musical and cultural practices relationally rather than hierarchically within an institutional setting,[45] Meeting of Knowledges makes space for conversations among and between people (learners, Masters, academics, apprentices, and others) belonging to dominant and marginalized groups alike. In turn, this space-making signals to everyone that the institution values diverse ways of being, knowing, and doing—an "important priority in pedagogy that supports cultural sustainability," claim education scholar Renae Acton and colleagues.[46] On these grounds, ethnomusicologists Beverley Diamond and Salwa El-Shawan Castelo-Branco believe that Meeting of Knowledges represents a model for "a radical political transformation in ethnomusicology and in academia more broadly, changing the rules and protocols that define the discipline and our role as teachers, researchers and activists."[47]

At its core, Meeting of Knowledges is a coalitional project. It offers a way for Masters to cultivate, celebrate, and explore their cultural practices with apprentices and among their own communities; for academic partner-lecturers and institutions to collaborate and learn from local Masters and their communities; for students of all cultural backgrounds to learn alongside each other on an equal footing; for students to forge new affinities with the Masters and their communities and cultures; and for Masters across Brazil, as culture-bearers of historically excluded groups, to work together toward common decolonial goals.[48] Together, these groups are empowered and enabled to counteract entrenched hierarchies of institutionalized power: between university and community, theory and practice, and local and Western knowledge systems. Through its coalitional approach, Meeting of Knowledges embodies and builds on the legacy of Brazilian critical educator and philosopher Paulo Freire—especially Freire's "pedagogy of love," which humanizes teaching and learning, implements liberatory pedagogies, and works to emancipate oppressed peoples.[49]

*

Given the catastrophic cultural losses that have resulted from cultural colonialism and cultural hegemony the world over, it seems reasonable to suggest that cultural equity is important for cultural sustainability—even perhaps, in today's interconnected world, a necessary condition for it. Educational efforts to honor and respect all cultures and cultural practices, like Meeting of Knowledges, thus play an important role in cultural sustainability, in addition to their contributions to educational and epistemic justice. Referring to the Australian context, where 98 percent of First Nations performance traditions are estimated to have been lost since colonization,[50] Renae Acton and colleagues claim that cultural sustainability largely hangs on educational practices "valuing localised and nuanced understandings of Indigenousness and Indigenous knowledges."[51] Ethnomusicologists Clint Bracknell and Linda Barwick concur, contending that music endangerment and cultural marginalization will only be repaired when equitable relationships between Indigenous music-makers and music education institutions significantly improve.[52] Although these scholars refer specifically to First Peoples in Australia, their theories about the local importance of cultural equity for cultural sustainability hold true for peoples around the world.

So, even though Meeting of Knowledges is primarily driven by concerns relating to educational and epistemic justice, it has made—and continues to make—significant contributions to cultural equity, cultural justice, and cultural sustainability in at least three ways. First, it begins to shift the lifelong attitudes and behaviors of participating students who belong to the dominant cultural group. By providing these students with humanizing ways to learn about unfamiliar local musics and cultures, the program fosters empathy for social and cultural "Others." Bengala explains how through Meeting of Knowledges, he first entered the world of the university and that of the students (whose immediate interest and receptiveness to learning about his culture was "a great surprise" to him), "but then the students started to come and visit my Arturos community; they wanted to learn more about Congado."[53] Some of Bengala's former students have maintained contact with him and his community beyond their graduation from university, and have been eager to forge ongoing creative collaborations (a proposition that Bengala and his community have wholeheartedly welcomed).[54] As Bengala's experience suggests, learning directly and experientially from culture-bearers increases the likelihood that students from the dominant group will become allies, over time, for the people and cultural groups they learn about and with. These students may be more inclined to attend performances or cultural events involving diverse music practices from their region, having become at least a little familiar with those practices during their education. They may be more confident to creatively collaborate with people from local cultural groups other than their own. Those who go on to teach may feel more inclined and equipped to respectfully introduce their own students to culture-bearers, knowledges, and pedagogies from their local area, having had that educational experience themselves. All these behaviors, in turn, help sustain local cultural practices, as those practices become an integral and integrated part of a healthy, diverse cultural ecosystem that values, engages with, and nourishes them.

A second way in which Meeting of Knowledges contributes to cultural sustainability is by expanding broad societal awareness, understanding, and valuing of diverse local cultures and peoples. As the program has spread across Brazil (and beyond), generating a substantial body of educational resources, it has advanced cultural documentation and mapping, too. An "archive of traditional knowledges" is developing, not least via a series of books, published by the Institute of Inclusion in Higher Education and Research at the University of Brasília, written by Masters themselves or based on interviews and transcriptions of their classes, symposia, and workshops.[55] As communities liaise with universities about the cultural practices to be represented in the curriculum, institutional awareness of local cultural diversity develops. As Masters and their apprentices build trusting relationships with partner-lecturers, students, and their institutions, opportunities grow for new research, supervision, teaching, and public-facing creative collaborations.[56] And as public awareness and interest in Meeting of Knowledges grows, the visibility of the Masters' communities and cultures is further bolstered, resulting (among other things) in public performance invitations, local print media features and broadcast appearances, and representation at community-based cultural and educational events.[57] A wider societal awareness of, and appreciation for, local cultural practices helps create a stronger cultural ecosystem for those practices.

Third, Meeting of Knowledges supports cultural sustainability through its positive resonances for and within the communities whose cultures are represented. Several universities bestowed on participating Masters the title of *Doutor por Notório Saber* (Doctor by Acknowledged Higher Knowledge), a measure of considerable esteem given to individuals who are socially recognized as holding exceptional knowledge in an area.[58] Usually, the title is bestowed on highly educated individuals, but the majority of the Masters are either illiterate or have very little schooling—including Bengala, who completed four years of primary education[59] (and worked as a municipal gardener most of his life).[60] The decision in 2022 of the Federal University of Minas Gerais to grant Bengala the *Doutor em Música* (music doctorate) sent a clear and strong message about the value of his cultural knowledge and skills—not only to people outside of his community, but also to those within it. Bengala reflects:

> I cannot even explain how much this means. It is a great step, because my community is also empowered by my receiving this title. My community made this, they made me, I am part of them; I am forged by the strength of our culture. So this title of *Doutor por Notório Saber* affirms my community, too.[61]

According to Bengala, Meeting of Knowledges has raised the perceptions and prestige of cultural practices within the community of Arturos:

> Even in my own community, where Congado has so much strength, my community didn't always understand its value. This understanding grew immensely through Meeting of Knowledges. I didn't just go to visit universities: I taught at them, and one of those universities has given me the title of *Doutor por Notório Saber*. Because of this, Meeting of Knowledges has transformed the way my community thinks about its own practices.[62]

Just as Meeting of Knowledges affords Masters, apprentices, and their communities a means to share musical and other cultural knowledge with students and others beyond their own communities, it also motivates the recollection, consolidation, and transmission of cultural skills, knowledges, and practices within their communities of origin. Some Masters have involved their communities in the process of creating curriculum content and resources for the university classroom; others have taken their teaching materials back to their communities, using them to teach younger community members about their cultural practices. Observing the Masters receive wider recognition—and remuneration—for their cultural knowledge and skills provides an incentive for the younger generations to learn. Observing the positive community-based outcomes of Meeting of Knowledges, Congado groups and Afro-Brazilian communities elsewhere in Brazil have asked Bengala for guidance on how they could achieve similar ends. Bengala reflects:

> Meeting of Knowledges and my *Notório Saber* title has sent a message to other Congado groups, to Maroon people and poor people, to other Afro-Brazilian communities, that they too have the capability to do as we did—that with humility, and by paying attention to culture, they too can follow this path.[63]

Evidently, when localized cultural knowledge, practices, and skills are recognized and valued in educational and other social institutions in respectful, relational, and contextualized ways—that is, when cultural equity pertains—cultural strength and sustainability can benefit too.

*

In recognizing and seeking to dismantle the "dishonest curriculum"[64] that presents Western knowledge and ways of knowing as unquestioned truth, Meeting of Knowledges values, nourishes, and sustains local knowledges and ways of knowing. It is one example of how institutions of higher music education can act decolonially and simultaneously advance cultural equity and cultural sustainability. The successes of Meeting of Knowledges suggest that when universities avoid reinscribing the Western epistemic tradition as normative, the result can be what Cameroonian political theorist Joseph-Achille Mbembe calls a "pluriversity:"[65] anti-oppressive, anti-colonial, anti-racist educational processes and systems that advance educational justice, epistemic justice, cultural diversity, cultural equity, and cultural sustainability.

Meeting of Knowledges is a method and a theory of decolonization, because to decolonize is to act to transform the colonized environment inherited from past generations.[66] In a sense, it is also a decolonial movement—that is, a holistic and action-oriented endeavor to "rehumanize[e] the world."[67] Decolonizing higher education—that is, completely liberating it from oppressive systems and structures of power—demands huge shifts in power relations, worldviews, and the very structure of the system.[68] The path ahead is long, considering the entrenched structural inequalities and injustices that still exist in music education institutions across the world. But, as Maldonado-Torres urges, decolonial efforts should be approached not so much in a spirit of perfectionism than as "an attitude" that keeps individuals and groups open to growth, to corrections, and to the unfinished project that it represents.[69] Welcoming the Masters as teachers transforms the staff of music institutions. Their new courses transform the curriculum. In turn, these transformations challenge existing musical hierarchies and sensibilities, including the institutional prestige associated with certain musical genres. Over time, this brings about broader change in musical and cultural values. In this way, step by step, educational institutions will transform.[70]

And that transformation, when it is achieved, will mean that learning environments will cater fully for all learners and teachers—including students like Marina, whose story opened this chapter. It will mean that students' academic success or failure will no longer be predicated on cultural, social, or economic factors. It will mean that educational biases, oppressions, and inequitable practices will have been eliminated. The transformation of the institution will forge and strengthen relationships between diverse social and cultural groups, while allowing all groups to celebrate, share, sustain, and take pride in their distinct cultural identities and expressions. Reflecting like this on the characteristics of a "transformed" (decolonized) institution can help us more clearly envisage what a socially just education looks, feels, and sounds like—and to identify educational practices, policies, and pedagogies that move toward that vision.[71] As Meeting of Knowledges suggests, the future of higher music education (and music education more generally) surely lies in transformative, pluralistic educational approaches, where diverse cultural practices and epistemic approaches sit alongside each other on equal footing, engaging and interacting freely and without hierarchy. This is no easy mission, but emphatically worth pursuing nonetheless, given what is at stake: an educational and social order that recognizes and celebrates the full humanity of all people.

Figure 4.0 Saurav Moni performing at a Patachitra (scroll-painting) Fair, Pingla village, Medinipur district, West Bengal, November 2011. Used with permission.

Introducing: Saurav Moni

Born in the riverine village of Hingalganj on the Bangladeshi border, Saurav Moni spent his childhood surrounded by water and by the sounds of villagers singing while rowing boats or pedaling rickshaws. When he moved to Kolkata to study history at university, Saurav started singing to share the songs of his locality; only then did he come to know that the name of the genre of boat songs he loved was bhatiyali. *Returning to his rural homeland, Saurav realized that many of the old folk repertoires sung by boatmen, peasants, and wandering minstrels were being forgotten. He began to document, learn, and perform the diverse music of his wider region. In time, Saurav formed the band Majhi-Mallah ("Band of Boatmen"), comprising musicians mostly from rural Bengal, who use traditional Bengali instruments and folk genres to explore the imaginary and metaphorical journey of a group of boatmen traveling along the river from north to south Bengal.*

Through his involvement in the Rural Craft and Cultural Hubs, Saurav has led local music workshops and training programs for children and youth, performed bhatiyali *and other genres at all levels from the village through to the international, taught dozens of students, and released albums that fuse* bhatiyali *and other rural folk traditions with contemporary sounds. His workshops, performances, and recordings have revived regional and national interest in the folk music of West Bengal. Regarding* bhatiyali, *Saurav is credited with introducing the boat songs to urban audiences and popularizing them among urban youth, as well as stimulating renewed interest in the genre within its riparian heartland. Along with a handful of other practicing artists, he is largely credited with securing the contemporary survival of* bhatiyali.

With its connections to the river, Saurav considers bhatiyali *to be the ideal cultural vehicle for helping younger generations explore and express the relationships between water, land, life, and environment. He played a leadership role in the "Climate Wall,"[1] an educational project based in his village that mobilized local schoolchildren to respond practically and creatively to local threats arising from the climate crisis. Among the project outcomes are new* bhatiyali *songs, composed and performed by the schoolchildren.*

4

Music for Life and Livelihood

With Saurav Moni

The southern coastal area of the state of West Bengal in eastern India is home to the music tradition *bhatiyali*, a genre of folk songs that reflects the changing character of the rivers that cross the landscape (see ▶ video Example 4.1).[2] Sung by boatmen at the helm of their boat while flowing down the river at low tide, the songs reflect philosophically on life.[3] Their lyrics are often simple, telling local folktales and stories of daily life; sometimes they are metaphorical too, with elements of spirituality, mysticism, and expressions of love. Traditionally, the songs are accompanied by instruments: the four-stringed plucked *dotara*, bamboo flute, the drums *tabla* and *dhol*, and sometimes harmonium.[4] Once popular not only in the Sundarbans but widely across Bengal, *bhatiyali* has influenced other Bengali musical practices, including the more well-known Baul-Fakiri tradition (a confluence of humanist Hindu and Islamic philosophies).[5]

Bhatiyali is inseparable from its riparian origins in the Sundarbans, a vast delta area that lies at the Bay of Bengal (see Figure 4.1). Comprising over 530 square miles (over 130,000 hectares) of mudflats, agricultural land, and the largest area of mangrove forests in the world, the Sundarbans hold UNESCO World Heritage status for their ecological significance. The forests and waters are habitats for hundreds of species of birds, reptiles, amphibians, fish, and mammals. Water is the defining feature of this unique landscape, crossed by a shifting network of channels and tidal streams. For its roughly 4.6 million inhabitants, this ecologically rich, ever-changing natural environment presents both challenges and opportunities. Recalling his childhood in Hingalganj village, Saurav Moni recalls: "Living life in the salty marsh land and deltas of the Sundarbans was a harsh reality: [it was] single-crop land, [with] Royal Bengal tigers roaming around [and] crocodiles and snakes as neighbors; we earned our livelihood by risking [our] lives in gathering honey and fishing."[6]

Sounding Good. Catherine Grant, Oxford University Press.
DOI: 10.1093/oso/9780197698433.003.0005

Figure 4.1 Map of West Bengal, India.

West Bengal is part of the geopolitical and cultural region of Bengal, one of the most densely populated regions in the world. Bengal comprises most of Bangladesh, which is predominantly Muslim, and West Bengal, which is predominantly Hindu. By population, West Bengal's state capital, Kolkata (formerly Calcutta)—one-time capital of British India and former trading post of the East India Company—is India's seventh largest city. Since India's independence from British rule in 1947, West Bengal's economy has been largely driven by agriculture (transitioning in recent decades from subsistence to commercial farming) and small-to-medium enterprises.[7] Some aspects of its economy are strong, and it boasts an economic growth rate higher than the national average. However, compared with other Indian states, West Bengal has limited local employment opportunities and poor per capita income.[8] Its Human Development Index value is slightly lower than that of India as a whole,[9] and around 15 percent of its people still live below the poverty line.[10] More than 91 million people live in West Bengal; around two-thirds of those live rurally, where poverty rates are higher than in urban areas.[11]

Culturally and linguistically, West Bengal is diverse. English and Bengali are the languages of administration, and Bengali is both the official language and the main ethnolinguistic group. Among the many other languages spoken are Hindi, Urdu, Santali, Nepali, and Kurrkh (the language of the Indigenous Oraon people). Local folk practices abound, including the songs and dances of the Baul-Fakiri, Jhumur, and Bhawaiya traditions,[12] and folk dramas from the Sundarbans (like *Manoshar Bhasan*, in praise of the Goddess of Snakes, and *Bonbibi Pala*, which tells stories of seeking protection from tigers).[13] Other cultural practices of West Bengal include embroidery, pottery, conch-shell engraving, scroll painting, puppetry, metalwork, and strong literary and filmmaking traditions.[14] Musically, perhaps the best-known repertoire of West Bengal is that of *Rabindra Sangeet*, or "Tagore Songs," comprising over 2,000 songs written by Bengali Nobel laureate and polymath Rabindranath Tagore (1861–1941), which demonstrate influences from Hindustani (north Indian) classical, Carnatic (south Indian) classical, Western classical, and Bengali folk music traditions.

The folk genre *bhatiyali* was at its peak from the 1930s to the 1950s, when some of its singer-exponents achieved some level of recognition for their artistry.[15] In the second half of the twentieth century and into the twenty-first, the tradition declined in popularity. Factors in its demise included rising poverty, industrialization, the introduction of motorized boats, and generally changing ways of life in the Sundarbans (and across Bengal and India) that left folk practitioners and their communities with little scope for cultural performance and practice.[16] According to ethnomusicologist Anna Morcom, socioeconomic pressures on the practice of folk genres like *bhatiyali* continue today: across India, she writes, "a great range of 'folk' performers struggle to subsist or to have their art validated. They are increasingly poor, due to exclusionary forces based variously on caste/class, nationalism, or the uneven economic development of neoliberalism."[17] In the case of *bhatiyali* and other traditions of West Bengal, environmental disasters have also inhibited their vitality. One notable example is Cyclone Aila in 2009, which impacted an estimated 100,000 people in the Sundarbans, devastating the lives of many artists and causing some to permanently leave the region.[18] Much as the natural ecology of the Sundarbans is being reshaped by these continual social and environmental changes, Saurav says, "so too are the lives of folk artist practitioners."[19] In 2022, an estimated fifty *bhatiyali* practitioners were active in West Bengal, making it among the most endangered cultural practices of the region.[20]

*

Since 2000, the social enterprise Contact Base (trading as "Banglanatak dot com") has worked across India to foster inclusive and sustainable development through culture. In 2004, Contact Base began researching the causes of rural poverty in West Bengal, finding that cycles of marginalization and deprivation were detrimentally affecting people's lives, that many rural villages lacked employment opportunities, and that many inhabitants lacked employable skills.[21] Local enthusiasm for folk arts and crafts was often high, but the practice of them was generally perceived to be unskilled labor. Artists typically had low income, low literacy, little or no home sanitation, and were prone to migrate from their rural villages to urban centers for employment. The low socioeconomic status of artists was one factor in younger generations' disinclination to learn these cultural practices. A lack of public interest combined with reduced opportunities for performance and public exposure had led to deterioration in the knowledge and skill levels of practitioners, leaving these traditions in jeopardy.[22] Contact Base began to develop and trial a framework for socioeconomic development and cultural sustainability that would generate "an eco-system for revival and rejuvenation of traditional art skills as livelihood."[23] Preliminary outcomes for the thousands of participating artists were promising, including increases in artists' income, performance opportunities, collaborations, and prestige.[24]

From these foundations emerged "Art for Life," a model for poverty alleviation and social inclusion through the arts, especially intangible cultural practices (see ▶ video Example 4.2). Launched by Contact Base in 2011 (with financial support from the European Union), the Art for Life model engages three key strategies: safeguarding cultural practices through cultural mapping, inventorying, documentation, and education; equipping artists with skills and resources, including in marketing, business management, and teamwork; and rebranding villages as cultural hubs, involving village festivals, folk art centers, and cultural education and transmission activities.[25] Through these three pillars—focusing respectively on art, artist, and village—Art for Life aspires to create cultural ecosystems that advance both socioeconomic development and cultural sustainability.

Art for Life served as the framework for Contact Base's flagship project, Rural Craft and Cultural Hubs, carried out in partnership with UNESCO

New Delhi, and funded by the Department of Micro, Small and Medium Enterprises and Textiles of the state government of West Bengal. The project aimed "to revive and safeguard intangible cultural heritage and equip traditional artists with the wherewithal to build sustainable cultural enterprises."[26] Through the project, artists received training in creative, technological, business, and collaboration skills, and were supported to develop and launch cultural micro-enterprises. Local cultural practices represented in the project include several vocal and instrumental music genres, folk and ceremonial dances, theater genres, martial arts, oral storytelling, puppetry, pottery, bamboo craft, metalwork, doll- and mask-making, scroll-painting, and various weaving and stitching practices. The scale of the project across West Bengal has been considerable: its first phase (2013–2016) involved around 3,000 artists across ten traditional cultural practices. In its second phase (2016–2019), formalized as the Rural Craft and Cultural Hubs, the project engaged an estimated 12,000 artists across fifteen practices, including *bhatiyali*.[27]

If one aim of the project was to bolster the cultural and socioeconomic viability of intangible cultural practices in rural West Bengal, another was to explore how cultural tourism could contribute to sustainable development in that area. With two World Heritage sites—the Darjeeling Himalayan Railway (part of UNESCO's "Mountain Railways of India" inscription) and the Sundarbans—West Bengal already had a relatively strong tourist presence, both domestic and international.[28] Through the infrastructure of the Rural Craft and Cultural Hubs, some villages began to develop and implement cultural experiences and products for tourists, gradually evolving as cultural tourism destinations where visitors could learn directly from local artists about the histories and contemporary practice of music and other local cultural expressions. As sites of collaboration between local artists and local businesses, the Hubs became places where collectives of artists could develop, produce, showcase, and sell cultural products, from music recordings to local handicrafts. Word of mouth spread, and tourism grew. Several villages introduced activities to share and celebrate cultural practices among locals (see Figure 4.2), as well as establishing multi-day festivals, cultural heritage tours, and other cultural education opportunities that attracted visitors from across West Bengal, India, and abroad. Artists, researchers, and enthusiasts from elsewhere in India and abroad began to take up residencies with local artists, generating a need for local accommodation facilities. Some villages established Folk Art Centers, which provided visitor accommodation as well as serving as venues for Hub-related cultural demonstrations, workshops, and performances.[29]

Against several socioeconomic measures, the Rural Craft and Cultural Hubs have resulted in positive outcomes for participating artists and their communities. Musicians and other participating artists developed transferrable creative, business, and digital skills that increase their capacity to establish or maintain a stable income and fulfilling livelihoods into the future, within or outside of the cultural sector. (Saurav, for example, believes he developed his skills as a teacher and cultural influencer through his work with the Hubs;[30] see Figure 4.3). These transferrable skills have expanded artists' socioeconomic opportunities in other ways, too—such as by enabling their greater participation in the digital environment, as artists use social media and other online tools to promote their cultural practices and manage their cultural activities.[31] Several musicians secured paid national and international music residencies and festival performances via their involvement with the Hubs. According to Contact Base, between 2016 and 2019 the arts-related income of performing artists involved with the Hubs doubled (meaning that those artists became more economically self-reliant, and were more likely to be receiving fair remuneration for their activities); and although not necessarily attributable only to the Hubs, over that same period the number of performing artists who had electricity and sanitation in their homes increased by 24 and

Figure 4.2 *Bhatiyali* artist Bishnupada Sakar (center) leads a community workshop on *bhatiyali* in the Sundarbans as part of the activities of the Rural Craft and Cultural Hubs, June 29, 2017. Photo: Banglanatak.

39 percent, respectively.[32] In all these ways, the activities of the Hubs represent a form of "cultural action," a process that ethnomusicologist Rebecca Dirksen defines as "putting culture in the service of the community, especially in the advancement of certain community-defined goals."[33]

In 2020, travel restrictions resulting from the COVID-19 pandemic saw domestic and international tourist numbers in West Bengal plummet. Even during this time, however, artists capitalized on the infrastructure of the Hubs to generate income, establishing Facebook Live streams for their performances and building new online audiences and markets. As the restrictions eventually began to ease, cultural tourism associated with the Hubs, which included local tourism, recuperated faster compared with tourism that relied heavily on national and international visitors alone.[34] These circumstances drew the attention of the state government of West Bengal, which saw that the Hubs afforded its local communities a degree of economic resilience against external shocks like the pandemic, as well as holding potential to further progress sustainable development in West Bengal. The government therefore introduced new policies and legal and regulatory frameworks to better support artists and micro-enterprises, ensuring their smooth integration with the cultural tourism activities of the Hubs. In this way, the Hubs have helped advance,

Figure 4.3 Saurav Moni leads a workshop on *bhatiyali* in his home region of the Sundarbans as part of the activities of the Rural Craft and Cultural Hubs, May 9, 2022. Photo: Banglanatak.

in West Bengal, UNESCO's recommendation that governments around the world implement policies and other measures (in areas of training, employment, social security, mobility, income, and tax conditions) that improve the social, economic, and professional status of artists.[35]

By developing their knowledge, skills, and capacities through the Hubs, artists have been enabled to grow their income, social participation, and social mobility.[36] Communities have increasingly come to recognize the contribution of artists to their local societies and economies. As artists, women, people with disabilities, and those belonging to other marginalized groups began to participate in training and in the production and marketing of cultural products, community perceptions of these individuals as unskilled began to shift. Artists and their communities began to develop a shared sense of purpose and social identity, and looked for ways to support each other in their cultural and economic activities. By connecting cultural enterprises and villages across West Bengal under a unified framework, the Hubs began to strengthen social and economic networks within and between villages. As artists gained access to domestic and international markets through the infrastructure of the Hubs, their social participation and mobility grew; thousands participated in regional festivals, and over 150 traveled abroad (mostly to Europe and elsewhere in Asia) for performances and other cultural activities.[37] In those regions hosting a Hub, Contact Base believes that outward migration from rural to urban areas has reduced since the Hubs were established.[38] These social wellbeing, social inclusion, and social empowerment benefits of the Hubs are self-reinforcing in their cultural and poverty-alleviating potential: when people are healthier and happier, they are more economically productive and better able to participate in meaningful cultural and social lives.

*

Poverty is a matter of social justice in the conventional sense of that term: it pertains to the fair and equitable (or unfair and inequitable) social distribution of resources, wealth, and opportunities among people and populations around the world. Poverty affects people of widely varying backgrounds and life circumstances, and in a variety of ways. It is exacerbated by war and conflict (cf. Chapters 1 and 5 of this book), imperialism and colonization (Chapter 2), and environmental and climate crises (Chapter 6), and it affects people's capacity to access education (Chapter 3). Globally, poverty rates in rural areas are more than three times higher than those in urban areas—a statistic that is key to understanding the socioeconomic rationale for the Rural Craft and Cultural Hubs.[39] Poverty also disproportionately affects women and children, Indigenous peoples, people with disabilities, refugees and people seeking asylum, and people from other socially marginalized groups.[40] When the United Nations designated "No Poverty" as the first of its 2030 Sustainable Development Goals, it insisted that economic growth alone would be insufficient; poverty alleviation measures, it urged, must encompass strategies that address a wide range of social needs, including in areas of education, health, employment, and environmental protection.[41]

The United Nations defines "extreme poverty" as living on less than USD$2.15 per day, an amount that leaves people unlikely to be able to meet their basic needs, like access to food and water, sanitation, healthcare, and education. By this definition, over 8 percent of the global population—around 670 million people—live in extreme poverty.[42] This percentage has decreased over the past three decades, but the pace of change decelerated and then, in around 2022, reversed for the first time in a generation. That year, the economic fallout of the COVID-19 pandemic, escalating inflation, and the Russian–Ukrainian war (among other factors) are estimated to have tipped an additional 90 million people into extreme poverty compared with pre-pandemic projections for the year.[43]

A low income in absolute terms, however, is only one way to define poverty. Other, perhaps more nuanced, dimensions that have been used to describe and measure poverty include a lack of a secure or sustainable livelihood, an inability to meet one's basic needs, or having a considerably lower standard of wealth, resources or living than is held by most others in a given society ("relative" poverty).[44] Economist Amartya Sen influentially described poverty as a lack of at least one "freedom"—freedom of opportunity, for example, or freedom of political rights, or freedom to develop individual capacities.[45] For Haitian filmmaker and economist Kendy Vérilus, an interviewee in Rebecca Dirksen's study about cultural richness and economic poverty in the Caribbean nation of Haiti, "[p]overty refers to an absence of possibility, an absence of means. It's not about whether someone is living on less than one dollar each day. Instead, it's the degree of well-being one can achieve with a dollar per day."[46]

These diverse ways of thinking about poverty are positive developments: for much of the last century (and to some extent still today), research and policy tended to oversimplify poverty and stereotype those experiencing it. (National governments, for instance, have sometimes failed to recognize that people who meet certain definitions of "poor" do not always conceive of themselves in that way, nor necessarily want governmental intervention.) While still recognizing and seeking to alleviate the generally damaging effects of poverty on people's lives, recent research and policy better acknowledge that poverty affects individuals and societies in multidimensional and dynamic ways. Moreover, poverty alleviation strategies now usually conceive of poverty in a way that, at a minimum, integrates deficit- with strengths-based models: that is, these strategies attempt to account for the assets, not only the paucities, of the people in question.[47]

In such models, local arts and culture are often prominent strengths.[48] One example is that of Leweton village in Vanuatu (see Chapter 6), whose inhabitants are drawing on their cultural practices to meet their economic as well as cultural and environmental needs. Another is a community-driven sustainable cultural development alliance in the municipality of Lautém, Timor-Leste, which aims to empower communities to practice and economically benefit from their cultural expressions amid rapid socioeconomic change.[49] Further examples of how cultural practices can economically empower people emanate from the Cultural Heritage Tourism Initiative, a program of the Smithsonian Center for Folklife and Cultural Heritage in the USA that designs and implements sustainable community-centered cultural tourist experiences. During its pilot program in Armenia (2015–2021), the Cultural Heritage Tourism Initiative created over a hundred new music, dance, food, and craft experiences for tourists. Much like the Rural Craft and Cultural Hubs, the pilot involved inventorying and documenting local cultural practices, designing tourism experiences and enterprises around them, training artists and linking them with markets, and ensuring appropriate policy support. The pilot has since expanded to Tunisia and Bosnia and Herzegovina.[50]

In similar ways, hundreds, perhaps thousands, of initiatives around the world are strategically drawing on intangible cultural expressions to counteract the barriers that attend socioeconomic disadvantage.[51] Given generally higher rates of poverty among rural populations, many of these initiatives focus on the economic empowerment of those living rurally. Such initiatives challenge the globally conventional view of the rural economy being heavily reliant on the urban economy, with the former existing to supply labor and primary products for the latter. As Contact Base founder Amitava Bhattacharya observes, the Rural Craft and Cultural Hubs demonstrate that the "cultural resources of rural India have massive economic potential on their own."[52]

The path to socioeconomic empowerment through arts and culture is not, however, always practically or ethically straightforward. The Art for Life methodology (on which the Hubs are based) gives a sense of some challenges. To be successful, the model requires artists, their communities, policymakers and other decision-makers, and local cultural and tourism industries to be open to experimenting with a social enterprise approach to culture and development. The success of the model hangs on the commitment and energy of artists and their communities, as well as the ideological and practical support of government and non-government agencies (like Contact Base, UNESCO, and the West Bengal tourism department, in the case of the Hubs). Such a model seems likely to work best when such agencies actively support the ideas and innovations of the participating artists and their communities, while remaining attentive to the risk of institutional regulations and processes constricting project content and delivery.

The matter of project sustainability also looms. When project funding ended in December 2019, the Rural Craft and Cultural Hubs effectively suspended operations. Plans to continue certain of its activities beyond the formal end date were soon interrupted by the onset of the COVID-19 pandemic. Some activities resumed in early 2022, and at the time of writing, Contact Base conceives of the Hubs as an ongoing project, though the shape it will take in the future remains unclear. A UNESCO-commissioned evaluation of the Rural Craft and Cultural Hubs found that the participating communities were "eager to re-invest and sustain the benefits gained;" it also acknowledged that the move toward self-reliance and sustainability for any given cultural practice or program "can take considerable time."[53]

Regarding the ethical complexities of culture-based socioeconomic empowerment initiatives, it may be instructive to turn first to the case of that highly publicly profiled anti-poverty music initiative El Sistema, founded in Venezuela in 1975 and later expanding to several further countries. Providing state-financed Western classical music education to socially disadvantaged children, the key aim of the program was to improve the socioeconomic opportunities and life prospects of its participants. Over the years, El Sistema has claimed impressive social, educational, economic, and health outcomes for participating children and their families—and by some accounts, the musical excellence emanating from the project has helped reshape certain prejudices of the privileged social class about the capabilities of those living in poverty. However, especially in the last decade or so, El Sistema has encountered hefty criticism, from the charge of "deficit thinking" regarding the capabilities of the child participants, to that of cultural colonialism in the program's emphasis on Western classical music (and much more besides).[54]

It would be difficult to raise those two charges against the Rural Craft and Cultural Hubs, which feature local cultural practices rather than Eurocentric ones, and which aim to keep the creative and commercial control of those practices invested in the artists and communities themselves. The Hubs raise other ethical considerations, however. One is that of cultural appropriation or exploitation, a risk perhaps especially acute for cultural development initiatives involving "folk" traditions, whose repertoire is aurally transmitted and whose composers or creators are usually unknown. For these cultural practices, conventional Intellectual Property (IP) rights (like copyright) offer limited protection over how those practices are used, now or in the future. A brief anecdote relayed in the external evaluation of Hubs suggests how even the perceived risk of economic exploitation can affect culture-based development programs. An older folk music practitioner reported that, upon first learning of the possibility for his community's involvement in the Hubs, he thought: "Oh yes, 'they' [Contact Base] are just going to take our recording and then sell our songs without our knowing." (As he and his community came to better understand the project's aims and approaches, and to see the positive outcomes, trust grew.[55])

From the inception of the Hubs, Contact Base used several strategies to ensure that control remained vested, as far as possible, in the communities themselves, tailoring approaches to suit each setting, and listening carefully to local voices. Further, recognizing the need to protect the rights of artists and communities associated with the Hubs, between 2018 and 2021, Contact Base conducted a project to investigate how heritage-specific IP protection strategies could give artists and communities greater control over the commercialization of their cultural practices. Focusing on three West Bengali cultural practices represented by the Hubs—Baul–Fakiri music, Chau dance, and Patachitra scroll-painting—the project Heritage Sensitive Intellectual Property and Marketing Strategies: India generated codes of ethics, case studies, policy briefs, toolkits, and a suite of other resources for artists, consumers, tourists, researchers, policymakers, NGOs, and creative industry bodies that aim to protect and safeguard the rights of artists.[56] Contact Base intends for these resources to be transferable across settings in India and beyond.

A further risk in communities regarding their music and other cultural expressions as cultural property marketable for tourists is the conflation of cultural and economic value—a conflation with potentially unsustainable consequences in cultural sustainability terms.[57] When cultural practices are transformed into commercial products for economic profit, their social functions and contexts change, as do the constructs and values that underpin them. Over time, artists and communities may question the cultural integrity and cultural value of the "sanitized" versions of their cultural practices adapted for tourists in the name of economic development,[58] which may bear little resemblance to their non-commoditized forms. Ethnomusicologist Helen Rees provides a case study of how the rise of the tourist industry in China from the late 1970s significantly changed folk arts practice, leading to the "cleaning up" of folk music genres and the loss of cultural meaning in the processes of commercialization.[59] (She also identifies various beneficial outcomes of rising cultural tourism, like wider recognition and appreciation of ethnic minority groups, cultural development, and economic gain to those groups.) Rebecca Dirksen raises further tensions in this regard: "Can seeming economic poverty be balanced against so-called cultural richness? Can the domains of economy and culture be reconciled as mutually useful? Specifically, can culture be exploited to enhance daily life and improve material existence?"[60]

As regards the Rural Craft and Cultural Hubs, some music genres have certainly undergone, and continue to undergo, significant changes to cater for tourist and outsider tastes, and to meet the requirements of the stage or festival circuit. However, as music education scholar David Hebert notes, the risk of cultural practices being unsustainably exploited for profit is lesser for those cultural initiatives where decision-making power remains vested with musicians and communities (compared with externally-led initiatives, such as might be prompted by the profit-driven music industry).[61] Furthermore, especially in the case of endangered genres like *bhatiyali*, their repurposing for cultural tourism (or some other socioeconomically profitable purpose) may be their best, or even only, prospect for a viable future. Another rejoinder to the concern about commercialization is a utilitarian one: if musicians and their communities choose to repurpose a music genre (like *bhatiyali*) for cultural tourism such that it no longer holds its "original" cultural value, at least the genre grows in economic value to them—and surely practitioners and their communities should have principal say in whether the cultural or economic value of a cultural practice takes precedence for them at any given time. But this functional argument may sometimes be moot in any case, since these two "values" are not always, or necessarily, in tension. Especially as artists and communities grow their socioeconomic capacity and resilience (through the arts and culture or in other ways), often they are thereby simultaneously cultivating the wherewithal to nurture both the cultural and economic value of their cultural practices.

*

This leads to the question of how cultural sustainability and economic poverty interrelate. Perhaps most obviously, the vitality of cultural practices simply depends on the socioeconomic capacity of artists and others within their community to engage in them.[62] Cultural participation often requires material resources: musical instruments and equipment, costumes or other paraphernalia, suitable performance spaces, perhaps an internet-connected device for creating and disseminating artistic products.[63] Sometimes, artists may bear the cost of these materials, potentially preventing those with fewer financial resources from engaging in cultural production to the same degree as those with more. In other instances, the financial burden of cultural participation may be shared across a community. Then, cultural vitality—especially as represented in communal cultural activities such as festivals, performances, rituals or ceremonies, and community events—depends on the economic circumstances of the community at large. Ethnomusicologist David Harnish offers the example of Lombok, Indonesia, where, in times of hardship, village communities have been compelled to sell their sets of shadow puppets or *gamelan* musical instruments to raise money for food for the residents.[64] Clearly, limited economic resources and capacity—not only of individuals, but of whole communities too—can act as barriers to a vibrant cultural life.[65]

This phenomenon exemplifies what ethnomusicologist Stefan Fiol terms *cultural poverty*: the reduction or absence of the means for people to express and engage in cultural practices.[66] The COVID-19 pandemic illustrates how cultural poverty can intertwine with socioeconomic (and health) challenges. In the first months of the crisis, cultural activities and performances were cancelled en masse around the world, including in West Bengal, out of concern for public health. Public health orders restricting artists and audiences from engaging in communal cultural activities quickly became entangled with the economic dimensions of poverty. Income and employment for musicians became precarious, especially for those (including many involved with the Rural Craft and Cultural Hubs) who had generated a high proportion of their income from live performances or collective music-making activities, like workshops or teaching. In 2020, the pandemic precipitated the loss of over 10 million jobs globally in the cultural and creative sectors.[67] The World Economic Forum estimates that in the first five months of the pandemic alone, revenue from global music industry performances dropped from over $50 billion to around half that.[68] Income and employment across many other sectors were destabilized too, reducing the economic capacity of the general population to financially support the arts and culture, even via non-live means (like purchasing recordings or attending paid livestream events). These circumstances surrounding the pandemic illustrate how the socioeconomic situation of local communities is not the only economic factor in the vitality and sustainability of "small," local cultural practices: much wider economic conditions also play a role.

In cases where economic poverty diminishes people's capacity to engage in musical or other cultural activities over a sustained period, the sustainability of cultural practices may come into jeopardy. Music scholar James Burns describes the economic hardship confronting Southern Ewe dance-drummers in Ghana: although appreciated by the broader population, their social contribution has been primarily acknowledged in non-financial ways, making it difficult for the artists to survive and to maintain their cultural practices in a cash-based society.[69] Even in wealthy Western countries, musicians may face relative socioeconomic hardship or income instability that jeopardizes their sustained livelihoods in the arts. (In my own country, Australia, the average income artists generate from their art places them below the poverty line.[70]) In some societies, the social prestige that artists garner for their artistry and creative skills—sometimes attracting high media attention, especially in the West—is not matched by the level of financial return that makes "artist" a lucrative, or even viable, livelihood. In turn, this can adversely affect the sustainability of the arts and even the arts sector at large, as some artists seek alternative, more stable livelihoods and income sources.

In the West, being a musician is generally viewed as a socially interesting livelihood, even if a low-earning one, but in other parts of the world—including much of rural West Bengal—musicians have historically experienced both low social status and low capacity to earn a livelihood. In these contexts, music-making may not generally be perceived as an acceptable, admirable, or sufficient source of employment or income, and this affects the capacity of musicians to practice their art or to earn sustainable livelihoods from doing so.[71] One example is the improvised bardic practice of *chrieng chapei*, one of the Cambodian genres promoted by the Khmer Magic Music Bus (see Chapter 1). Historically, playing the lute *chapei* was considered appropriate for, and within the capabilities of, people who were blind, who were therefore able to reap a modest income through street performances. For much of the twentieth century, the *chrieng chapei* tradition relied almost completely on these individuals for its perpetuation[72]—an example of how, in certain settings or for certain music genres, socioeconomic disadvantage can facilitate, rather than impede, cultural participation. However, the ongoing stigma surrounding the *chapei*, a musical instrument and cultural practice so closely associated with both poverty and disability, is a primary reason for its precarious contemporary situation. (In 2016, UNESCO deemed it "in need of urgent safeguarding."[73]) In West Bengal, Saurav Moni believes that, especially prior to the work of the Rural Craft and Cultural Hubs, the social stigmatization and marginalization experienced by folk musicians—who were typically members of lower social castes—made it difficult for them to thrive.[74] In turn, this affected their capacity to practice, teach, learn, and otherwise promote their traditions.

If economic poverty often jeopardizes cultural sustainability, alleviating poverty can benefit it. The cultural sustainability outcomes of the Rural Craft and Cultural Hubs have perhaps not been as extensively evaluated as the socioeconomic ones, but multiple indicators suggest that the Hubs are having positive effects on the practice and sustainability of folk traditions in West Bengal.[75] Practically, the Hubs have provided much-needed infrastructure and resources (like musical instruments, physical spaces, and technology) for the documentation, practice, and intergenerational transmission of cultural practices.[76] Through the project, over 1,800 folk songs have been documented—an estimated 1,000 *Baul*, 250 *jhumur*, 450 *bhawaiya*, and 100 *bhatiyali* songs[77]—forming an important resource for current and possible future efforts to maintain and revitalize these genres. Musicians and other artists have been supported to develop curricula to help them teach folk traditions to visiting outsiders and local youngsters, and these curricula form another resource that supports the viability of the cultural practices they relate to.[78] In a further promising sign for sustainability, artists associated with the Hubs, including Saurav Moni, are adapting musical traditions for contemporary contexts: Saurav's band *Majhi-Mallah* fuses folk genres with contemporary "world music" sounds (see ▶ video Example 4.3), and a Coke Studio video featuring Saurav "recreates" a *bhatiyali* song "in a mellow rock and reggae groove yet retaining its folk tune" (see ▶ Example 4.4). As artists innovate these genres to make them better suit the stage, festival scene, and tourist taste, cultural practices like *bhatiyali* whose original popularity, contexts, or functions have waned, are given a new lease of life.

Perhaps the Hubs' greatest contribution to cultural sustainability in West Bengal, however, is simply to provide rural artists and communities with a social and economic motivation to engage, or re-engage, with folk practices. Younger generations have a social and economic reason to learn, and older generations to teach. In itself, this has led to a degree of revival of certain traditions (like *bhatiyali*) and musical instruments (including the stringed *sarinda* and *dotara*).[79] As artists share their artistry at all levels from the village to the international, they gain greater social recognition within their communities; in turn, this has lifted the prestige associated with folk practices and practitioners. Local, regional, national, and international "consumers" of these cultural practices have grown, raising the chances that these practices will have a sustainable future. The profiling of the Hubs in the mass media, the domestic and international tourist industry, and the regional and international cultural sector has helped educate policymakers and other stakeholders about the rich diversity of cultural practices across West Bengal and the role those practices can play in sustainable socioeconomic development. This greater awareness has flowed into new state governmental policies that support the secure livelihood of artists and the sustainability of the cultural practices themselves.

As Rebecca Dirksen has argued, putting culture at the service of a community's socioeconomic goals—taking "cultural action," in her terms—"has potential as a low-cost, high-impact, locally defined economic model to development, providing a pathway for the slow climb out of poverty."[80] It is the central premise of this chapter that cultural approaches to poverty alleviation can have cultural benefits as well as economic ones. The Hubs demonstrate how cultural action advances cultural rights:[81] that is, how cultural action grows the capacity of artists and their communities to sustain their cultural practices and pass them on to future generations. If the Rural Craft and Cultural Hubs tell us anything about the connections between economic poverty and culture, it must be that cultural sustainability and poverty alleviation can be mutually reinforcing.

*

The success of the Rural Craft and Cultural Hubs has attracted wide national and international attention, from an endorsement by Indian Prime Minister Narendra Modi (who publicly encouraged people to visit the Hubs)[82] to a commendation by the United Nations World Tourism Organization (UNWTO).[83] By demonstrating how "poor" people from rural areas can generate thriving lives and livelihoods through culture, the Hubs are helping change widespread preconceptions about the capabilities of such people and their communities. Through their profile, they are also raising national and international awareness about the social, economic, and cultural benefits of strengths-based, cultural approaches to reducing poverty. The Hubs exemplify how music and other cultural expressions can be integrated into socioeconomic development initiatives in a way that is meaningful and sustainable for local communities. They demonstrate how such approaches can help pursue two important goals: the sustainable future of local cultural practices, and economic justice.

The Hubs hold high potential as a model for projects in other contexts, in India and beyond. Contact Base recently launched a new project in the western Indian state of Rajasthan, modelled on the Hubs and their Art for Life methodology. In collaboration with UNESCO New Delhi and the Rajasthan government tourism department, *Promoting Intangible Cultural Heritage (ICH) and Developing Cultural Tourism in Jodphur, Barmer, Jaisalmer and Bikaner Districts in Rajasthan* aims to promote the performing arts and handicrafts of Rajasthan's western desert region through responsible, community-led cultural tourism. A preliminary evaluation carried out for UNESCO showed promising socioeconomic and cultural outcomes (Gupta 2021, 18–19).

Music and other intangible cultural practices can play a distinctively human-centered role in reducing poverty and boosting the socioeconomic prosperity of individuals and communities, as the Rural Craft and Cultural Hubs demonstrate. Those cultural practices can reduce poverty in several of its dimensions, enhancing the health and wellbeing, freedoms, capabilities, and capacities of individuals and societies. They can build transferable skills that enable people to secure employment and generate income, whether within or outside of the cultural sector. They can contribute not only to the improved livelihood circumstances of individuals but also to a thriving local economy; in turn, this further improves the socioeconomic conditions of individuals and their communities. They can drive sustainable economic growth by creating employment, boosting tourism, strengthening creative industries, building community capacity, and enabling communities, cultures, and regions to become more visible in the national and international arenas.[84] They can advance social and political resistance against the systemic disadvantage and other societal barriers that arise from poverty. By helping artists recognize their potential to improve their lives and those of their community, projects like the Rural Craft and Cultural Hubs align with a "capabilities" approach to poverty reduction.[85]

The cultural sustainability gains from integrating culture into poverty alleviation and socioeconomic development efforts are also strong. The Rural Craft and Cultural Hubs illustrate how cultural approaches to socioeconomic development create the conditions in which cultural practices can flourish. When the cultural sector offers artists like Saurav Moni the potential to build livelihoods from their cultural practices, the demand for learning those art forms grows. This increases the demand for teaching, further increasing the avenues for generating income through cultural practice.[86] When the cultural practices and cultural ecosystem of a community are strong, artists have the best chances of developing a sustainable livelihood. Especially in contexts of socioeconomic disadvantage, it makes sense for cultural sustainability efforts to not only support cultural practices directly but also to attend to the "cultural soil" around them, including the socioeconomic wellbeing of culture-bearers and the cultural ecosystem at large.[87] As communities and regions achieve a socioeconomic situation in which people have the resources and capacity to engage with cultural practices, those practices are able to thrive. Empowering artists to develop, implement and maintain sustainable, income-generating cultural enterprises has dual benefit, then: it supports sustainable economic growth and sustainable cultural lives, with each of these working in the service of the other.

Figure 5.0a Violeta Ruano Posada. Used with permission.

Introducing: Violeta Ruano Posada

A specialist in the music of the Bidhân region of northwest Africa, Spanish researcher, writer, and musician Violeta Ruano Posada (PhD) has spent over a year living and working with the Saharawi people of Western Sahara. In the refugee camps in southwest Algeria, Violeta collaborated with local Saharawi cultural authorities, non-government arts organizations, and the Saharawi people on projects that have promoted Saharawi music, culture, and the Saharawi cause. Her doctoral research at the University of London's School of Oriental and African Studies (2012–2015) investigated the relationship between music, culture, resistance, and exile for the Saharawi people. In partnership with the British Library and the Saharawi Ministry of Culture, Violeta led Portraits of Saharawi Music *(2013–2014), a collaborative project (featured in this chapter) supporting the Saharawi people to document and preserve their musical heritage, and promote it to an international audience. Since then, Violeta has been involved with establishing music education and empowerment programs for Saharawi children and adults through the non-government organization Sandblast.*

Now returned to Spain, Violeta remains an advocate for Saharawi music and culture. She reflects:

> *My involvement with the Saharawi people and their music, culture, and struggle was, from the beginning, about justice and human rights. When I first learnt as a university student about the historical politics of the Saharawi struggle, I couldn't believe that I knew nearly nothing about my own country's colonial history. Throughout the following years, my research projects and other collaborations with the Saharawi people were a way for me to offer them a platform for them to use as they liked. I noticed that when Saharawi people talked about music and culture, they forgot about their personal struggles, and remembered why they were fighting, and that was really magical to see. This is why I believe that Saharawi music is inextricably linked with their human rights: for the Saharawi people, making themselves heard through music, through culture, is their way of telling the rest of the world: we are here.*[1]

Figure 5.0b Mohamed Sleiman Labat. Used with permission.

Introducing: Mohamed Sleiman Labat

Mohamed Sleiman Labat is a visual artist, filmmaker, and writer, born and raised in the Saharawi refugee camps in the hamada *desert, Algeria. His multidisciplinary arts practice investigates the political, cultural, social, and environmental issues that affect his Saharawi community and the world at large. Mohamed writes:*

> *My art draws upon the past and present life of the Saharawi people. I've been exploring these interconnected topics through different visual arts, films, writing and community-based art. After graduating from Batna University, Algeria, I returned to Samara Refugee Camp to help support my family and community with the arts and education I received. In 2016, I built Motif Art Studio in Samara Camp (www.motifartstudio.com), an art space built entirely from discarded materials; the studio is now a creative hub for art creation and art education. My art practice also includes collecting and preserving the oral heritage of the Saharawi. In 2015, Sam Berkson and I co-authored* Settled Wanderers, the Poetry of Western Sahara, *the first collection of Saharawi poems to be translated into English. In 2020, Motif Art Studio published* Nomadic Seeds, *an artist book I co-authored with Pekka Niskanen, written in English and Hassānīya, the oral language of the Saharawi.*[2]

For Mohamed, "art is not for entertainment; art has a mission to get us to experience things in a way that helps us ask questions, solve problems, create abundance, team up with each other, learn from one another, and enjoy what we have been offered in this short journey we call life."[3]

5

Music for a Desert Homeland

With Violeta Ruano Posada and Mohamed Sleiman Labat

On November 6, 1975, some 350,000 Moroccan civilians, backed by the government and military, marched into Western Saharan territory in northwest Africa and claimed it as part of Morocco.[4] Over a period of months, as the Moroccan army attacked, around half the indigenous Saharawi[5] population of Western Sahara—somewhere between 40,000 and 50,000 people—fled across the border into neighboring Algeria.[6] Near the southwest Algerian town of Tindouf, in the harsh *hamada* landscape of the Saharan desert, they set up camps (*wilayas*) (see Figure 5.1). In February the following year, with Algerian backing, the Saharawi people proclaimed an independent Western Saharan nation they called the Saharawi Arab Democratic Republic (SADR), which they then proceeded to govern in exile from the camps (see Figure 5.2).

For centuries, the Saharawi people had lived in nomadic and pastoral kinship groups or "tribes" (*qabâʿil*) extending across the vast arid territory of northwest Africa they called Trab el-Bidhân, which encompasses Western Sahara, Mauritania, and parts of Morocco, Mali, and Algeria.[7] Western Sahara came under Spanish colonial control in 1884, leading to rapid urbanization and modernization of Saharawi society. By the mid-1960s, Spain had accepted the principle of self-determination for the Saharawi people, though it procrastinated in organizing the referendum that could bring it about. Not coincidentally, Saharawi nationalism intensified in the 1970s, a time that also saw Spain's intensified exploitation of Western Sahara's natural resources, including its plentiful phosphate deposits, iron ore, and coastal fishing.[8] In 1973, the Saharawi people launched the Polisario Front, a mostly student-led liberation movement that demanded greater economic and political rights for Saharawi people—and above all, independence from Spanish rule. When Morocco invaded two years later, the existence and vigor of the Polisario Front was a major reason for Spain's near-immediate relinquishment of its colonial control over Western Sahara.

Sounding Good. Catherine Grant, Oxford University Press. © Oxford University Press 2025.
DOI: 10.1093/oso/9780197698433.003.0006

Figure 5.1 View of Boujdour refugee camp near Tindouf. Credit: Violeta Ruano Posada. Reprinted from Ruano Posada (2019). CC BY-SA 4.0 via Wikimedia Commons.

So Spain left, and Morocco came. In the 1980s, Moroccan forces built a 2,700-kilometer-long minefield-flanked defensive wall running roughly north to south through Western Sahara. The Moroccan Western Sahara Wall (or "Berm Wall") separated those Saharawi who had stayed in Western Sahara from those who had fled, and effectively brought around three-quarters of Western Saharan territory under Moroccan control. With heavy fighting interspersed with periods of relative calm, the war between the Moroccan army and the Polisario Front would continue for sixteen years. A ceasefire was finally negotiated in 1991, when the two sides agreed to resolve the territorial dispute through a United Nations-brokered referendum on independence. For its part, the UN had long backed the "inalienable right" of the Saharawi to self-determination and independence; during its General Assembly the previous year, with specific reference to Western Sahara, it had adopted a resolution titled *Importance of the Universal Realization of the Right of Peoples to Self-Determination and of the Speedy Granting of Independence to Colonial Countries and Peoples for the Effective Guarantee and Observance of Human Rights.*[9] Despite the 1991 agreement, the UN's efforts to implement the referendum on the independence of Western Sahara have not yet come to fruition: at the time of writing, its mandate to support a referendum has been extended over fifty times.[10]

Thus, after nearly fifty years, the Saharawi people are still seeking independence and self-determination. They have had (and continue to have) limited

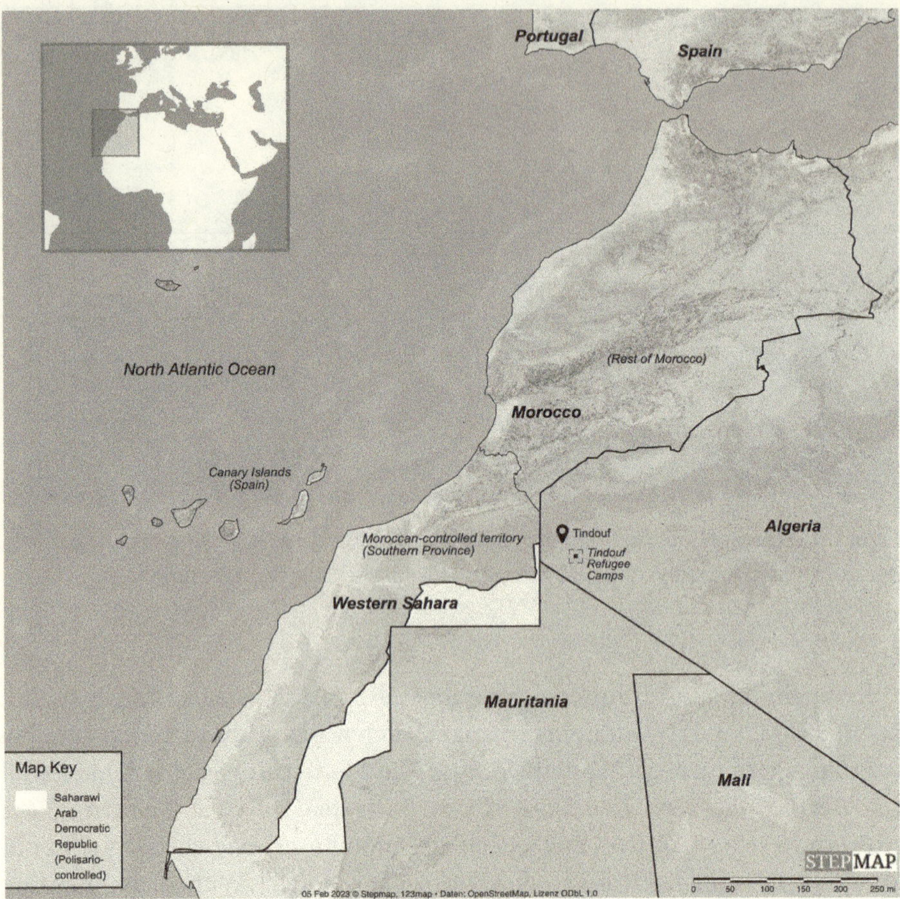

Figure 5.2 Polisario-controlled Saharawi Arab Democratic Republic (SADR) of Western Sahara, and the location of the Tindouf refugee camps in Algeria, the site of its government in exile.

access to conventional methods of seeking justice, for reasons including the contested status of the SADR as an internationally recognized state, the challenges presented by governing it as refugees in exile, and the many social and legal impediments that attend forced displacement.[11] Those more than 600,000 Saharawi people who remain in Moroccan-occupied Western Sahara[12] are treated, at best, as minority second-class citizens. Many have endured—and continue to endure—a multitude of human rights violations, including "disappearances," arrest and imprisonment, intimidation and torture, withdrawal of education and work opportunities, withholding of medical treatment, cultural repression, and the abuse of laws in such a way that excludes, discriminates against, and oppresses them.[13] Those living in the

Tindouf refugee camps in Algeria face multidimensional challenges too, albeit different ones: limited access to education, employment opportunities, and health services; water and electricity shortages; extreme weather conditions; and reliance on international aid for food, shelter, and medical care, among others. The matter is gendered: of the more than 173,000 people in the camps, around 80 percent are women and children.[14]

The hardship of life in the Tindouf camps and the persecution of those who remain in Moroccan-occupied Western Sahara have given rise to a third group of Saharawi people: those who have sought asylum further afield—many in Spain, Western Sahara's former colonizer. Both those who flee from Moroccan-occupied Western Sahara and those who feel compelled to leave the Tindouf camps (the latter displaced twice over) face a difficult and often dangerous journey abroad. For those who safely reach Spanish (or other) land, their Saharawi national identity may not officially be recognized, due to the internationally contested status of the SADR (see map Example 5.1 ▶).[15] While Spain allows people it considers stateless to claim asylum, this can be an inordinately protracted process. Work and travel rights are restricted while claims are in process, meaning that Saharawi people are prohibited from visiting family in the Tindouf camps (or elsewhere) during that time.[16] Even for those ultimately granted asylum, that status is accompanied by considerable social barriers, as in so many countries around the world—from curtailed work rights and temporary residency permits through to limited access to legal aid and other services.

Back in Western Sahara, the political situation remains unstable, and the trajectory unclear. Detractors of the Polisario Front have suggested that the liberation movement is "caught up in a revolutionary vision that may no longer be viable,"[17] especially given heightened international concerns about stability and security in the region. The Saharawi situation remains only minimally visible on the international arena—partly a result of Morocco persistently blocking international media, independent researchers, and other countries' government representatives from entering occupied Western Sahara.[18] In their policy brief to the European Council on Foreign Relations (ECFR) in 2021, Hugh Lovatt and Jacob Mundy opined that "self-determination for the Sahrawi people appears more remote than when MINURSO [the United Nations Mission for the Referendum in Western Sahara] was first launched in 1991."[19]

In November 2020, the ceasefire between Morocco and the Polisario Front broke down after twenty-nine years, when Moroccan troops crossed into a UN-patrolled buffer zone to remove unarmed Saharawi demonstrators.[20] The following month, contravening international law, then-US President Donald

Trump recognized Morocco's claim to Western Sahara (a political maneuver made in exchange for Morocco establishing full diplomatic ties with Israel), marking the first time any nation recognized Morocco's sovereignty over Western Sahara.[21] A further setback to the Saharawi cause came in March 2022, when Spain yielded to Morocco's claims to sovereignty over Western Sahara. The collapse of the ceasefire in 2020 has intensified Morocco's watchfulness and repression of the Sahrawi people in occupied areas,[22] and Amnesty International has since recorded human rights violations in the form of torture or other ill treatment against dozens of Saharawi activists, journalists, human rights defenders, and children.[23] Across the Algerian border in the Tindouf camps, the effects of the COVID-19 pandemic, the Israel–Gaza and Russia–Ukraine conflicts, and the global rise in food and fuel prices are jeopardizing humanitarian support for the Saharawi refugee people, who are facing increased food insecurity and malnutrition.[24] Meanwhile, the political impasse continues.

*

Songs, storytelling, poetry, and other oral traditions have been an important part of Saharawi culture for centuries. Saharawi artist Mohamed Sleiman Labat emphasizes the importance of poetry to Saharawi culture, and its intimate connection with song.[25] A rich repertoire of Saharawi spiritual songs (*medeh*) has long held the function of praising the Prophet Mohammed (the Saharawi being predominantly Muslim of Arab-Berber or Moorish descent), and *thaydin* songs have long been a way to remember and share epic tales and war stories. In nomadic times, the Saharawi people drew on *atlal* songs (about the landscape) to navigate and carry knowledge about the territory they roamed, looking for water and pasture for animal herding.[26] Another genre, *haul* (or *el hawl*), traditionally accompanied daily activities, weddings, and other festivities; it employs a modal system (*azawaan*) that dates to at least the sixteenth century.[27] *Haul* features poetic lyric forms in the variety of Arabic known as Hassānīya, the language of the Saharawi people, as well as distinctively Saharawi rhythms and instruments (especially the four-stringed lute *tidinit* and calabash harp *aardin*).[28] These instruments notwithstanding, Saharawi music-making was primarily vocal: as Mohamed explains, as a nomadic people, "you could only own what your camel could carry."[29]

Performing *haul* and other musical genres was customarily the domain of the *iggâwen*, professionalized hereditary musicians of low social status who were hired for their services, like the *griots* of other Western African cultures.[30] Historically, *iggâwen* travelled from one nomadic camp to another throughout the Trab el-Bidhân region. Most commonly, *iggâwen* frequented the permanent settlements of the south (now Mauritania), where both money and resources were found in greater supply than in the north (now Western Sahara), where people were almost exclusively nomadic.[31] Still today, some Saharawi cultural practices are similar to, and in certain ways indistinguishable from, those of Mauritania. When opportunity permits, Saharawi musicians living in the Tindouf camps sometimes still travel to Mauritania for paid performances at weddings and other social events, making the most of the greater financial opportunities and freedoms there.[32]

In Western Sahara, through the nine decades of Spanish colonization (1884–1975), social contexts and functions for Saharawi performance traditions shifted. By the early 1970s, Saharawi activists for the Polisario Front were adapting the lyrics of well-known Saharawi songs, especially *haul*, to propel the revolutionary and decolonial cause. No longer confined to specialized families of *iggâwen*, music-making became a predominantly political act. Now that nearly everyone was singing or making music for the political struggle, the social stigma of being a musician began to weaken. At the same time, longstanding conventions of musical patronage were shifting: it became considered shameful for musicians, *iggâwen* or not, to accept payment for performing.[33] In addition to economic implications, the heightened emphasis on the political cause had gender implications for musical (and other cultural) practices too: breaking with prior codes of modesty, women were encouraged and motivated to join the revolutionary activities, including public acts of political expression through poetry and song.[34] Sometimes these activities would be carried out clandestinely, regardless of gender: revolutionary songs would be performed at secretive social events, for example, or recorded and distributed on smuggled cassette tapes, with the goal of rousing more Saharawi people to join the cause.[35]

Following Morocco's invasion of Western Sahara and the displacement of tens of thousands of people to the refugee camps in Algeria, traditional *haul* continued to be taught and learnt in the camps to some extent, and spiritual *medeh* were still practiced too.[36] But the focus of musical activity was the new revolutionary genre of songs, which became known as *nidal* ("struggle"). *Nidal* served to promote a national ideology, to rally commitment to the revolution, to help the Saharawi people better understand their political situation, and to encourage and inspire those fighting at the front.[37] In the camps, the newly established SADR Ministry of Culture formed and supported groups dedicated to performing *nidal*. Over time, *nidal* became institutionalized as the Saharawi national musical genre: it began to be performed in social and official contexts, featured on local radio in the camps, and even supported through regular *nidal* competitions.[38] Its practitioners introduced Western instruments (including keyboards, drum kits, and electric guitar), as the *haul* foundations of the genre became fused with a more global and contemporary aesthetic, symbolic of the revolution.

In this way, the trajectory of *nidal* (and indeed of *haul*) in recent decades must be understood in the context of the development and promulgation of a Saharawi social and political discourse, a "liberation struggle" through which a national consciousness is forged.[39] Amid the rising nationalist sentiment of the 1960s and early 1970s, old Saharawi traditions took on new meaning, as the people drew on pre-colonial cultural practices to create a distinct syncretic music genre. At the same time, a new way of thinking about musical expression arose, in which music was never merely entertainment but always emphatically contributed social, cultural, political, and nationalist value to the causes of decolonization, independence, and self-determination for Western Sahara. In the nearly five decades since the Moroccan invasion, *nidal* has continued to evolve in response to changing political and socioeconomic realities. Following the 1991 ceasefire, for example, the tone of its lyrics shifted to reflect the increasingly diplomatic and peacefully resistant political tactic of the Polisario Front.[40] In the late 1990s and through the 2000s, promoted by Spanish music label Nubenegra, it became commercialized as world music and garnered an international following.[41] At the time of writing, *nidal* endures as a vibrant musical genre—as does the idea of it necessarily serving a political end. Contemporary *nidal* songs continue to reflect contemporary Saharawi political and social concerns, including national unity and the ongoing struggle for human rights.

Especially in the last couple of decades, Saharawi musicians and music groups living outside of occupied Western Sahara have extensively promoted, on the international arena, the message of Saharawi independence and self-determination. Saharawi-Spanish singer-songwriter Suilma Aali, whose music incorporates jazz, soul, Spanish, and Saharawi influences, advocates for the Saharawi cause through her music;[42] Saharawi rapper Yslem Hijo del Desierto, now living in Spain, uses his music for political and social activism too.[43] Music and dance group Tiris, which formed in 2005 in the Tindouf camps, vigorously promoted the Saharawi culture and cause through festival performances, international tours, and their album *Sandtracks*, integrating *haul* with reggae, blues, worldbeat, and other genres.[44] Perhaps the two most internationally prominent Saharawi musicians are singers Mariem Hassan and Aziza Brahim. Hassan (1958–2015) incorporated both traditional *haul* and revolutionary *nidal* styles in her music (as well as jazz, blues, and others); in her third and last solo album *El Aaiún Egdat* (El Aaiún on Fire) in 2012, she sang: "I am Saharawi and I want to live in my free land."[45] Brahim, born in 1976 in one of the Tindouf refugee camps and resident in Spain since 2000, combines Saharawi *haul* and *nidal* with contemporary globalized music styles, including rock and blues, to promote political messages of Saharawi freedom and aspirations for independence.[46] Brahim has toured widely, released several albums, and continues to pursue the cause of justice through her art. All these Saharawi artists are expanding notions not only of what Saharawi music can be, but also what it can do.

*

People who experience forced displacement,[47] like those Saharawi who fled Western Sahara when Morocco invaded, do so in widely divergent ways. Their experience will depend on where they come from and where they seek to be, their age, gender, culture, religion, educational background, and other facets of their backgrounds and identities. Those who are permanently settled, those temporarily settled, and those in transit will experience forced displacement differently. Yet practically all individuals who become forcibly displaced—whether due to conflict, violence, persecution, discrimination, human rights violations, natural disaster, and/or other serious social disruptions—face a multitude of challenges, including risks to their wellbeing and human rights. Various instruments seek to safeguard the rights of these people. The 1951 United Nations Convention Relating to the Status of Refugees, initially limited to include only those people fleeing pre-1951 events within Europe, was amended in 1967 to give it universal scope.[48] In this revised form, this Convention remains the bedrock of international protection for those who are forcibly displaced. It is supported by the 1948 Universal Declaration of Human Rights, which recognizes the right of people to seek asylum from persecution[49] and is supplemented by numerous national, regional, and international protection policies and laws.

Despite these instruments and measures, forced displacement has recently escalated across the world, fueled by political instability and conflict such as that in Afghanistan, Burundi, the Central African Republic, Gaza, Iraq, Myanmar, Nigeria, South Sudan, Syria, Ukraine, and Yemen. Within just a few months of Russia's 2022 invasion of Ukraine, the number of people forcibly displaced across the world reached 100 million—more than 1 percent of the global population, and more than double the number of people forcibly displaced only ten years earlier.[50] Especially on such a scale, forced displacement precipitates further social unrest, including disputes over national identities, politics, borders, economics, and resources. If the present trajectory of an increasing number and intensity of conflicts continues, warns the United Nations High Commissioner for Refugees (UNHCR), still greater numbers of people will be forcibly displaced. Accordingly, the UNHCR urges greater international cooperation to resolve existing conflicts (like that in Western Sahara), to address root causes of social and political unrest (like a lack of political self-determination), and "to deliver sustainable opportunities at the scale required to allow forcibly displaced people to live in safety and with dignity" (such as might be secured for the Saharawi people in exile, whether in the Tindouf camps or elsewhere).[51]

Forced displacement—itself a matter of social injustice—is often caused by social injustices and precipitates further injustices, including several of the kind explored in this book. Forced displacement can result from conflict and genocide (cf. Chapter 1 on Cambodia, and this chapter on Western Sahara), domination and oppression (Chapter 2 on colonization and land dispossession in Australia, and again this chapter), poverty and global economic inequality (Chapter 4 on artists in rural India), and the intensifying effects of the climate crisis (Chapter 6 on a village community in Leweton), as well as various other social, political, economic, and environmental factors (such as religious and ethnic politics, or natural disasters). Often, experiences of forced displacement begin with the status of escapee, as they did for those Saharawi who fled Western Sahara upon Moroccan invasion. This status inevitably entails some degree of dependence on others; in turn, that dependence heightens risks to security and safety, especially for women, children, the elderly, those with disability, those who are gender diverse, and those who belong to (other) marginalized or stigmatized groups. Maintaining continuity of education (cf. Chapter 3 on epistemically just education) or employment is often difficult or impossible for those who flee their homes or homeland; so too, accessing appropriate healthcare, legal services, or travel documentation. In short, forced displacement often considerably constrains the rights, opportunities, resources, and civil liberties of those who experience it, jeopardizing everything from food and shelter, health and wellbeing, to stable livelihood, freedom of movement, and the capacity to vote.

Alongside the immense social, economic, and psychosocial challenges of forced displacement are its cultural dimensions, which may play out in several ways.[52] First, a person's cultural identity may have been a factor in their displacement (as it was for the Saharawi people fleeing from Moroccan invasion). Cultural identity may also lead to racist or dehumanizing treatment in the process of seeking refuge, for example, when a receiving country lacks humane refugee policies or processes, or its population exhibits hostility toward people seeking asylum. For these (and other) reasons, individuals may choose to suppress their cultural identity or refrain from cultural practices during the experience of displacement. At the population level, this may affect the sustainability of musical and other cultural practices. Second, cultural pursuits may simply not be a priority for a time (as was almost certainly the case for many Saharawi people during the war in the late 1970s and 1980s), as people contend with the challenges of fleeing and establishing a new temporary or permanent home. Third, once people leave their homes, the physical infrastructure needed for cultural practices—musical instruments, ceremonial paraphernalia, public or shared performance spaces, and so forth—may simply no longer be accessible, as was (and to some extent remains) the case in the Tindouf refugee camps. Fourth, members of a cultural group may disperse in the process of seeking safety elsewhere, meaning fewer opportunities for individuals to engage in shared cultural practices. In such cases, the challenges of cultural maintenance may be particularly acute, especially if the displacement lasts years or decades, or is permanent.[53] (Given the mass resettlement in the Tindouf camps, population dispersal has been less of a factor in Saharawi cultural endangerment than it has for many other forcibly displaced groups.) This list could go on, but the implications are clear: cultural participation and practice are often difficult or even impossible for those experiencing forced displacement, at least in the nature or to the degree that characterized cultural activity prior to the displacement.

But forced displacement is not always, or exclusively, culturally disruptive. It can be culturally generative, especially for refugees who establish themselves in a new place as a consolidated community, as tens of thousands of Saharawi refugees did in the refugee camps in Algeria in the immediate aftermath of the Moroccan invasion. In such newly formed communities, music that requires few tangible resources (such as song repertoires) can readily adapt to the new context, transforming over time to explore and express the experiences, circumstances, and newly forming identities of their human bearers.[54] In such situations, the often radically changed relationship between music, culture, and community life may lead to new contexts and functions for musical practices, and new modes of musical participation. Although some practices may be left aside, no longer serving a useful purpose, others may be maintained as valuable markers of identity (like Saharawi *haul*). Still others may germinate anew or change trajectory altogether (like revolutionary *nidal*). Sometimes, too, the music of the host setting becomes incorporated into that of the displaced people (and vice versa), stimulating new musical creativities.[55] Mohamed Sleiman Labat observes the rising popularity of the Algerian music genre *raï* among young Saharawi people, who "listen to it in their cars, in the markets, in the streets, or when they hang together;" some are starting to incorporate the sounds of *raï* into their music.[56] As Saharawi youth travel to Algeria, Spain, Cuba, or elsewhere to study, the musical styles and instruments of those countries are finding a way into Saharawi musical practice too.[57]

The Saharawi case illustrates the complex dynamics of cultural sustainability in situations of forced displacement. Those Saharawi who sought refuge over the Algerian border in the Tindouf refugee camps have faced (and continue to face) considerable constraints on their musical and other cultural activities. The difficulties include accessing and maintaining musical instruments and other resources; the need to prioritize basic chores of daily life; the population's dispersal across the five camps, with unreliable transport between them; and the prohibitive daytime temperatures, which can reach as high as 122 degrees Fahrenheit (50 degrees Celsius). With weddings and other social gatherings severely disrupted during the war between Morocco and Western Sahara, and with even the function of music itself largely shifting to serve the revolutionary cause, traditional *haul* lost ground. As themes like love, landscape, epic tales, and religious praise fell out of favor in preference for songs with a revolutionary message, *haul* songs on those themes were gradually forgotten. This has been of concern for some Saharawi musicians, including Mariem Hassan: "Since we are so invested in our political situation and above all we sing songs of denouncement and resistance, usually more traditional songs are left on the side."[58]

For the Saharawi people, any degree of cultural loss is a cause for political as well as cultural concern, especially since a long-standing strategy of occupation has been for Morocco "to deny the existence of a Saharawi identity that is distinct from Moroccan identity."[59] Strong cultural practices equate to a strong cultural identity, and a strong cultural identity is understood to be crucial if the Saharawi struggle for decolonization and independence is ever to succeed. Thus, over the years, the cultural authorities in the Tindouf camps have spearheaded various measures to maintain, stimulate, and transmit Saharawi cultural practices of all kinds. One such measure is the International Observatory for the Protection of the Cultural Heritage in the Western Sahara, established by the SADR Ministry of Culture in 2008 to protect tangible and intangible Saharawi culture.[60] Another key government strategy for cultural safeguarding has been to support local festivals involving *haul* and *nidal*, dancing, and other Saharawi cultural activities. These festivals continue to be features of life in the camps, as well as in the Polisario-controlled parts of Western Sahara east of the Berm Wall. By stimulating cultural activity, the festivals help maintain, showcase, and celebrate Saharawi cultural practices and cultural identity. Where possible, the festivals in the Tindouf camps are scheduled to coincide with the arrival of international visitors to the region, such as for the popular Sahara Marathon or Western Sahara International Film Festival. In this way, in addition to their cultural maintenance function, the festivals also serve to expand international awareness of the Saharawi political situation.[61]

By contrast, for those Saharawi who remained in Western Sahara, the practice and transmission of Saharawi music of any kind was severely inhibited following Moroccan occupation, and remains so to this day. As an expression of Saharawi identity, Saharawi music is considered a provocation against the occupying force—intensely so when it promotes the Saharawi political agenda. In Morocco and the occupied parts of Western Sahara, Moroccan authorities continue to censor the music of Saharawi artists, both those residing in occupied Western Sahara and those in exile; those who perform or listen to it face possible torture or arrest.[62] Over the five decades of occupation, the sustained repression of Saharawi culture has led to considerable cultural losses, exacerbated by the forced displacement and prolonged exile of those who fled their homeland, as well as the passing away of many older Saharawi musicians (both those in exile and those who remained). Notwithstanding the various government strategies for cultural survival, local estimates place the loss of Saharawi musical and cultural heritage since the mid-1970s at around 60 percent.[63]

However, by other measures, Saharawi music has survived, even thrived. A whole new musical genre effectively sprang from the circumstances surrounding displacement: *nidal*, the revolutionary music of the Polisario Front and the SADR government-in-exile, which co-opted features of traditional *haul* music for its political purposes. *Nidal* has been a culturally and politically important resource for Saharawi people, largely supplanting *haul* as the bedrock of Saharawi musical practice and cultural identity.[64] As the decades passed, Saharawi music has developed in new directions, increasingly drawing on both traditional and revolutionary styles as signifiers of Saharawi identity, while engaging emotionally, socially, and politically with the experience and causes of forced displacement. Among the foremost recent exponents of Saharawi musical innovation have been Western- and world-music-influenced international artists like those mentioned earlier (Hassan, Tiris, Brahim), who have expanded notions of what is considered "Saharawi music."

Notwithstanding the cultural losses precipitated by war, oppression, and exile, in many ways, Saharawi cultural practices are thriving. Mohamed Sleiman Labat believes that creative innovation and creative responsiveness to ever-changing circumstances are key ingredients of this cultural survival and resilience—that fixing static traditions would "kill" them.[65] Reinventing and redefining Saharawi cultural identity, Mohamed maintains, is not a matter of merely replicating historical traditions from nomadic life in Western Sahara, but rather of "understanding the essence of being a Sahrawi and a nomad and bringing that sense of understanding to life through new means and processes."[66] In this sense, cultural sustainability is a resource for the future:

> The past Saharawi nomadic knowledge is still relevant to the social and environmental challenges we face today. Reclaiming and revisioning traditions are possible if we understand their essence and know which parts we keep and which parts we leave. If we understand the wisdom of yesterday, it can help us not only see the untold fate of tomorrow, but actually create it.[67]

*

For decades now, from Liberia to Syria to Vietnam, non-government organizations, other cultural agencies, and applied researchers have developed and delivered music programs to refugee peoples.[68] These programs (sometimes called "interventions") aim to ameliorate refugee lives in some way: perhaps by promoting the profile of refugee musicians or helping them generate income, by fostering wellbeing through musical activity, by supporting the musical and general education of the children and youth, or by raising awareness of their community's socioeconomic or political circumstances. Often, such interventions are led by non-government organizations based in relatively wealthy Western countries, with the obvious benefit of unlocking access to funding and resources that may be difficult or impossible to come by locally. They therefore tend to take place in resettled communities or refugee camps with relatively easy access for outsiders (and not, for example, in situations of internal forced displacement where access may be challenging).

Historically and often still today, these kinds of music programs have largely drawn on the musical skills and knowledge, approaches to teaching and learning, and modes of musical participation most familiar to those who deliver them—that is, predominantly Western ones. Critics have observed that such programs risk reinscribing the power hierarchies and lack of agency that are all too familiar to people with a refugee experience.[69] Recognizing the problems with such an approach, some cultural agencies are transforming their programs to center the cultural and musical identities, knowledges, interests, and skills of the people they aim to serve. This approach has better odds of not only improving lives but also of supporting cultural sustainability and cultural justice. In one of the Tindouf refugee camps (Boudjour), for example, the UK-based NGO Sandblast launched a program in 2016 called Desert Voicebox, an after-school music and English training project for primary school-aged Saharawi children. Initially, the program was delivered by English-speaking outsiders and provided only Western music education. From the start, though, it aimed to train Saharawi people to deliver it, and the program is now taught by local Saharawi women; the music education aspect also now involves local musicians and incorporates local musical instruments and styles alongside Western ones. In these ways, Desert Voicebox is strengthening its potential to advance its cultural and educational justice objectives, as well as better acknowledging and valuing the lived experiences of those it seeks to support.[70]

The remainder of this chapter explores the cultural sustainability and social justice contributions of another project undertaken with and for the Saharawi people: *Portraits of Saharawi Music*, which took place in the Tindouf camps in 2013 and 2014 (see ▶ Example 5.2). *Portraits of Saharawi Music* represented a partnership between three parties: the SADR Ministry of Culture, with its concerns to maintain and sustain Saharawi cultural practices and activities, and to promote a distinct Saharawi cultural identity; the World and Traditional Music Department at the British Library, with its documentation and archiving remit; and Spanish researcher-academic Violeta Ruano Posada, at the time a doctoral candidate at the University of London. Together, these parties identified three key project aims: to identify and better understand the musical practices of the Saharawi community in the camps; to document and safeguard Saharawi musical heritage by generating a publicly available corpus of music recordings; and to promote Saharawi culture and build greater international awareness of their political situation, especially among the Anglophone world.[71] The British Library provided modest funding and the SADR Ministry provided practical and ideological support. The *Portraits* project is relatively unusual among refugee-related music projects with an activist or advocacy agenda—not so much in involving external partners and researchers, but in co-designing the project with the refugee participants, and in exclusively centering the music, and the cultural and political interests, of the refugee community it involves (see ▶ Example 5.3, a reflective statement by Violeta on her role and relationship with the Saharawi people and cause).

Between September 2013 and April 2014, Violeta worked with a small project team of Saharawi people, and the Saharawi musicians living in the camps, to generate 133 audio and video recordings of Saharawi music. Forty-two musicians participated from all five Tindouf camps, around half of them women. Some of the recordings were made in the camps' designated cultural spaces, others in people's homes. Choosing music they considered most representative of Saharawi culture, the musicians performed traditional *haul*, instrumental improvisations (*azawaan*), spiritual songs (*medeh*), landscape songs (*atlal*), and—by far the most well-represented category—nationalistic *nidal*, all sung in the Saharawi language, Arabic Hassānīya. The instruments the musicians played included various forms of percussion, from the traditional Saharawi *tbal* to improvised instruments such as plates, buckets, and plastic bottles, as well as electric keyboard, accordion, and acoustic and electric guitars. Once the recordings were complete, the project materials—audio and video recordings as well as photographs and metadata—were made available on the British Library website,[72] as well as to the Saharawi people directly via the cultural institutions in the camps.

In effect, with the local and international deposit of the project recordings, *Portraits of Saharawi Music* generated a national music archive for the SADR. Through its documentation and archiving, Saharawi musical heritage (as it was at the time of the project) should remain accessible to Saharawi people (and others) now and into the future, regardless of the threats presented by ongoing exile, protracted conflict, or regional instability. But the project has contributed to cultural safeguarding not only in its documentation and archiving outcomes, but in its processes too. The recording sessions brought musicians together, sanctioned and encouraged musical activity, and provided a focus and purpose for music-making in the camps.[73] They also stimulated musical and cultural discussion and debate between the participating musicians and other cultural mediators and authorities in the camps.[74] According to Violeta, the sessions (and the resulting recordings) captured a wide spectrum of musical styles, cultural identities, and political perspectives within the Saharawi refugee society—unified, however, by a denouncement of Moroccan occupation and a call for Saharawi independence and self-determination.[75] Since being made publicly available, the project recordings have featured in locally and externally produced radio shows, news media, compilation records, creative projects, and educational materials, and have been the topic of several scholarly articles and presentations.[76] In these ways, the project has raised awareness of Saharawi music, as well as the situation, even the very existence, of the Saharawi people. This very book chapter is evidence that, a decade on, the project continues to raise awareness of the Saharawi cause, countering its "extreme invisibility" on the international arena.[77]

In one of the project recordings, singer and percussionist Mariem "Habuza" Mohamed Lamin sings "Climbing the Mountain," a *nidal* song she first sang forty years earlier (see Figure 5.3 and ▶ video Example 5.4). The description for this recording in the British Library project archive reads in full:

Figure 5.3 Mariem "Habuza" Mohamed Lamin, singer and percussionist. Photograph taken by Violeta Ruano Posada during recording session in El Aaiún refugee camp, October 17, 2013. British Library website (n.d.(a)).

> This song belongs to the national repertoire of early revolutionary music composed before exile between 1973 and 1975 by Polisario Front founder El Uali Mustapha Sayed and other friends. This music was a re-adaptation of traditional music with revolutionary lyrics and new instrumentation such as the guitar. It had the function of spreading the message of the anti-colonial revolution throughout the Saharawi population. This song talks about continuing the revolution. The performance occasion [for this recording] was a private session in the house of the musician. Habuza was one of the first revolutionary singers to join the anti-colonial revolution in 1973. She was playing percussion on a metal plate because she doesn't own a drum.[78]

This description, like Mohamed Lamin's performance, draws the listener's attention to the political struggle of the Saharawi people. While this struggle is most obvious through the lyrics of the song, it is made poignant in several further ways: the performer's close personal connection to the song and to the revolution; the song's continued ideological relevance, decades after this singer first sang it; and even the metal plate as percussion instrument, suggestive of the continued economic hardship and limited resources available to the Saharawi people in exile. Many further recordings in the *Portraits of Saharawi Music* project likewise address and oppose the social and political challenges and injustices facing the Saharawi people.

*

Recent scholarly studies on the role of music in war, conflict, and forced displacement have explored how music may assist in transforming or resolving conflict, in providing respite or relief from trauma, and in advancing diplomacy and peace.[79] But music is not always a "medium for compromise" that strives for conflict resolution or transformation.[80] Sometimes, as in the Saharawi case, music forms a locus for resistance against political hegemony and social injustice: empowering the dispossessed, performing their ideologies. In such settings, music can occupy a "paradoxical position" where it is simultaneously used to perpetuate conflict and to promote its resolution.[81] When conceived as a manifestation of Saharawi music-making in the Tindouf refugee camps, *Portraits of Saharawi Music* embodies this paradox: it represents the kind of engaged activist research that does not seek to mediate or reconcile, but rather to join with the disempowered in moving toward political and social justice. Violeta describes the project as "a political act of cultural advocacy."[82]

Evidently, music has been, and continues to be, a vital resource in the lives of the Saharawi people, through their experience of conflict and displacement. For those who fled and established new lives in the Tindouf camps in Algeria, and for those younger Saharawi who were born and have grown up in those camps, music has been a way to process loss and displacement, bear witness to grief and injustice, keep alive the memory of the homelands, reconstruct individual and collective identities, and explore and share experiences of life in the camps. When little else has seemed within control, making music has been an act of Saharawi defiance and self-determination—a commanding and empowering way to bring the Saharawi political cause and Saharawi human rights into the international spotlight. Saharawi musical practice over the last half-century demonstrates Saharawi resilience, determination, innovation, creativity, and humanity, countering the dehumanizing deficit narratives that often feature in refugee discourses. Despite the cultural losses that have occurred through the decades of conflict, war, and exile, Saharawi musicians continue to practice, transmit, share, and celebrate their rich cultural knowledge and skills.

As the Saharawi people reach fifty years in exile, what trajectory might their music take? National independence and a return to the Western Saharan homeland would effectively mean that *nidal* will have fulfilled its *raison d'être* and might cede ground over time to other Saharawi musical expressions. (In that case, the *Portraits* project would remain as a historical repository, a musical reminder, of historical Saharawi struggles for recognition.) Conversely, and somewhat ironically, ongoing displacement and dispossession under occupation may mean that *nidal* continues strong—even if it continues to shapeshift, reflecting and influencing the ever-changing social and political realities of its Saharawi bearers. A multitude of other scenarios are possible. One thing seems sure: until some semblance of justice is achieved, Saharawi music will continue to play a key role in the struggle.

Figure 6.0 Sandy Sur. Photo: Jacintha Bezgovsek.

Introducing: Sandy Sur

Sandy Sur is a community leader of Leweton, a small village on the outskirts of Luganville township, on the island of Espiritu Santo in Vanuatu. Sandy is founder and director of Leweton Cultural Village, a local cultural tourism enterprise that features the traditional cultural practices of the ni-Vanuatu[1] islands of Gaua and Merelava. As culture-bearer, community advocate, and cultural researcher, Sandy has travelled internationally, often with members of his community, to participate in festivals and cultural events, artistic residencies, congresses and conferences, and research and policy discussions. At home in Leweton, Sandy coordinates an ongoing project to document, transmit, and promote the rich cultural knowledge and cultural practices of his community.

Central to Sandy's understanding of culture is its relationship to the surrounding environment. Water is especially important to life and culture in Leweton. In Sandy's words, "Water is the connection between human life and the earth. Therefore, Water is sacred."[2] For Sandy, the cultural practice of etëtung, *or Vanuatu Women's Water Music, has helped his community convey to outsiders the living nature of water, and its deep connections with human and other life on earth. In collaboration with his community and researchers in Australia, Sandy is exploring the potential for new technologies (like virtual reality) and interdisciplinary partnerships to advance the international reach of* etëtung; *to share widely the message of the interconnectedness of land, water, nature and culture; and to propel climate action. Sandy recognizes* etëtung *and other cultural practices of his community as useful means to promote wider awareness of the ramifications for his community of the warming climate. Sandy explains, "Government officials think climate change is about sea rise, but I think it's about culture, language, way of life."*

6

Weaving Sound through Ocean and Land

With Sandy Sur

On April 6, 2020, Tropical Cyclone Harold made landfall on the South Pacific island of Espiritu Santo, the largest of eighty-three islands that constitute the nation of Vanuatu (see Figure 6.1).[3] Harold had just strengthened into the most severe possible category of cyclone. In the main township of Luganville (population around 18,000), sustained winds roared at more than 200 kilometers per hour, with gusts of nearly 300 kilometers per hour. The cyclone tore roofs off homes, uprooted trees, and severed the island's power and communications. Roads became blocked by flash flooding, landslides, and debris, and the pelting rain threatened to contaminate water supplies. Two days later, by satellite phone, the mayor of Luganville implored the international community: "We urgently need water, food and shelter . . . Many have lost their homes. Schools are destroyed. Electricity is down. I'm urgently calling for help."[4] Reports soon emerged that the cyclone had destroyed up to 70 percent of buildings in Luganville,[5] ruined crops and farms across the nation,[6] and left 160,000 people—roughly half the nation's population—homeless.[7] International aid efforts were hampered by impassable roads and other damaged infrastructure, as well as by the challenges and risks posed by the escalating COVID-19 pandemic. By the end of 2020, over a third of the population of Vanuatu was facing food insecurity due to the cyclone.[8]

The people of Vanuatu have dealt with cyclones for generations: the nation falls in the path of tropical cyclones for several months of the year. But with the climate crisis generating more frequent and more extreme weather events, the risks are intensifying. Cyclone Harold was the second strongest cyclone ever recorded in Vanuatu. The strongest, Cyclone Pam, had decimated the nation only five years earlier, in March 2015, leaving two-thirds of the population in need of urgent humanitarian assistance, and destroying up to 90 percent of infrastructure in the worst-affected areas.[9] Like Cyclone Harold, Pam devastated the nation's key agricultural, forestry, and fisheries sectors.

Sounding Good. Catherine Grant, Oxford University Press. © Oxford University Press 2025.
DOI: 10.1093/oso/9780197698433.003.0007

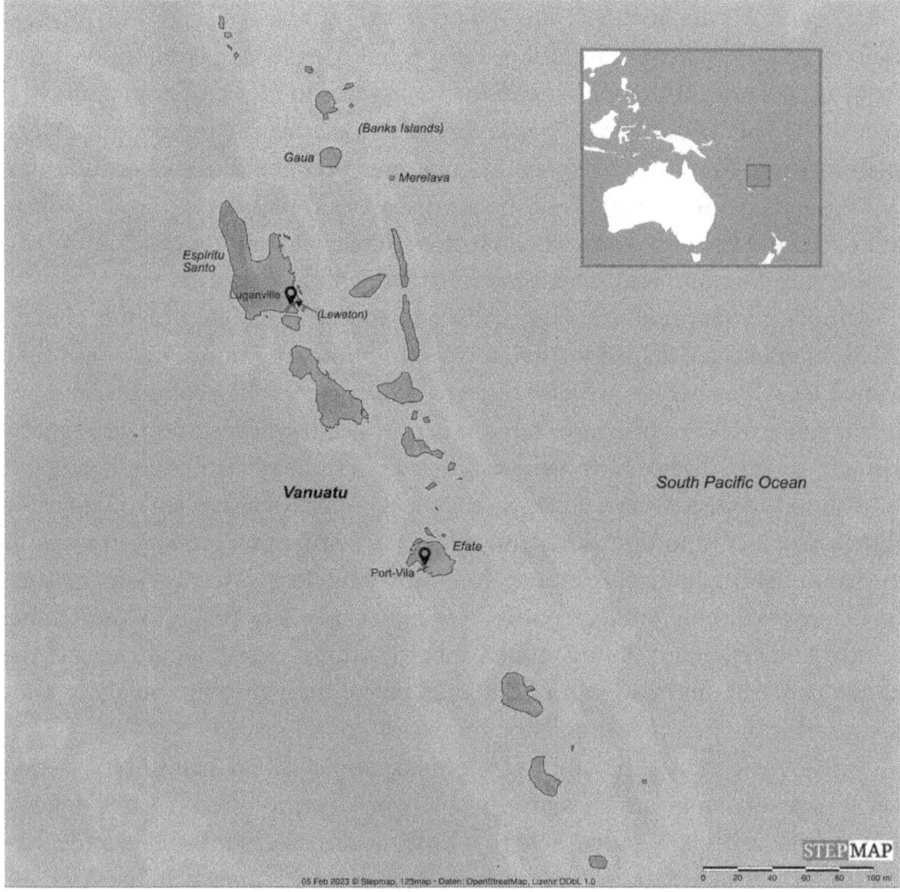

Figure 6.1 Vanuatu showing location of Leweton village on Espiritu Santo.

It also demolished its biggest industry, that of tourism—something Harold would undoubtedly have done too, except that the COVID-19 pandemic had already brought the sector to its knees by the time Harold made landfall.

More frequent and severe cyclones are only one of many threats Vanuatu faces due to the climate crisis. Coastal erosion, saltwater intrusion into land and freshwater ecosystems, damage to coral reefs and island ecologies, landslides brought about by more intense and prolonged rainfall, and more frequent and severe weather events (including flooding, drought, heat waves, fires, and storm surges) all carry the real risk of damaging Vanuatu's major tourism and agricultural sectors,[10] in turn jeopardizing livelihoods and holding serious ramifications for the social and economic wellbeing of individuals and communities. The World Bank Group warns that in this way, the climate crisis is likely to exacerbate inequality and poverty in the nation.[11]

Water quality is already declining, and water resources are becoming increasingly scarce.[12] Internal migration is expected to rise, as people move away from their communities in search of social, economic, and environmental security.[13] The risk of vector-borne diseases (like malaria and dengue fever), malnutrition, food insecurity, and temperature-related illnesses are all high, while the risk of water- and food-borne disease outbreaks is "extreme."[14] Soon after Cyclone Harold, when 181 countries were evaluated for the 2021 World Risk Index, Vanuatu was assessed as having the highest disaster risk.[15]

Although everyone will eventually feel the ramifications of the climate crisis, its effects are disproportionately felt in poorer regions of the world (like Vanuatu), where people are least resourced to cope. Social, economic, and political vulnerabilities of poorer regions exacerbate the devastation wrought by climate-related disasters; those existing vulnerabilities also make it difficult to respond to disasters in a satisfactory way. Moreover, as the climate crisis intensifies, it compounds other mounting environmental crises—from globally diminishing natural resources to biodiversity loss—that are similarly set to disproportionately affect poorer regions, especially those in the Global South. And yet, people living in the Global South have contributed least to the climate crisis: comprising around 88 percent of the world's population, they are responsible for only 8 percent of its excess emissions.[16]

Native American (Spokane) ethnomusicologist Chad Hamill states that for Indigenous communities around the world—who often inhabit delicate ecosystems especially vulnerable to a heating climate, like small islands, riverine and lake areas, desert peripheries, high-altitude zones, and the Arctic—accelerating climate change "amounts to a crisis that is every bit as threatening as the legacy of European colonialism."[17] But (as Hamill also notes) the association is not only figurative: the climate crisis interlocks in very real ways with the global colonial project, including the latter's historical and persisting patterns of imperialism, racism, slavery, genocide, linguistic and cultural oppression, land dispossession, and resource extraction.[18] In 2022, for the first time, the report of the Intergovernmental Panel on Climate Change recognized colonialism as a major historical and ongoing driver of environmental and climate destruction.[19] Further, legacies of colonialism continue to obstruct efforts to draw on Indigenous and local knowledge systems to understand and tackle the climate crisis from different perspectives—an endeavor that Western powers are gradually recognizing as being in everyone's best interest, including their own.[20]

The uneven historical, socioeconomic, and geographical causes and impacts of the global climate crisis are matters of *climate justice*.[21] Climate justice is about the multiple interlocking socioeconomic dimensions of the climate crisis, and their unequal manifestation across societies and nations. The economic dimensions of the climate crisis, for example, undermine local and global poverty reduction efforts and compound socioeconomic inequalities within and between nations. Its racialized, gendered, and ableist dimensions meant that Indigenous people, women, those with disabilities, those forcibly displaced, and other socially marginalized groups disproportionately bear its consequences.[22] The climate crisis has health and wellbeing dimensions too, as individuals and communities, especially those who are under-resourced or disempowered, struggle to cope physically and psychosocially with climate-related disease, disaster, and loss. It compounds forced displacement, as residents of local communities—even of whole nations—seek to migrate before their homelands are inundated by rising seas, extreme heat, or other climate-related adversities.[23] It has intergenerational dimensions, because it endangers the safety, security, and prosperity of children living today, now and throughout their lives, as well as those who are yet to be born.[24]

And climate justice has cultural dimensions too. When climate-related diseases or disasters strike, people's capacity to engage in cultural practices is reduced. When local ecosystems degrade due to climate stress, associated cultural practices weaken or disappear along with them. When populations are displaced due to climate-related adversities, the usual contexts and functions for cultural practices are often disrupted or disappear altogether, and the cultural practices may be jeopardized or lost.[25] Again, it is those more vulnerable communities and countries that are at greatest risk of major cultural losses. Since climate justice intersects with other issues of social justice, considering the impact of climate justice on cultural sustainability means also considering an array of other matters relating to social justice, from capitalism, colonialism, and neo-liberalism to land ownership, economic precarity, and political corruption.[26] Ethnomusicologist Michael Silvers summed up this intersectionality of climate justice and cultural sustainability in his investigation into the impact of drought on *forró* music of the *sertão* (backlands) of northeastern Brazil, when he concluded: "The story of music and drought is inherently a story of structural inequality—between nations, regions, knowledge-bearers, social classes, and sectors of society."[27]

Who gets to decide on responses to the climate crisis, and who should? Historically, those who have held most sway in international climate policy decisions are those with the most economic and political power—that is, elites and powerbrokers of the Global North who stand to gain the most by perpetuating the imperialist and capitalist status quo. The social paradigm of the Global North especially values economic advancement. Exploiting environmental resources for economic development ("progress") is seen as both reasonable and justifiable by this paradigm; climate mitigation and adaptation strategies are only seen as acceptable to the extent that they do not unduly jeopardize economic growth. When this worldview dominates international climate debate and decision-making, both the processes and outcomes risk perpetuating the racism, nationalism, colonialism, imperialism, capitalism, elitism, and (other) "neo-colonial mythologies" that precipitated the climate crisis in the first place (and that have long plagued Western environmentalism).[28] One example (relevant to Chapter 5 of this book) is the proposal to cover large swathes of the Saharan desert in solar panels, a proposition founded on the idea of *terra nullius*—"that the desert is just empty space in which European and US companies could generate energy for consumers back home in the Global North."[29] In short, like all environmental and social problems, the climate crisis can be framed in different ways according to different value systems, and these different framings and value systems lead to different solutions.[30] Political solutions to the climate crisis that are legitimate are those that are fair, and fairness is only possible with the equal—arguably the prioritized—political representation and participation in the debate of those most affected by the crisis, who will offer different framings of both the problems and their solutions. This is the procedural dimension of climate justice.

Procedural justice is important at all levels, from the local and national through to the regional and international. For example, within Vanuatu, national consultation processes on climate matters have at times involved only experts and government senior officials, failing to take into sufficient account the knowledge and priorities of local communities. One risk here is that decisions misalign with local needs, such as when environmental resource protection is prioritized over the needs of communities whose livelihoods and cultures rely on those resources.[31] The top-down, minimally consultative nature of certain previous climate processes and outcomes in Vanuatu may at least partially explain why researchers and policy experts have encountered reticence, unenthusiasm, and even apathy among ni-Vanuatu communities about externally driven climate adaptation and mitigation strategies.[32]

This is despite environmental issues, including the climate crisis, being a cause of significant concern among many ni-Vanuatu people. In a study involving 444 residents of the island of Espiritu Santo, environmental law and climate researcher Kirsten Davies found that participants reported significantly greater concern about environmental issues (including climate change) than other locally relevant social, cultural, or economic issues.[33] Participants referred to the challenges that increasingly unpredictable rainfall, temperatures, and seasonal changes presented to their food security; they spoke of coastal and riverine flooding and erosion affecting their mobility, farming land, coconut plantations, and road infrastructure; and they described the broader effects of these climate-related challenges on their personal economic security, their access to education, and their health (the latter the result of an increase in mosquitoes and malaria). Of any age group, children under ten years old reported the highest rates of "extreme concern" about the impacts of global climate change on their environment and lives on Santo.[34]

Climate response efforts in Vanuatu that embrace procedural fairness and principles of climate justice are best positioned to succeed. Such efforts are those driven by the wishes and needs of local communities. They integrally involve and build the capacity of those communities, respect and engage local cultural and environmental knowledges, and uphold and value local cultural practices.[35] Considerations of procedural fairness pertain not only to climate response efforts, but to cultural sustainability ones too, where community agency, self-determination, and meaningful participation are similarly key.[36] The rest of this chapter explores a local initiative exhibiting procedural fairness in both climate justice and cultural sustainability terms: the Leweton Cultural Village, featuring the cultural practice *etëtung*.

*

The village of Leweton lies on the periphery of Luganville, the township on the island of Espiritu Santo that was so hard hit by Cyclone Harold (see Figure 6.1).[37] The twelve or so families who comprise the community originally came from the islands of Gaua and Merelava in the northern Banks Islands group of the Vanuatuan archipelago. In the 1970s and 1980s, these families were among many ni-Vanuatu people who moved from more remote areas of the archipelago to urban centers, seeking education, employment, and other opportunities afforded by metropolitan life.[38] Some older people of Leweton still speak to each other in *Mwerlap*, the indigenous language of Gaua and Merelava (and one of over 100 languages spoken across the small nation),[39] but most converse in Bislama, Vanuatu's lingua franca. As in many small-island communities around the world, water is central to culture, society, and economy in Leweton, being a source of food (fish, shellfish), livelihood (fishing, tourism), trade (via small boats), and leisure (swimming, bathing). It is also an inspiration and site for cultural expression. Ethnomusicologist Philip Hayward characterizes the people of Leweton as inhabiting an *aquapelago*, navigating both freshwater and saltwater aquatic spaces in and around it in a manner "fundamentally interconnected with and essential to the social group's habitation of land and their senses of identity and belonging."[40]

Following relocation to the place they called Leweton, these families continued to maintain *kastom*, a ni-Vanuatu term roughly translatable as *tradition* or *traditional culture*, though with a strong sense of its dynamic, living nature.[41] In addition to cultural practices, *kastom* incorporates religious beliefs and traditional customs, and "informs environmental protection, attitudes, values, family and community structures, behaviours and participation."[42] However, as was the case for many ni-Vanuatu communities at that time, the people of Leweton soon found that the practice and transmission of *kastom* in their new village home were being disrupted by several intersecting factors: among them, new livelihoods, the cash economy, changing food-sourcing practices, and the growing influence of Western culture. Sandy Sur and other cultural leaders of Leweton began to consider explicit grassroots strategies to help preserve, promote, and transmit to younger generations the cultural and linguistic knowledge and practices of their homelands.

Thus, in 2008, under Sandy's leadership, the community launched the enterprise Leweton Cultural Village, whereby tourists and other visitors would be able to learn about and experience first-hand the *kastom* music-making, singing, dancing, weaving, cooking, storytelling, kava-drinking, and other cultural practices of the Leweton people. One rationale was economic: through cultural tourism, it was hoped the enterprise would expand livelihood prospects for individuals and boost the economic capacity of the whole community.[43] Cultural sustainability was the other key driver: through the enterprise, Sandy and others involved hoped to enable and encourage the continued practice, across all generations, of *kastom*.

Featuring prominently in the activities of the Leweton Cultural Village right from the start was *etëtung*, known in English as "Vanuatu Women's Water Music" (also "liquid percussion" or "water percussion"). In this cultural practice common to several ni-Vanuatu communities, a small group of girls and women stand in a circle or semicircle in waist-deep water and rhythmically slap or scoop its surface to create a diverse repertoire of rhythms and pitches (Figure 6.2; see ▶ video Examples 6.1 and 6.2). According to local lore, women in the Banks Islands had engaged like this in playful, spontaneous, improvised percussion games with water "since time immemorial."[44] On Merelava and Gaua, when women went from their village to the ocean, rivers, or creeks to wash, bathe, or collect food, they began to recreate in the water the natural sounds around them. Girls, often as young as five or six years old, would watch, listen, learn, and join in. Thus, over time, *etëtung* became a *kastom* practice.

Figure 6.2 The women and girls of Leweton Cultural Village perform *Etëtung* in the coastal shallows near Leweton village on the island of Espiritu Santo, Vanuatu. Photo: Ashley Burgess, November 17, 2017.

According to late Leweton cultural leader Warren Wevat Wessergo, the contemporary development of *etëtung* was started by a group of Mwerlap-speaking women in the 1970s. These women began to creatively codify the sounds they made, including the solo and group singing that sometimes accompanied the percussion, with the intention of teaching them to other local women and girls.[45] In Wessergo's version, a key impetus for this codification was the keen interest shown in *etëtung* by two European yachting tourists, who "provided various gifts, and later cash, to the performers to show their appreciation."[46] This was likely the first instance of *etëtung* being a source of income for its practitioners. In its contemporary form, with an extensive repertoire, *etëtung* continues as a commercial activity across Vanuatu. More than a decade ago, music researchers Brian Diettrich, Jane Freeman Moulin, and Michael Webb wrote that visitors to Vanuatu could "be entertained in resorts by girls and women performing unique ensemble music involving the unison rhythmic beating of hands on water in swimming pools."[47] The ongoing intersections of *kastom* with the tourist industry and the cultural economy (explored further later in this chapter) resonate with the notion of Leweton Cultural Village as a "transitional society," where *kastom* practices and institutions sit alongside, and interact dynamically with, market forces.[48]

Etëtung forms part of the Leweton people's "Indigenous ecology"—a holistic framework that embraces and connects cultural expressions, spiritual phenomena, and understandings of the surrounding world.[49] *Kastom* practices like *etëtung* carry profound local environmental and social knowledge—of place, plants, animals, landscape, seascape, nature, weather, seasons, climate, ecologies, medicines, disasters, threats, local histories, and more. As the women of Leweton recreate in the water various sounds familiar to them—a dolphin, rain falling on taro leaves, thunder, a waterfall, whale fish, skull fish, certain local species of birds, water ebbing back through the rocks at high tide—they are embodying and sharing local knowledge built up over generations, as well as continuing to dynamically explore the world around them. Ways of living and being in places with significant water resources—which geographers Philip Steinberg and Kimberley Peters refer to as "wet ontologies"—enable and require constant reformation, regeneration, and adaptation.[50] As the world and their experience of it evolves, the girls and women of Leweton constantly explore and introduce new sounds into their practice of *etëtung*. In recent years, the sonic repertoire has expanded to include "*sogor* (the sound of fish chasing baitfish); *worworok* (rhythmic creek noises) and *ne-lea* (water flow resonating in cave spaces),"[51] among other sounds. "Water Music is alive," Leweton woman Martha Rowan Wevales told me; young performer Delite Ron added, "Every day the earth is changing; by playing Water Music we are sharing a message about these changes."[52]

In this sense, *etëtung* is an *acoustemology*, a sonic way of knowing and understanding the world.[53] Examples abound of Indigenous ecologies and acoustemologies around the world that integrate cultural practices with environmental knowledge, that lend the natural environment significance through culture, and that interact dynamically with local environments and their features (like water). Writing about the Columbia Plateau region in the interior northwest USA, Chad Hamill describes how for millennia, the Spokane and Columbia rivers "have been the lifeblood of the Spokane people, the heart-center from which culture is nourished and sustained. Like the rivers, our songs inhabit the landscape; the rivers fed our bodies, the songs feed our souls."[54] Saurav Moni, exponent of *bhatiyali* boat songs (see Chapter 4), speaks in similar terms about the rivers, estuaries, mangroves, and songs of his West Bengal river-delta homeland. In reminding us how inextricably connected are cultural and environmental sustainability,[55] these examples suggest that the matter of environmental sustainability may be at least as much a cultural as an environmental one.

In reflecting on Indigenous ecologies, Chad Hamill underscores the importance of stories: "Indigenous landscapes [and waterscapes] are brought to life through stories," he writes, stories that form "ontological bonds" through culture, and that "reflect unique ways of knowing and being in the world."[56]

Sandy Sur echoes this sentiment: "Stories are knowledge, knowledge is culture, and culture is water and land." Describing *etëtung* as "a message," Sandy explains: "The sound weaves through the ocean and the land, weaving our stories as it goes;" through *etëtung*, "our stories are told through the water like a book."[57] Pacific anthropologist Chris Ballard and colleagues offer the model of "People, Place, and Story" as a way to understand ni-Vanuatu epistemologies and ontologies like this one: the physical world of landscapes, seascapes, and environments ("Place") is made meaningful through local knowledges and narratives about it ("Story"); these stories are developed by, and shared among, individuals and communities ("People") through cultural practices such as *etëtung*.[58] Each time the women and girls of Leweton perform *etëtung*, they strengthen their relationship to Place—both their ancestral homes on the islands of Merelava and Gaua, and their new home of Leweton. For them, Place is inseparable from understandings of sociocultural identities, kinship groups, and cultural expressions; it has "spiritual and cosmological significance, which underpins the community's relationship with the ancestral world in continuity between the past, present and future."[59] Story helps the People of Leweton live in Place safely and sustainably. Story and Place—culture and nature, sound and water—are life-sustaining resources.

A substantial body of ethnomusicological scholarship explores interconnections between culture and nature, and between environmental and cultural sustainability. It has come to be known as *ecomusicology*—the study of the intersections of music/sound, culture/society, and nature/environment.[60] One matter afforded particular attention among ecomusicologists is the threats the climate crisis presents to musical and cultural sustainability (and those posed by related environmental crises such as land degradation, deforestation, and biodiversity loss). These studies inevitably underscore the intersections of climate and culture with a range of other social matters in areas of the economy, health, wellbeing, food security, gender, politics, education, and more.[61]

Research in ecomusicology and cognate fields (such as that of biocultural diversity[62]) suggests that the cultural sustainability implications of the climate crisis are particularly acute for Indigenous peoples, whose cultural practices and knowledge systems are intimately interconnected with the natural environment. When that environment comes under pressure or is degraded, cultural practices are often at risk. In Vanuatu, a national pilot study completed in 2012 found that nearly half the 800 ni-Vanuatu respondents had relatively little knowledge or understanding of *kastom* stories, songs, dances, and games[63]—a circumstance partly attributable to "forces of colonisation, globalisation and modernity,"[64] but almost certainly exacerbated by environmental changes. An even earlier study (from 2007) of a ni-Vanuatu community on Tangoa Island, which is particularly affected by cyclones, found that its people believed themselves to be less resilient to climatic stress than in the past; they attributed that fact to the increasing prevalence of "Western" or "modern" values and systems, including capitalism and the cash economy, over *kastom* practices.[65] When Indigenous cultural practices are lost, whole repositories of local knowledge, often formed over tens of thousands of years, disappear along with them. Communities are left with fewer cultural resources through which to understand, process and respond to the climate crisis. Beyond the major cultural, social, economic, and wellbeing implications of cultural loss for Indigenous communities, and the aesthetic loss for humankind, losing the vast stores of ecological, environmental, medicinal, historical, and other knowledge contained in Indigenous cultural practices lessens the capacity of all humanity to respond and adapt to future threats (such as unforeseen health or climate dangers).[66]

But if culture is under siege from the climate crisis, it also offers a way to respond to it. A theme arising from Kirsten Davies' study of Espiritu Santo residents was the strong local belief that *kastom* was fundamental to ensuring the local sustainable use of natural resources, and that *kastom* knowledge could assist in the sustainable management, monitoring, and governing of the community and the environmental ecosystems it formed a part of.[67] The climate crisis being anthropogenic, human responses through cultural expression are powerful; and since its effects are felt locally, local responses (like those afforded by *etëtung* and other cultural practices) are especially meaningful. Around the world, individuals and communities are "performing environmentalisms" through sonic, musical, and other forms of cultural expression,[68] thereby consolidating their relationships to the world around them, responding to unfolding environmental and climate crises, exposing environmental and climate injustices, and issuing calls to action.[69] So it is for the people of Leweton. In every manifestation of *etëtung*, its performers are maintaining and passing on *kastom*, the embedded environmental and cultural knowledge that forms a rich resource for the community's efforts to adapt to their changing world. In this way, each performance of *etëtung* builds the collective resilience of the community.[70] Each performance counteracts the threats that climate injustice presents to cultural sustainability, and to the lives and futures of the Leweton people. Maintaining *etëtung* as a dynamic contemporary practice is, in itself, an act of cultural resistance and climate justice.

*

With Vanuatu's tropical climate, attractive beaches and coral reefs, active volcanos, and striking topography, tourism is one of the nation's largest industries. Over the last two decades, perceiving tourism to be an especially promising industry for growth, the Vanuatuan government has channeled substantial resources into the sector.[71] As part of these efforts, ni-Vanuatu culture has been increasingly recognized and promoted as an integral part of what the nation has to offer. Tourists arriving by plane and cruise ship are offered opportunities to peruse and purchase cultural handicrafts and to join cultural workshops, performances, excursions, and tours.

Since its founding in 2008, Leweton Cultural Village has become one of the most well-known and successful of these cultural tourist attractions in Vanuatu. Most visitors are funneled to the Village from the cruise companies that dock nearby. Since cruise-ship tourists typically only visit the Village for an hour or two, a concrete pool has been constructed within its bounds, eliminating the need for the women performers (and the tourists) to make the trip to the ocean or another natural water source for performance. Substantial attention has gone into curating these performances for tourist taste. The women performers replace their contemporary dress with customary grass-woven costumes from Gaua and Merelava, sometimes with armbands and headwear of woven leaves, flowers, coconuts and pandanus.[72] The performances consistently attract high-rating reviews on tourism websites, the reviewers often enthusiastically referring to the "wonderful" or "magical" Water Music that forms the central showpiece.[73] The women of Leweton regularly receive invitations to perform in tourist resorts elsewhere on Espiritu Santo and other nearby islands, too.

Over the years, thousands of tourists have experienced *etëtung* and other *kastom* practices, performed by the Leweton villagers, at the Leweton Cultural Village and elsewhere in Vanuatu. Numerous benefits have accrued to the people of Leweton. The pooled revenue from the enterprise has enabled new infrastructure to be built in the village, including new homes (huts) and toilets, modestly improving the quality of life for its inhabitants. The gendered nature of the practice has expanded employment prospects and financial independence for the women of Leweton, in an otherwise restricted local employment context.[74] The success of the enterprise has incentivized the women to teach *etëtung* to younger generations, and the girls to learn it, and the community at large now sees value in supporting and encouraging its practice and transmission. The Leweton Cultural Village has focused the community's efforts to maintain and promote *kastom* practices more generally, too. It has enabled them to share their cultural heritage with international visitors, to teach those visitors about the significance of ni-Vanuatu culture, and to educate them about local environmental and other challenges, including those wrought by the climate crisis.

However, in Vanuatu, as in many other parts of the world, relationships between culture, tourism, and the natural environment are uneasy ones. For starters, the cruise and airline industries are hefty carbon polluters.[75] On the island of Espiritu Santo, tourism has degraded beaches, coral reefs, and water quality in lagoons; it has led to rivers and mangroves being dredged, vegetation being cleared, and people being dispossessed of land.[76] Leweton Cultural Village founder Sandy Sur has long been dismayed about certain harmful local impacts of tourism, including the damage to coral reefs near Leweton caused by the massive cruise liners that dock there. At the same time, he recognizes the paradox: these same liners feed the Leweton Cultural Village with tourists, generating income for the village, providing direction to their practice of *kastom*, and enabling the community to educate the visitors about the local ramifications of the climate crisis.[77]

If tourism entails environmental harms, the climate crisis in turn jeopardizes the tourism industry and thus Vanuatu's economic stability at large. Extreme weather events (like Cyclone Pam) damage infrastructure and inhibit tourism.[78] Declining average rainfall, combined with the tourism sector's "voracious consumption" of water, has left tourists and locals alike struggling to access a reliable supply of safe drinking water, especially in rural areas.[79] Over time, coral bleaching, coastal inundation and erosion, and other types of environmental degradation reduce the nation's attractiveness to tourists. Thus, a perilous cycle is in motion: the local ramifications of the climate crisis are hampering a healthy tourism industry; ni-Vanuatu people are left with less capacity to convert their rich cultural and environmental resources into income through cultural tourism; and this circumstance further exacerbates the economic and cultural threats the climate crisis poses to the nation and its people.

In tourism terms, one possible response to this cycle is for local communities to develop environmentally responsible tourism opportunities that build on Vanuatu's strengths, reduce its vulnerabilities, and seek to mitigate climate harm. Through the Leweton Cultural Village enterprise, the people of Leweton are striving to leverage their key strengths—local environmental and cultural assets—to respond to three local vulnerabilities: cultural endangerment, environmental degradation, and economic instability. In this endeavor, the villagers are positioning *etëtung* as distinctive and meaningful not only despite the climate crisis, but because of it. "The sounds of Water Music are still the same, but the meaning of Water Music is different now, because of climate change," performer Cecelia Lolonun told me; "climate change changes everything about nature and us. We have to keep on teaching traditional ways of looking after things. If we keep these ways strong, we can keep our nature alive."[80]

The process of *etëtung*'s commodification has not always been straightforward. Following some disagreements (partly over pricing) between Leweton Cultural Village and the major cruise company that channeled tourists there, a nearby village began to offer commercial *etëtung* performances too, for a time leading to some inter-village tensions around which individuals and communities have the right to perform *etëtung*, in which settings, and under which terms.[81] Though this matter was eventually resolved, contestations around cultural property rights and cultural ownership are ongoing for Leweton Cultural Village as they are throughout Vanuatu, a predictable and perhaps inevitable consequence of the commercialization of *kastom*.[82]

*

Etëtung enjoys what scholars have called "inherent portability:"[83] it can be performed in any waist-deep water, is not tied to any specific cultural site, and requires little infrastructure or resources beyond the water and the performers' bodies, knowledge, and skill. This physical portability makes *etëtung* economically and practically attractive to international event and festival organizers. Inasmuch as it features water, *etëtung* is psychologically portable too: people and cultures around the world recognize that water is essential for survival. The combined physical and psychological portability of *etëtung* is perhaps one reason that the tradition has proven more easily mobilized in the service of climate justice than many other cultural practices.

Since the founding of the Leweton Cultural Village in 2008, *etëtung* has facilitated the Leweton people's participation in national and international dialogue on cultural sustainability and climate justice. Operating as the "Leweton Cultural Group" (a sub-entity of the Leweton Cultural Village), women from the Leweton community have performed *etëtung* around the world, promoting their *kastom* and raising awareness of the importance to their local community, and more broadly, of healthy water, land, ecosystems, environment, and culture. Over the past decade, the women have appeared at world exhibitions and festivals in Spain, Malaysia, Australia, and several diplomatic functions of the European Union, as well as various national and regional events in Vanuatu. In 2014, in collaboration with the Australian label

Wantok, the Leweton Cultural Group produced the DVD *Vanuatu Women's Water Music* to critical acclaim; the product, which includes a thirty-two-page print and e-booklet describing the genesis and practice of *etëtung*, aims to promote awareness of the value of culture and environment to the people of Leweton.[84] Awareness-raising is important for many villagers: "Water Music is my identity, my culture," young performer Vanessa Nilson told me; "I hope [it] teach[es] people overseas . . . about changes in the lives of people and the environment in Vanuatu."[85]

While it is true that Leweton's international touring, recording, and performing of *etëtung* can be understood as their exporting a world music product for the arts and music festival and film circuits,[86] this is not the full story. As its community members travel nationally and internationally to perform *etëtung*, they are also staking a firm claim to their participation in the global climate discourse, informing and educating their audiences about the deep relationships between people, culture, water, environment, and climate. Ethnomusicologist Brian Diettrich and colleagues warn that in Small Island Developing States in the Pacific, music as a tourist product can "support and maintain a power system wherein Islanders are the suppliers of services but seldom the ones who control and reap the power on a global, or even national, level."[87] This vulnerability is redolent of the procedural injustices of the climate crisis described earlier in this chapter, where Indigenous peoples in developing countries are among those most affected by climate change, but have held little sway in international decisions about how to address it. By contrast, the case of Leweton Cultural Village, a project fully initiated and driven by the community to further its own cultural, economic, and environmental goals, illustrates how one small Indigenous community of the Global South is turning the tide on these injustices. The very nature of *etëtung* as an attractive cultural expression makes it a powerful tool in climate justice efforts: persuasive and compelling to outsiders (whether tourists, festival audiences, diplomats, or policymakers), it lacks any semblance of the dominance or protectionism that have misguidedly characterized many externally led climate response tools or initiatives in Vanuatu.

Further to Leweton Cultural Village's performance and recording activities, founder Sandy Sur has profiled *etëtung* at over a dozen international conferences and symposia over the last decade or so, often in collaboration with Australian researchers (including this writer). By delivering conference papers, participating in panel discussions, and even performing a "virtual opening ceremony" from Leweton for one conference,[88] Sandy has shared with thousands of people around the world how sounds and stories are key to his community's understandings of place, and how culture is proving a catalyst for exploring and responding to environmental and climate crises. Sandy's ongoing commitment to maintaining and promoting *etëtung* is driven by several factors, including his personal conviction about its cultural importance for his community, his recognition of its role and potential as a renewable local socioeconomic resource, and increasingly, his awareness of how *etëtung* may advance climate justice for his community (and in this way, for other Indigenous and small-island communities around the world).[89] In this pursuit, he is not alone. Through the efforts of Indigenous people the world over, Chad Hamill writes, Indigenous cultural practices and their embedded environmental knowledge are helping Indigenous communities adapt to the effects of the climate crisis, inform and influence Western-dominated decisions about climate adaptation and mitigation, and unify with other communities to strengthen Indigenous self-determination around the globe.[90]

Although *etëtung* has become an iconic cultural attraction and a formidable tool in the pursuit of climate justice, it retains its identity as a *kastom* practice. The international profile of the Leweton Cultural Village has reinvigorated local interest in *etëtung* (and other *kastom* practices), encouraging Leweton villagers of all ages to learn, learn about, teach, participate in, and support its practice. Moreover, the success of the enterprise has motivated other communities in the Banks Islands group and beyond to learn more about their own *kastom* activities and to renew their practice of them. Several of these groups of girls and women are now re-engaging in local Water Music traditions, resulting in "pride and pleasure amongst the Leweton community based on the fact that people in the Banks Islands are performing this music again."[91]

7
The Eyes of All Future Generations

"You say you love your children above all else," sixteen-year-old climate activist Greta Thunberg rebuked distinguished delegates at a 2018 United Nations convention, "and yet you're stealing their future in front of their very eyes."[1] At the UN Climate Action Summit in New York later that year, she chided world leaders:

> How dare you! You have stolen my dreams and my childhood with your empty words. . . . You are failing us. But the young people are starting to understand your betrayal. The eyes of all future generations are upon you.[2]

The young Thunberg's impassioned words and actions mobilized millions around the world to join her in calling for urgent climate action.[3] Arguably Thunberg's greatest contribution as a teenaged climate activist was to place on the global stage, loud and clear, the voice of children and youth—the age group set to be most affected by the climate crisis. Now in adulthood, Thunberg continues to assail world leaders for what she calls their "thirty years of blah, blah, blah" on climate change, and to advocate for immediate and strong climate action.[4]

While the climate crisis (a theme of Chapter 6 of this book) is probably the most palpable example of a social justice concern whereby today's decisions chart a course for tomorrow, the future is deeply implicated in all manner of social justice concerns. The present-day freedoms and resources people have (or do not have) to express their cultural identities will determine how their children and grandchildren develop and express their own identities (Chapters 1, 2, and 4). Government policies and practices determining who may live safely and permanently in a given country (and who may not) will affect individual and family trajectories for generations to come (Chapter 5). The inclusiveness (or not) of educational institutions will affect lives and livelihoods long into the future (Chapter 3). And so on, across healthcare, food security, gender

Sounding Good. Catherine Grant, Oxford University Press. © Oxford University Press 2025.
DOI: 10.1093/oso/9780197698433.003.0008

equality, disaster prevention, disability support, and many other areas. In short, present-day decisions and actions expand freedoms and opportunities for some and limit them for others—not only now, but long in the future. We might therefore hope and expect of today's decision-makers that they consider the consequences for tomorrow of their decisions.

Too often, though, political decisions prioritize the short game. According to the globally prevailing political and economic paradigm, the greatest financial and political rewards for those in positions of power derive from their increasing today's financial profit, maximizing short-term economic growth, and growing the prosperity of individuals (especially those who are already wealthy). Often, these goals are attempted—and sometimes achieved—through strategies that deprive future generations of resources, opportunities, or other advantages like a stable climate, arable soil, unpolluted seas, or the integrity of political borders. Russia's 2022 invasion of Ukraine is one egregious example (among many), representing the attempted theft of the nationhood, sovereignty, land, culture, and identity of the Ukrainian people, now and for generations to come. Political activist and journalist George Monbiot maintains that this whole paradigm is founded on looting: "looting from other people, looting from other nations, looting from other species, and looting from the future. . . . Everything we take for ourselves we take from someone else."[5] The World Future Council contends that in certain cases—like that of willful climate inaction—such looting amounts to crimes against future generations: that is, actions (or inactions) that risk causing "serious, widespread and long-term harm to the health, safety, or survival of future generations."[6]

The opposite of intergenerational theft is *intergenerational justice.* Intergenerational justice can be a retrospective affair, as when present generations seek reparation for injustices of the past. (Consider Cambodia's efforts toward restorative justice in the decades following the Khmer Rouge genocide, mentioned in Chapter 1.) But when intergenerational justice is forward-looking, it becomes *future justice*, the kind of social justice that strives for safety, fairness, and prosperity for present and future generations alike. If social justice attends "to how people, policies, practices, curricula, and institutions may be used to liberate rather than oppress those least served by our decision making,"[7] future justice is concerned with how to liberate both those who are alive now and those who will live in the future. It is about making economic, social, and cultural advances for present generations while securing and strengthening the life quality and conditions of future generations too.[8] Future justice has been an implicit theme of this book so far, one that this closing chapter now makes explicit—because when we think about cultural sustainability, social justice, and their intersections, we are also thinking about tomorrow's chances of a better world.

*

In the introduction to this book, I invited the reader to reflect on what social justice might look like in reality. How would a socially just world differ in practical terms from the world we inhabit? The practice of comparing present with possible realities is a subjective affair—it engages our "*beliefs* about inequality and *perceptions* of justice"[9]—and is therefore also contestable. Each person could reasonably hold a quite distinct impression of a socially just world. Some might envisage a globally interconnected, tolerant, peaceful world order where resources are freely and equitably shared, according to need, among and between peoples and nations. Others might picture a world without borders or nations at all, where a multitude of societies live largely self-sufficiently according to their own practices and institutions in a sustainable global ecosystem. Whenever we compare what people have with what we *believe* they should have, or what they experience with what we *believe* they should experience, we are reflecting on social justice.[10] This practice of comparing contemporary realities with contemporary ideals can help us to know what we are striving for when we strive for social justice.

The distinction might seem subtle, but envisaging possible futures, not only possible contemporary realities, is worthwhile, too. What might the world look like, in social justice terms, fifty or a hundred years hence? A small thought experiment in "futures thinking" might help.[11] Imagine a young girl living in a rural village in the year 2075. Perhaps she lives in Romania, or the United States, or South Sudan—it doesn't really matter. If the intergenerational theft of economic and environmental resources is left unchecked, how might this young girl's life be? By the 2070s, perhaps decades of efforts to maximize individual wealth have meant that economic disparities in her country have continued to grow. At the same time, geopolitical power struggles around the world have exacerbated differences in security and wealth between nations. In statistical probability, the family of this rurally dwelling child finds itself at the wrong end of these measures, and they begin to sense their economic and personal security jeopardized. Moreover, because governments and billion-dollar businesses have continued to expend global resources unabatedly, the climate crisis is in full swing; recent cycles of severe drought and floods are compounding the family's poverty. Unable to grow sufficient food or earn a reasonable living, the girl's family are forced to move to an urban area, where life is even more expensive and unstable, and where the family members cannot easily practice the cultural traditions of their home village. In the city, the girl is unable to access schooling in her first language and begins to fall behind in standard educational measures of success. Her minority cultural status means that she experiences racial discrimination, its effects compounded by gender discrimination. Increasingly restrictive global migration policies, founded on fear over scarce resources and jobs, mean the girl and her family have no freedom of movement outside their country. This child's prospects for personal health and wellbeing, a successful education, a stable livelihood, and a proud and robust cultural identity seem uncertain, to say the least. (For some children alive today, this scenario is already a reality. For them, the future is now.)

Now consider what life might look like for this young girl if the lives of children in the future are prioritized more than they are currently (even if not on fully equal standing with those currently in authority, in case that seems a little *too* utopian). By 2075, people in positions of power, at least in some parts of the world, will have gradually implemented structural measures that empower those with less and oblige those with more to act responsibly and fairly. For the young girl in this thought experiment, these measures have resulted in greater local social equity, bringing greater stability, safety, and security to life in her rural village. Concerted global greenhouse gas reduction efforts, over some decades now, have meant that her family's crops remain a fairly reliable source of food and income, at least for now. The girl and her family can afford to access local health services, which are provided in their own language. At the village school, the girl learns from a teacher of her own ethnolinguistic and cultural background. Economic security, general health and wellbeing, an inclusive education, and a safer society enable this child to develop a strong sense of personal and cultural identity within her community. All things considered, life is good.

Envisaging possible futures engages our worldviews, perceptions, and experiences. It also demands our creativity. When we try to imagine a socially just world, "the end point, a new order, cannot be fathomed from our current vantage point."[12] This shouldn't stop us trying. Envisaging socially just futures can encourage and inspire us. It can help us reassess the prevailing social contract between generations. It can remind us that the future costs of policy inaction on matters of social justice may considerably outweigh the costs of preventative or corrective action.[13] And it can prompt us to consider, or reconsider, the legacy we wish to leave for those on this planet after us.

*

Imagining a socially just world can remind us of something further, too: that cultural sustainability is a matter of future justice, much like economic, social, and ecological sustainability is. To date, future justice hasn't featured much in rationales for supporting cultural sustainability. For much of the twentieth century, in anthropological and ethnomusicological circles, cultural "traditions" were largely viewed and valued as time-honored inheritances through the ages—a trait, it was reasoned, that bestowed them present-day worth. This trope certainly had benefits: among other things, it encouraged critical consideration of how the past is represented in the present (including whose cultural histories are told, and how). It also helped rationalize the efforts of UNESCO and other cultural agencies to "preserve" and "safeguard" what came to be known as "intangible cultural heritage."

Around the turn of this century, the past began to loosen its grip on matters of cultural sustainability. In 1997, UNESCO's *Declaration on the Responsibilities of the Present Generations towards Future Generations* urged current generations to protect and safeguard their cultural heritage, so as to pass it on to future generations.[14] Scholars in critical heritage studies started to shift away from characterizing cultural heritage chiefly in legacy terms, and began to recognize it as a process that depended on, and responded to, human actions and agency in the present.[15] Ethnomusicologists and folklorists began to frame musical and other cultural traditions not as artifacts, but as responsive processes situated within complex, dynamic sociocultural ecosystems. By these new framings, cultural sustainability mattered not so much because of the intrinsic or inherited worth of any given tradition, but because of the social, cultural, economic, educational, political, or environmental value of cultural practices to individuals and communities. In this way, a "human dimension" was introduced into cultural sustainability scholarship,[16] whereby the wellbeing of individuals and communities took precedence over concerns about the prospects of any specific cultural practice. This human dimension remains prominent in contemporary ethnomusicological and folklore thinking about cultural sustainability.[17]

The future is gradually becoming recognized as an integral component of this human dimension to cultural sustainability, too.[18] Cultural practices themselves have long been valued as a way to envisage and bring about better possible futures: music and other arts have been understood as a realm where the impossible, non-existent, or ideal "is imagined and made possible," and where new possibilities lead to new lived realities.[19] Ethnomusicologist Deonte Harris observes that this is especially true for marginalized and oppressed groups, for whom cultural expressions can be a way to explore the gap between what is, and what is possible.[20] If this is true, then the sustainable future of cultural practices will not only be important for people alive now, but also for those who live in the future. Moreover, maintaining a rich global diversity of cultural practices expands possibilities for everyone, not only now, but for generations to come.[21] Folklorists Michael Mason and Rory Turner argue that expansive, holistic, future-oriented thinking is a crucial part of what it is to "do" cultural sustainability—that cultural sustainability should engage "the whole social and cultural ecosystem and its current actors to chart a course for self-conscious cultural change."[22] These future justice orientations are an exciting development in the area of cultural sustainability.

But it is worth remembering that applying a future justice lens to cultural sustainability is a means, not an end. Seeking to better understand (as this book does) the present and potential benefits of sustainable cultural practices lays the *groundwork* for acts of future justice. It is not, itself, an act of future justice (and nor is this book). The acts of future justice come when policymakers and governments, researchers and funding bodies, teachers and lecturers, educational and social institutions, and all other advocates, activists, and powerbrokers across the breadth of cultural and social spheres incorporate a future justice lens into their policy and practice: that is, when we—all of us—make decisions that consider not only the short-term benefits (and costs) of our actions, but also the likely benefits (and costs) for those who will live on this planet after we are gone.

*

The case studies in this book illustrate how, when musicians make music, they are not only maintaining cultural practices: they are also often engaging in acts of social justice, including future justice. Music-making is not only a cultural or an aesthetic act: it is also often a political one, proffering a way to reflect on society, and to reconfigure it. When a young girl tries out a traditional musical instrument at a workshop of the Khmer Magic Music Bus in the Cambodian countryside (Chapter 1), or a Saharawi mother teaches her son a revolutionary Saharawi *nidal* song (Chapter 5), or an Indigenous cultural elder in Brazil steps in front of a university lecture-room for the first time (Chapter 3), these people are participating in and enabling the advancement of cultural, educational, political, racial, economic, and gender justice (and more besides), for themselves and those who will come after them. As music researchers Tia DeNora and Gary Ansdell discern, it is not "the music itself" that accomplishes social change for the better, "but rather what is done with, done to, and done alongside musical engagement." In this sense, they quip, "music can do nothing and everything."[23] The case studies in this book illustrate how music—or more precisely, what people do with, to, and alongside music—can play considerable roles in advocating for, and advancing, more prosperous and equitable societies.

What might we do with the new understandings of music, cultural sustainability, and social justice gained through this book? In one sense, generalizing an answer to that question would be problematic. Music education researcher Juliet Hess reminds us that considering the social and cultural particularities of each local setting is not only a matter of good research practice, but also one of ethics. When researchers recognize and acknowledge the specificity of their findings, they honor the distinctiveness of the contexts they study and prompt other researchers to "only implement strategies that pertain to their specific place and time."[24] Instead of pursuing "mythical objective truth," then—which music education scholar Leigh Patel reminds us is "on the side of coloniality"—it is better to ask: "What knowledge might be useful at this moment, in this place?"[25] I therefore leave others to decide how the findings of this book may be relevant for specific local cultures and communities.

I do, however, wish to comment on the possible implications of this book for broader efforts to promote cultural sustainability and social justice. First, I want to emphasize that the relationships between cultural sustainability and social justice are not always as positive as the case studies presented in this book suggest. As explained in the Introduction, this book deliberately focuses on musical examples where cultural sustainability and social justice are directly correlated—that is, where cultural loss and social injustice go hand in hand (whichever the causality), as do cultural sustainability and social justice. In Cambodia, the Khmer Rouge genocide led to the massive loss of cultural practices; their contemporary revitalization represents a form of cultural justice (Chapter 1). For the Leweton people of Vanuatu (Chapter 6), climate injustices (and other challenges) jeopardize the viable future of certain cultural practices; those same cultural practices are now helping progress climate justice for that community. Similarly, the Meeting of Knowledges in Brazil (Chapter 3) and the Rural Craft and Cultural Hubs in India (Chapter 4), on educational and economic justice, respectively, illustrate direct correlations between cultural sustainability and matters of social justice.

The cases of the Australian First Nations' mission songs (Chapter 2) and the music of the Saharawi people (Chapter 5) are perhaps a little more complex in this regard. The direct social justice–cultural sustainability correlation is still evident: the contemporary revival of the mission songs through the Mission Songs Project advances racial and cultural justice for First Australians, and the Saharawi people's maintenance of their traditional music and creation of new revolutionary music genres in the Algerian refugee camps is a step toward political and cultural justice for a displaced people. And yet, these cases suggest that the social justice–cultural sustainability relationship is not always as straightforward as it may seem. The mission songs show how creativity, cultural resourcefulness, and cultural vitality sometimes go hand in hand with social *in*justice: this musical practice arguably only emerged and thrived *because of* circumstances of racial and cultural oppression on the missions. For the Saharawi people, too, the genesis and practice (over five decades now) of *nidal*, the repertoire of political revolutionary songs, has been borne of land dispossession, cultural and political subjugation, and forced displacement.

Cultural sustainability and social justice, then, are not always easy bedfellows. Ethnomusicologist Ruth Opara writes about how girls of Igbo ethnicity in southeastern Nigeria are exposed to (and resist) gender-based violence through their practice of the pot drum dance *Avu Udu*—and how recent well-meaning efforts to sustain the dance have exacerbated the violence.[26] Michael Silvers describes how the impressive poverty alleviation achievements of the leftist Brazilian government at the start of the second decade of this century were sometimes paradoxically at odds with the sustainability of local music practices.[27] Kirsten Dyck explores how neo-Nazi and white-power music incites racist hate and harm, and how its rising profile and popularity in several countries is being actively suppressed by public authorities.[28] Further examples are not difficult to come by.[29] In my editorial introduction to a recent compilation of articles on social justice, human rights, and the sustainability of traditional arts, the only conclusions I could safely draw were about the complexities of their interconnections—to wit:

> that vibrant and viable traditional arts practices can be formidable instruments in the pursuit of social justice and human rights, but can also work against them; that human rights violations and social injustices can threaten the sustainability of traditional arts, but perhaps counterintuitively also underpin them; and that local, regional, and national cultural sustainability initiatives and interventions can have beneficial, but also multifaceted and complex, ramifications for human rights and/or social justice.[30]

As researchers and other stakeholders seek to better understand the dynamics of cultural sustainability and social justice, remaining alert to these complexities could help avert any glib claims about the unadulterated benefits of social justice pursuits for cultural sustainability, or vice versa.

While this book has primarily explored correlations in the cultural sustainability and social justice relationship, much could be gained from further efforts to understand causality—although the likely challenges of that task are prefigured by existing research that attempts to understand the social impact of arts-based interventions.[31] For some case studies in this book, the direction of causality seems relatively clear. In West Bengal (Chapter 4), the efforts of the Rural Craft and Cultural Hubs to advance economic justice for artists and their communities have precipitated the renewed vitality of local musical and other cultural practices—that is, social justice actions have resulted in cultural sustainability gains. In the case of the *Portraits of Saharawi Music* project (Chapter 5), the directionality could be understood in reverse: the project's cultural documentation and maintenance goals have contributed to Saharawi political and cultural justice—that is, cultural sustainability actions have resulted in social justice gains. For some other cases in this book, the directionality is less clear. While the Mission Songs Project (Chapter 2) is certainly a cultural sustainability initiative (in that it revives a musical tradition that had fallen away as a living practice), Jessie Lloyd conceived of the project as having both social justice and cultural maintenance intentions. The cultural tourism enterprise of the Leweton Cultural Village (Chapter 6) is another example of equivocal causality: the endeavors of the Leweton community to revitalize *kastom* practices including *etëtung* have (somewhat unexpectedly) advanced climate justice for the community—but in parallel, its climate advocacy is stimulating new contexts, functions, and opportunities for *etëtung*. From the cases presented in this book, perhaps it can only safely be surmised that the causality between social justice and cultural sustainability depends on the context. Better understanding causality (and the correlations more generally) may guide practical, context-specific decisions about whether to primarily attend to cultural sustainability concerns for the sake of social justice outcomes, or the converse. (If the case studies in this book are indicative, the answer will almost certainly lie in a balance of the two.)

As understandings grow about the relationships between cultural sustainability and social justice, cultural advocates and scholars should guard against any tendency to assume that injustices are at the root of all circumstances of cultural endangerment, or that advances in social justice always hold the key to the survival of at-risk practices. Some cultural practices may die away for quite innocuous reasons. The corpus of Māori rowing-songs mentioned in the opening chapter, for example, no longer held a meaningful function for its practitioners, as technologies and lifestyles changed.[32] As that example suggests, not all impending or actual cultural losses necessarily warrant intervention, especially if the practitioners and their communities are not particularly concerned about the loss. And yet, those cultural losses most likely to cause concern, harm, or suffering to practitioners and their communities—whether in the present or in the future—are undoubtedly those occasioned by inequity or injustice, since it is inequity or injustice that leads to people losing their agency to participate freely in the cultural practices and cultural lives of their choosing. (Here I remind the reader of my definition of cultural sustainability from the Introduction: individuals and social groups having agency over which cultural practices they engage in, and how).

Perhaps that last point sounds depressing, and in a way it is: social injustice leads to cultural losses that further harm people. But for those concerned with cultural sustainability and global cultural diversity, it is also immense grounds for optimism—because precisely there, where cultural sustainability matters most, are we most likely to have the capacity to do something about it. Arguably, something can always be done to advance social justice (even if that "something" takes months, years, or generations to bear fruit). When we engage our creativity, imagination, and hope—all admittedly in good measure—social justice is achievable. If we believe that to be true, we are in luck on two counts, because then cultural sustainability is achievable too.

How could it be done? To date, the cultural sustainability strategies associated with UNESCO's 2003 Convention on the Urgent Safeguarding of Intangible Cultural Heritage have largely focused on protecting or supporting specific at-risk cultural practices directly, often through targeted local- or national-level interventions: festivals and performances, documentation and archiving projects, cultural education programs, and so on. Many of these activities have brought temporary or sustained improvement in the vitality of certain cultural practices; some have brought concomitant social benefits too (such as those resulting from bringing people together to express and celebrate a shared cultural identity). However, in situations (like those presented in this book) where some or other social injustice has threatened cultural sustainability, cultural interventions that narrowly seek to support a specific cultural practice or practices merely address the symptoms of cultural endangerment, not its root cause. Moreover, as I have just argued, it is precisely such circumstances involving injustice or inequity where cultural endangerment is most likely to aggrieve culture-bearers and their communities, and therefore where achieving cultural sustainability is most important. Yet without overcoming (or attempting to overcome) the social impediments ("unfreedoms," to use economist Amartya Sen's term[33]) that result in the need for cultural safeguarding in the first place, narrowly conceived cultural sustainability interventions in settings such as these seem precisely those least likely, ironically and unfortunately, to succeed in the long term.

Instead, in such circumstances, the interests of cultural sustainability would seem best served by nurturing the social preconditions that allow cultural practices to thrive, now and in the future. Sometimes, for example, cultural sustainability may be best supported by reforming social institutions and practices to be more equitable (as does Meeting of Knowledges, Chapter 3). At other times, it may be best supported by empowering those who experience poverty or other unfreedoms—as in the Rural Craft and Cultural Hubs (Chapter 4), the social enterprise in rural communities of West Bengal that cultivated the socioeconomic "soil" from which local cultural practices could begin to regenerate. In considering how culture should be integrated into sustainable development, economist and philosopher Amartya Sen encouraged such holistic thinking, arguing that culture should not be understood as something that works in isolation, but rather as only one of many dynamic and interactive influences on society.[34]

Attending to the wider ecosystems in which cultural practices operate characterizes what I call a "future justice orientation" to cultural sustainability work. A future justice orientation considers the future implications of decisions about cultural support strategies. It recognizes that cultural sustainability initiatives that advance social justice yield social *and* cultural gains now and in the future—gains likely exceeding those produced by measures that focus narrowly on the viability of specific cultural practices. Adopting a future justice orientation could help practitioners and communities, researchers and policymakers, cultural agencies, and other changemakers, from the grassroots to transnational, develop more effective cultural support strategies that simultaneously address social and cultural concerns. Attending to the wider causes of cultural precarity greatly expands the options for supporting cultural practices; focusing on causes rather than symptoms increases the chances of long-term success. Some scholars are already advocating for such an integrated, future-justice approach to cultural sustainability. Tan Sooi Beng's engaged activist research on the endangered Chinese globe puppet theatre *potehi* in Penang (Malaysia) is a leading example, driven not only by cultural sustainability objectives, but also by Tan's stated commitment "to a larger struggle for minority rights and cultural equity."[35] Her project has produced inspiring outcomes in both cultural sustainability and future justice terms.

One implication of a future justice orientation to cultural sustainability is that no single scholarly discipline, or even worldview, is likely to hold all the solutions to cultural sustainability concerns. Cultural sustainability researchers and advocates whose work and lives are founded on Western epistemologies will need to look beyond their own sociocultural norms and values, and beyond the conventional bounds of their areas of expertise. This means that collaboration with practitioners and communities, as well as with experts across a range of disciplinary areas, will be key. So too will thinking outside of disciplinary confines. In the realm of cultural policy, for example—which Anthony Seeger identifies as one where ethnomusicologists should continually strive to be influential[36]—UNESCO has come to recognize that policies to protect and promote cultural practices can and should be made not only *qua* cultural policies, but also as policies across a range of areas: gender equality, climate change mitigation, decent employment, sustainable economic growth, social inclusion, and more.[37] In bringing our expertise to bear on policy decisions relating to cultural sustainability, researchers and other cultural agents should consider social concerns (and their possible cultural implications) in addition to cultural concerns. This flips on its head the more common trope in cultural policy debate, which maintains that culture holds the key to solving economic, social, cultural, and environmental challenges.[38] Here, my point is not that cultural policy could inform social policy or address social concerns (true through that may be); rather, it is that culturally-informed social policy could advance cultural sustainability, in addition to the social concerns it seeks to address.

And, of course, a future justice orientation to cultural sustainability not only increases prospects for keeping cultural practices strong, but also expands opportunities to progress social justice. To make this case, I turn to the United Nations' Sustainable Development Goals (SDGs), adopted by UN Member States as part of the 2030 Agenda for Sustainable Development.[39] Sustainable development is about more than just economic growth; Amartya Sen influentially defined it as the expansion of human freedoms.[40] To be sustainable, development must not only address the needs of present generations, but also allow future generations to meet their needs too. By expanding the freedoms of people now and in the future, sustainable development is a means, according to UNESCO, "to achieve a more satisfactory intellectual, emotional, moral and spiritual existence."[41] Thus, embracing a future justice perspective, the UN's seventeen SDGs are intended to guide and mobilize all countries toward greater social inclusion, economic prosperity, environmental sustainability, good governance, and effective partnerships (Figure 7.1; for color figure, see ▶ Example 7.1).[42]

Though none of the SDGs centers on culture, the UN acknowledges that culture will be important to achieving them (and much applied research bears this out).[43] UNESCO aims to ensure that culture is incorporated into all development policies—whether related to education, science, health, environment, communication, or tourism.[44] And yet, culturally integrated approaches to

Figure 7.1 United Nations Sustainable Development Goals. https://www.un.org/sustainabledevelopment/news/communications-material/

realizing the SDGs are yet to gain wide traction, and so their potential to accelerate sustainable development remains largely unrealized.[45]

The case studies in this book illustrate how vibrant musical practices, and initiatives that aim to support their sustainability, advance the SDGs (see ▶ Example 7.2). All six case study projects are locally advancing (or have advanced) three of the Goals: *SDG 3 Good Health and Wellbeing*, by promoting cultural participation, cultural strength, a sense of cultural identity, and better social and cultural conditions; *SDG 10 Reduced Inequality*, by progressing the causes of fairness and equity across cultural, racial, economic, educational, climate, and refugee domains; and *SDG 16 Peace, Justice and Strong Institutions*, by promoting just, peaceful, and inclusive societies and, in some cases, building more effective and inclusive institutions (such as Meeting of Knowledges strengthening educational institutions, and Rural Craft and Cultural Hubs strengthening governmental policy).

Each of the case studies contributes to further SDGs, too. Meeting of Knowledges promotes culturally inclusive tertiary education (*SDG 4 Quality Education*). Leweton Cultural Village empowers women and girls to generate income and participate in international climate advocacy for their Indigenous community (*SDG 5 Gender Equality* and *SDG 13 Climate Action*). Leweton Cultural Village and the Rural Craft and Cultural Hubs are raising awareness of the social and cultural value of water and water ecologies, through the water-related cultural practices *etëtung* and *bhatiyali*, respectively (*SDG 14 Life Below Water*). The Rural Craft and Cultural Hubs have enabled artists and other community members to participate in training and education (*SDG 4 Quality Education*); they have also raised the social mobility, cultural participation, and income of women (*SDG 5 Gender Equality*), expanded industry and infrastructure in participating communities, especially in the tourism and cultural sectors (*SDG 9 Industry, Innovation and Infrastructure*), and promoted the ethical consumption and production of cultural goods and services (*SDG 12 Responsible Consumption and Production*). The Khmer Magic Music Bus, Leweton Cultural Village, and Rural Craft and Cultural Hubs are all helping make rural or peri-urban settlements (in Cambodia, Vanuatu and India, respectively) more resilient and sustainable, by expanding opportunities for people to participate meaningfully in the social and cultural lives of their communities (*SDG 11 Sustainable Cities and Communities*). Those three initiatives, as well as Meeting of Knowledges, employ artists of traditional cultural practices in their programs, thus contributing to poverty alleviation (*SDG 1 No Poverty*) and helping to grow the local economy (*SDG 8 Decent Work and Economic Growth*). The Rural Craft and Cultural Hubs and *Portraits of Saharawi Music* mobilize and strengthen partnerships between local communities, public institutions, governmental departments, and non-profit organizations (*SDG 17 Partnerships for the Goals*). *Portraits of Saharawi Music* has also contributed to *SDG 11 Sustainable Cities and Communities*, even if the eventual goal is for the camps to disband as Saharawi people return to their homeland: the project established safe spaces for music-making in the Tindouf refugee settlements, providing opportunities for Saharawi people to build connections, express their shared political aspirations, and reflect together on experiences of refugee life.

In sum, through their "inclusive, people-centered and context-relevant approach" to sustainable development,[46] the case study initiatives in this book demonstrate how advancing social justice can sustain culture; how sustaining culture can progress the cause of social justice, including future justice; and how music can be central to these efforts.

*

It is not only big cultural or social institutions like the UN or UNESCO that are key players in matters of social justice and cultural sustainability. All of us who engage with music or the other arts, or who aspire to create rich cultural lives and cultural futures for ourselves and others, can help reform institutional structures so that they are more socially just, and so that they support a rich and sustainable local and global diversity of cultural practices. Mason and Turner encourage us: "Those interested in the project of cultural sustainability have every reason to hope that they can influence [its] arc in positive ways through projects that cultivate the capacity for and realization of self-determined cultural representation and production."[47] Given the affordances of the interconnections between cultural sustainability and social justice, cultural scholars, activists, and advocates might be encouraged to be aspirational not merely in the cultural objectives of our efforts, but in the social and political ones too.

Researchers incur obligations through the very act of encounter with marginalized and oppressed communities.[48] A growing number of ethnomusicologists are calling for a move away from "conventional neutral methods" in that field, in favor of problem-centered, socially and politically engaged research that actively seeks to influence political realities and address sociocultural concerns.[49] Ursula Hemetek and colleagues argue that we should carefully consider how ethnomusicological work can become "a political intervention in the interests of social justice,"[50] for example, working with marginalized or disempowered social groups to generate knowledge that advances the capacities and interests of those groups.[51] In such an activist ethnomusicology, musical activity is mobilized as "oppositional and emancipatory knowledge in the pursuit of social justice and the common good."[52] The time for activist agendas in music research, argues David McDonald, is now:

> At a time of widespread global conflict and violence, economic inequity, environmental devastation, and unprecedented forced migration, our training as critical scholars who uncover and strive to redress structural inequalities rooted in personal experience has never been more needed.[53]

And what of the mindset of those who would seek to advance cultural sustainability through social justice, or social justice through cultural sustainability? Inevitably limited in our abilities to effect systemic change—limited, that is, not only as musicians, researchers, or social activists, but simply as individuals often working against the immense tide of institutional power—we will likely struggle at times to reconcile our desire for social transformation with our capacity to bring it about. Each of us will need to pave our own way forward. Nevertheless, it seems safe to propose that compassion, humility, and humanity will be useful assets—not so that we forgive or forget the world's injustices and inequalities, but so that we can clearly recognize its imperfections in the human experience, accept them with equanimity, and cultivate the wisdom and strength to do what we can to address them, individually or (better) together with others. In the words of Black feminist scholar bell hooks: "The heart of justice is truth telling, seeing ourselves and the world the way it is, rather than the way we want it to be."[54] Over and over, in the writings of great thought leaders, love surfaces as key to advancing the human condition. Philosopher Martha Nussbaum believes that empathy and love, as central human capabilities, are fundamental to practicing and advancing social justice.[55] Educator and philosopher Paulo Freire writes: "No matter where the oppressed are found, the act of love is commitment to their cause—the cause of liberation.[56] And bell hooks again, on "an ethic of love": "The moment we choose to love we begin to move against domination, against oppression. The moment we choose to love we begin to move towards freedom, to act in ways that liberate ourselves and others."[57] If, as educator and social justice ally Veronica McDermott proposes, "love on a social scale is social justice,"[58] the converse is a useful idea too: that social justice on an individual scale is love. Perhaps that simple conceit could help orient our actions—as individual artists, researchers, activists, advocates, and educators. As humans.

*

Like Mark Pedelty does of his book on musical performance and environmental activism, I view this book as "a segue rather than an end point."[59] The case studies presented here only touch on the depth, breadth, and nuances of relationships between cultural sustainability and social justice. They represent a tiny fraction of the communities and places around the world where people are drawing on creativity and resilience to advance the strength of their cultures and societies in remarkable ways. I hope that this book inspires greater attentiveness to, and celebration of, such cases. I also hope that it may provide intellectual, ethical, and practical stimulus to embrace a future justice orientation in cultural sustainability work, and to explore new culturally led ways to progress the causes of social justice. But most of all, I hope this book inspires bold action spurred by optimism, for buried at the nexus of cultural sustainability and social justice lies a magnificent opportunity: to capitalize on their interconnectedness for the dual social and cultural benefit of present and future generations.

A quarter-century ago, David Miller concluded his book *Principles of Social Justice* by declaring that "the pursuit of social justice in the twenty-first century will be considerably tougher than it has been in the last half of the twentieth."[60] His prediction seems prescient. Across a multitude of economic, political, and social measures, the principles and realities of social equity and social justice seem distant, and at times receding. Much is at stake, especially for marginalized and disempowered groups, including the future of countless cultural practices and cultural lives around the world. But this century still has some course to run, and there is time to change the trajectory. Imagination and courage are called for: imagination to envisage what it would take for sustainable cultures and equitable social worlds to become reality, and the courage to believe—and act—as if it could be so. That belief, it must be said, may ultimately prove overly optimistic. But even if so, if it edges us even a little closer to a culturally rich, sustainable, equitable, and prosperous global future, it will have been worthwhile.

APPENDIX 1

Case Studies

Table A.1

Chapter	Initiative	Country	Theme	Musical practice
1	Khmer Magic Music Bus	Cambodia	Cultural justice	"Traditional" Cambodian music
2	Mission Songs Project	Australia	Racial justice Cultural justice	Australian First Nations *Mission Songs*
3	Meeting of Knowledges	Brazil	Educational justice Epistemic justice	Music of the Indigenous, Black, and Afro-Brazilian people of Brazil
4	Rural Craft and Cultural Hubs	India	Economic justice	*Bhatiyali* songs of West Bengal
5	Portraits of Saharawi Music	Western Sahara/ Algeria	Political justice Justice for those forcibly displaced (refugee justice)	Saharawi *haul* and *nidal*
6	Leweton Cultural Village	Vanuatu	Climate justice	*Etëtung* (Vanuatu Women's Water Music)

APPENDIX 2

Map of Case Study Locations

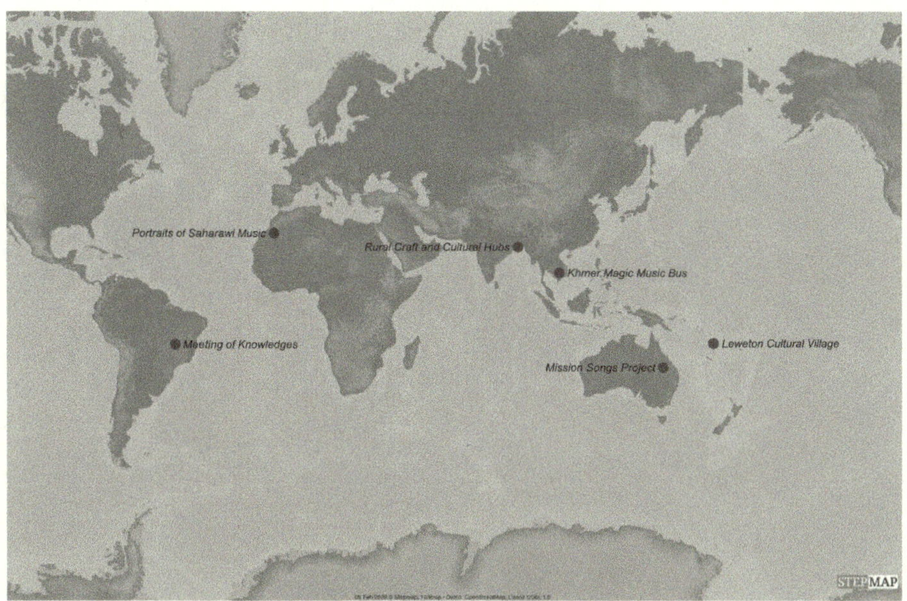

Figure A.2 Case study locations.

Notes

Preface

1. UNESCO (2003, opening section).

Introduction

1. Titon (2008–2022); see also Titon (2020).
2. Schippers and Grant (2016).
3. Stobart (2017), Alfaro Rotondo (2020).
4. Lettau, Mtaku, and Otchere (2022).
5. Gillespie (2017, 2022). Among other relationships, Gillespie notes the irony in there being available "ample wealth and infrastructure to undertake cultural heritage projects to support culture that is seen to be at risk precisely because of the [mining] industry's inherent process of wealth creation" (2017, 94).
6. Bendrups (2019), Silvers (2018), and McConnell (2019) respectively.
7. See for example Harrison (2014), Pettan and Titon (2015), Foster (2016), and Romero et al. (2022). Major philanthropic and funding agencies have sought to amplify the roles of music and other cultural practices in revealing and responding to inequalities and injustices (for example, see Walker 2015). Cultural organizations, research centers, and professional associations too are supporting research and action that address social injustices through cultural means (for example, see the ongoing *Music and Social Justice Resources Project* of the Society for Ethnomusicology, n.d.).
8. For example, contributions to the edited volume of Bartleet and Higgins (2018).
9. For example, Levy and Byrd (2011), Benedict et al. (2015).
10. Hemetek, Kölbl, and Sağlam (2019, 7).
11. Snyder and Best (2022, xi). Scholars of other forms of cultural expression, including dance and theater, are adopting similar perspectives; see for example Bell and Desai (2011), Schmidt-Pirro and McCurdy (2005), Auclair and Fairclough (2015), and Foster (2016).
12. They are the subject of Grant, Opara, and Dyck (2024). Allen acknowledges these negative correlations, commenting that even though we surely do not want to sustain environmentally harmful cultural practices or those that "condone exploitative economic and social practices . . . that exacerbate inequities and human life," some methods and musical practices attended to by ethnomusicologists "can be correlated with negative outcomes we would rather not support" (2019, 45). See also Harrison (2020a, 84).
13. Pedelty (2016, 17, 8).
14. Lorde (1984, 138). From Lorde's speech "Learning from the 60s," delivered at Harvard University in 1982.
15. Goldbard (2017, 7).

16. Ethnomusicologist Michael Silvers evidently met with this challenge in writing about the politics of environment and music in northeastern Brazil: "Just as environmental crises threaten ecologies," he writes, "they also result in forced migration, poverty, and limited access to water and other resources for the poor;" and these realities are intensified by "prejudice, corruption, unfettered capitalism, and expanding neoliberalism" (2018, 6). Similarly, Angela Impey's book *Song Walking* (2018) engages not only with gender and environmental justice (in southeast Africa), but also with colonialism, racism, land dispossession, rural-urban inequities, and other intersecting matters of human rights and social justice.
17. Sunderland et al. (2023, 7).
18. In their relationship to cultural sustainability, both disability and gender justice are considered in Gerald Groemer's stimulating historical ethnography about *goze*, blind itinerant female musicians from Japan whose traditions date back to the seventeenth century and eventually fade away in the late twentieth (Groemer 2016).
19. Taket and McKay (2020).
20. See for example Weintraub and Yung (2009), Porsdam (2019), and Sunderland et al. (2023).
21. In this book, I use the terms *cultural practices* and *musical practices* to refer to discrete genres, repertoires, or traditions (in this way, avoiding the preservationist bearing often associated with *traditions*).
22. Following international human rights instruments, in this book *community* denotes "[I]ndigenous, tribal, minority, migrant, local or other communities [groups of people] formed in accordance with criteria such as language or ethnicity" (United Nations General Assembly 2016, 5). Communities can be formed according to criteria such as age, religion, ability, and gender, too. Because individuals in a community may hold disparate views and experience their society differently, for example due to intersectional factors, I sometimes refer to *groups of people* instead.
23. McLean (1996).
24. Sethi (2001, 85).
25. See Titon (2021, 26).
26. Scholarly arguments have been mounted for decades (for example in zoomusicology) about the existence of cultural practices in the animal world (such as among whales and songbirds) and the threats to their sustainability. Jeff Todd Titon reminds us that it is possible to consider "the application of justice within a broader ecological context including the interrelations among animals, plants, landforms, forces of nature, etc." (2021, 45), an undertaking he calls *ecojustice*. Lamenting that "most music and sound scholars are unapologetically anthropocentric," ecomusicologist Aaron Allen maintains that "for successful advocacy of cultural sustainability, we must continuously make, analyze, and articulate the fundamental connections between culture and nature" (2019, 56). While this book focuses on human cultural practices, human social justice, and the intersections of each with the world around us, I fully acknowledge the immense importance of ecojustice and of the sustainability of more-than-human cultural practices, both as areas of scholarly enquiry and as practical pursuits. Chapter 6 touches further on these matters.
27. Some of these are outlined in Titon (2009), Grant (2014a), Schippers and Grant (2016), Cooley (2019a), Allen (2019), and Schippers and Seeger (2022).
28. Frandy (2022). See also Allen (2019, 45).
29. Cooley (2019b, xxv).
30. Mason and Turner (2020, 88).
31. Miller (1999), Alwin (2000, "Social Justice Research" section).

32. Rinehart, Barbour and Pope (2014, 5).
33. Reisch (2014, xxiv).
34. These "levels" of social justice are deeply intertwined, of course: the attitudes and behaviors of individuals influence institutional policies and practices, and are in turn influenced by them.
35. Charmaz (2014, 326).
36. Sensoy and DiAngelo (2019).
37. Alwin usefully distinguishes between "micro justice" that relates to a person's immediate circumstances, and "macro justice" that relates to justice for groups, or society as a whole (2011, "Perceiving Justice" section).
38. Reisch (2014, 9).
39. Throughout this book, "West" or "Western" denotes the worldview emerging from the dominant cultures and institutions in Europe and North America, as well as those English-speaking countries (like Australia and New Zealand) whose political, social, cultural and educational traditions draw substantially on Europe (after Ford 2021, 178).
40. Koger and Winter (2010).
41. See for example several chapters in Reisch (2014). Sen's *Development as Freedom* addresses this matter (2001).
42. Hopgood (2014) exposes the distinction. For the Declaration, see United Nations (1948).
43. Reisch (2014, 3).
44. Weintraub (2009, 2).
45. Rees (2009, 44).
46. Robinson (2020, 10).
47. Noting the lack of consensus in politicized contexts about capitalizing W in White (as a parallel to the now common practice of capitalizing B in Black to refer to the history, culture, and identity of people of African ancestry), Susan Asai maintains that capitalizing White acknowledges Whiteness as a racial identity, thereby embedding the racial identity and privilege of White people "in a discourse of inequality and exclusion" (2022, 280). Nell Painter (2020) advances further arguments to this end. I adopt the practice in this book, except in direct quotes where the author chooses not to capitalize the term.
48. Capeheart and Milovanovic (2007, 2).
49. Walzer (1983).
50. Harris (2022, 229). On speaking for "Others" in music research, especially oppressed populations, see also Hofman (2010) and Hess (2018, 577–578).
51. McDonald (2022, 4).
52. Wong (2021, 188).
53. Shao (2021, 88).
54. Whitmarsh and Kreil (2022, 2).
55. Grant (2018).
56. On scholarly co-publications between local experts and outsider-scholars (still "a relative rarity in ethnomusicology"), see Diamond and Castelo-Branco (2021, 20); also Bakan with Chasar, Gibson, Grace, Hamelson, Nitzberg, Peterson, Pytlik, Rindale, Sequenzia, and Silar (2018). I too have taken this approach in some of my research publications.
57. McDonald (2022, 4).
58. Asai (2022, 279, 280).
59. The sole exception is Chapter 5, where, for reasons detailed there, Mohamed Sleiman Labat's positionality is that of a Saharawi artist with lived experience of the desert refugee

camps that this chapter describes, rather than of one direct involvement in the case study project at hand.

60. Our Race (n.d.).
61. Our Race (n.d., "What is a Story?" section). Though they do not belong to the minoritized cultural groups featured in their respective case studies, José Jorge de Carvalho (Chapter 3) and Violeta Ruano Posada (Chapter 5) are Story Holders too, in as much as they spearheaded and led (with others) the initiatives represented in those chapters.
62. Ware and Dunphy (2020, 16).
63. McDonald (2021, 78). See also Harrison (2020a, 76–77) in relation to value alignment between researchers and the communities they research, including the matter of the diversity and complexity of values within communities.
64. Despite my sustained efforts through the publication process for this book—and the ideological support and advocacy efforts of my editorial team at Oxford University Press—my request to feature the Story Holders' names along with mine on the front cover of this book was ultimately unmet "for legal reasons."
65. Forsyth and Dick (2021, 6).
66. De Sousa Santos (2016, 238).
67. Harris (2022, 229).
68. Fraser (2012, 50).
69. World Economic Forum (2022).
70. Bromham et al. (2021).
71. Fraser (2012, 50)
72. Brooks (2018, subtitle).
73. McDonald (2022, 11–12)
74. Clammer (2015, 1).

1 This Music Is Magic Music

1. Glatzer (2003).
2. Arn Chorn-Pond and Thorn Seyma (personal communication, 3 July 2019).
3. Wight (2013, para. 16).
4. Wight (2013, para. 17).
5. Arn Chorn-Pond (personal communication, 3 July 2019).
6. Yale University (2019).
7. Sam (2016). According to Kallio and Westerlund, the figure may have been as high as 95 percent (2016, 91).
8. Visiting Arts (2001, 13).
9. Chorn-Pond and Ungar (2012, 100).
10. Chorn-Pond and Ungar (2012, 103–104).
11. Cohen (2005).
12. Chorn-Pond and Ungar (2012, 105).
13. The term is used in Cambodia to refer to those artists, now few, who learnt their skills prior to the Khmer Rouge era.
14. Cambodian Living Arts (2017).
15. United Nations Development Programme (2020).
16. Kallio and Westerlund (2016, 91).

17. World Bank (2019).
18. Grant (2017).
19. World Bank (2023).
20. Grant (2015).
21. Cronin-Furman (2018); see Anonymous (2021) on implications for intangible cultural heritage. Uyghur musicians have resisted State control in various ways (see Wong 2017).
22. Freemuse (2020); see also Freemuse (2022, 9).
23. IFACCA (2023, 7).
24. IFACCA (2023, 7).
25. UNESCO (2019, 2).
26. Office of the High Commissioner for Human Rights (2019, clause 62).
27. Freemuse (2022, 6).
28. Freemuse (2022, 8, 13–14).
29. United Nations (1948); see also UNESCO (2001, 2005). Fifer et al. (2022) offers case studies on intersections of music and human rights, including in relation to artistic freedom.
30. Office of the High Commissioner for Human Rights (n.d., "What Are Cultural Rights?" section, para. 1).
31. Office of the High Commissioner for Human Rights (n.d., "What Are Cultural Rights?" section, para. 2).
32. Weintraub and Yung's (2009) edited collection on music and cultural rights offers some examples, including the chapters by Rees and Stillman.
33. United Nations (1948, Article 27).
34. Office of the High Commissioner for Human Rights (1966).
35. UNESCO (2001, Article 5).
36. Office of the High Commissioner for Human Rights (2007, Articles 11, 31, et al.).
37. Findings are presented in Grant (2014b, 2015, 2016).
38. Links between poverty and cultural endangerment, and between socioeconomic empowerment and cultural sustainability, are further explored in Chapter 4, a case study from West Bengal, India.
39. Afghanistan National Institute of Music (2021).
40. World Bank (2015).
41. Khalil (2015).
42. Garrison (2017).
43. Zemaryalai and Geddie (2021, para. 5).
44. King (2021).
45. Zemaryalai and Geddie (2021).
46. UNESCO (2005, Article 2).
47. Arn Chorn-Pond (personal communication, July 3, 2019).
48. Khmer Magic Music Bus (2019). For the project's latest website, see Khmer Magic Music Bus (2022).
49. Arn Chorn-Pond and Thorn Seyma (personal communication, July 3, 2019).
50. Chorn-Pond and Ungar (2012, 105).
51. Wight (2013, para. 21).
52. Thorn Seyma (personal communication, July 3, 2019).
53. Pann (2019).
54. Pann (2019).
55. Scheidel (2015).

56. Thorn Seyma (personal communication, July 3, 2019).
57. Arn Chorn-Pond (personal communication, July 3, 2019).
58. Pann (2019). In early 2023, Doung was still teaching a little, as his health permitted (Thorn Seyma, personal communication, May 23, 2023).
59. Musicians Without Borders (2022, para. 3).
60. Koehler (2019).
61. Cohen (2008, 27).
62. Bingley (2011, 60), Gberie (2005, 6).
63. Bingley (2011).
64. Rush and Simić (2014).
65. Office of the High Commissioner for Human Rights (2023).
66. For example, Urbain (2007), O'Connell and Castelo-Branco (2010), Howell (2018), Cohen (2020), Phillips-Hutton (2020), Jeffery (2021).
67. Impey (2021, 173).
68. Impey (2014).
69. Impey (2021, 169, 172–3).
70. Pann (2022).
71. Thorn Seyma (personal communication, May 23, 2023).

2 Oh Give Me a Land

1. Rowatt (2022, para. 6).
2. Watson (1995, 149). Australia's First Peoples comprises two distinct cultural groups: Aboriginal and Torres Strait Islander peoples. In this chapter, following guidance from the national First Nations agency AIATSIS (n.d.(a)), I use the terms *First Nations* and *First Peoples* largely interchangeably to refer to Aboriginal and Torres Strait Islander peoples (also *First Australians*). I reserve use of the adjective *Indigenous* (as in "Indigenous Australians") to quoted sources that use that term, to proper nouns (as in "National Indigenous Television"), and to contrast with *non-Indigenous* (as in "Indigenous and non-Indigenous Australians"). In these cases, as is standard practice in Australia, *Indigenous* is capitalized as a mark of respect.
3. Watson (1995, 154).
4. Queensland State Parliament (1897, clause 9).
5. Queensland Government (2018, "Palm Island Aboriginal settlement" section).
6. Australian Human Rights Commission (1997); AIATSIS (n.d.(b)).
7. AIATSIS (n.d.(c)).
8. Thaiday (1981, 33) provides these names and a first-hand account of the strike in a chapter of his book *Under the Act*.
9. Lloyd (2017a).
10. Watson (2010, "We Couldn't Tolerate Any More" chapter).
11. Thaiday (1981, 36). Thaiday wrote about the incident: "We sing like anything in the military patrol boat . . . The policemen are on top and machine gun is pointed down to us but while we are in front of machine gun we sing like anything."
12. Watson (1995, 163).
13. Watson (1995, 164). Watson (2010, 102–120) provides an in-depth account of the circumstances surrounding the strike.

14. Townsville Bulletin (2015, 26).
15. Truth and Reconciliation Commission of Canada (2015).
16. Hilder (2015).
17. Australia-New Zealand Regional Committee of the ICTM (2011, paras. 1 and 3). Context is provided by Corn and Bracknell (2020).
18. UNESCO (n.d.(a), "Threats" tab).
19. Lloyd (n.d., "Blog" page: "What Is a Mission Song?").
20. Australian Institute of Aboriginal and Torres Strait Islander Studies (n.d.(c), "Control" section); Franklin (2016, 45).
21. Lloyd (n.d.(a), "Videos" page: "The Irex").
22. Watson (2010, 108).
23. According to contemporary First Nations accounts, missions could be sites of joy as well as suffering. Growing on the Swan Reach Mission in the 1940s, Agnes Rigney had memories of a stress-free, fun, and happy childhood despite poor living conditions, little material wealth, and authoritarian control (in Anderson, Rigney, and Hunter 1997).
24. Fraser (1995). Chapter 5 of this book, on the Saharawi people's struggle for cultural justice following colonization of their Western Saharan homeland, provides another case in point.
25. Webb (2019, 466).
26. Webb (2023).
27. Franklin (2016, 45).
28. Skelchy and Taylor (2022, 3).
29. Lloyd (2017b).
30. In Wood (2017, "Finding Forgotten Songs" section).
31. Lloyd (n.d., "Videos" page).
32. Lloyd (n.d., "Videos" page: "The Irex").
33. In schools, national standards for general learning outcomes relating to Aboriginal and Torres Strait Island Histories and Cultures were established only in 2010. See Australian Curriculum, Assessment and Reporting Authority (n.d.).
34. Birtles (1935, 149).
35. Hilder (2015).
36. Amnesty International (2021, paras. 6, 7).
37. Race Forward (2014, vol. 1, 1).
38. Nussbaum (2003). In turn, this implies that decolonization is a necessary condition for social justice, because colonization is centrally about maintaining an imbalance of power between colonizer and colonized, and decolonization is about dismantling that imbalance of power. See Reisch (2014, 13); also Weaver (2014, 120).
39. Race Forward (2014, vol. 1, 1).
40. Lloyd (n.d., "Videos" page: "NITV—Songstress Jessie Lloyd Takes Music on a Mission," 1:19–1:22).
41. Lloyd (n.d., "Videos" page: "The Irex"); also Lloyd, in Reigersberg (2017).
42. Cohen (2008, 31).
43. Race Forward (2014, vol. 1).
44. Weaver (2014, 120–121).
45. Race Forward (2014, vol. 1, 2–3).
46. As one example, First Nations Australians are jailed at thirteen times the rate of non-Indigenous Australians (Allam et al. 2021).

47. Several scholars' work lies at the intersection of all these areas. Tan Sooi Beng (2008), for example, describes how her collaborative, socially engaged ethnomusicological research with young people in Malaysia is revitalizing music, dance, and theater traditions in ways that bridge cultural barriers, maintain cultural diversity, and promote tolerance in a multiethnic society.
48. AIATSIS (2022). The second edition of the Guidelines was released in 2010 and revised in 2012. In 2020, the Guidelines were superseded by the *Code of Ethics for Aboriginal and Torres Strait Islander Research.*
49. Treloyn and Goonginda Charles (2021, 136). Native Hawaiian scholar Amy Ku'uleialoha Stillman (2009) describes how her privileged status as researcher permitted her to access historical records relating to Hawaiian music housed in museums, archives, and libraries, whereas Native Hawaiian practitioners were denied access to those same records.
50. Garma Statement on Indigenous Music and Performance (2002, 1). Sunderland et al. (2023) articulate how musical activity can be a resource for culturally safe, strengths-based health promotion for and with First Nations people, and how First Nations musical activity functions as a cultural determinant of health.
51. Office for the Arts (2023, para. 1).
52. Corn (2011); see also Corn and Bracknell (2020).
53. I use quotation marks because the binary is misleading: "First Nations music will always be inherently contemporary, because creative innovation is intrinsic to sustaining even the most stable song traditions" (Sunderland et al. 2023, 3). Bracknell and Barwick (2020, 72) make the same point. Also relevant to this discussion of the mission songs is the argument of Sunderland and colleagues that although Western music was deployed during the colonial era "as a form of settler-colonial indoctrination," popular music is "neither exclusively Western nor colonial" (2023, 3).
54. Diamond and Castelo-Branco (2021, 15).
55. UNESCO (n.d.(b), "Ethical Principles for Safeguarding Intangible Cultural Heritage" section, #6).
56. Cooley (2019a); Frandy (2022).
57. Flexner and Spriggs (2015).
58. Flexner and Spriggs (2015, 203).
59. Australian Human Rights Commission (2018).
60. Hooper (2006, para. 2).
61. National Archives of Australia (n.d.).
62. Chen (2018, "Police Response Was Racist, Court Found" section).
63. Brisbane Times (2016, para. 12).
64. Brisbane Times (2016, paras. 1–2), Australian Human Rights Commission (2018), Queensland Government (2018, "Deaths in Custody" section).
65. Australian Human Rights Commission (2018).
66. Australian Human Rights Commission (2018).
67. Brisbane Times (2016, paras. 4–5).
68. Brisbane Times (2016, paras. 8–9, 16).
69. Nothling (2018).
70. Anti-Discrimination Commission Queensland (2017, updated July 25, 2018, 45).
71. Roberts (2021, 128).

3 Masters in the Academy

1. Maroon people are descendants of Africans in the Americas and the islands of the Indian Ocean who, from the early sixteenth century, escaped from enslavement by Spanish captors and established their own settlements, often forming close ties with local Indigenous peoples (Diouf 2016).
2. Also known as *Reinado*, or more fully, *Reinado de Nossa Senhora do Rosário* ("Reign of Our Lady of the Rosary"). For more on Congado and its relationship to popular Catholicism, saints, slavery, ancestors, Blackness, and racial justice, see Lucas (2002), Clayton (n.d.), and Dempsey (2016, 2017). Dempsey provides further detail on terminology (2017, 7), explaining that *Congado* "can refer to the community as a whole, the songs, dances, parades, and rituals themselves, as well as the groups of around 15 to 150 musicians who are accompanied by royal entourages" (2017, 4).
3. Bengala (Zoom interview, August 25, 2023); see also Dempsey (2017). Throughout this chapter, English translation of Bengala's interview is by José Jorge de Carvalho.
4. Pacelli (2019, "The Origin" section).
5. Bengala (Zoom interview, August 25, 2023).
6. José Jorge de Carvalho (personal communication, August 24, 2023).
7. José Jorge de Carvalho (personal communication, August 24, 2023).
8. Rawls (1971).
9. McClary (2001).
10. Asea (2022, 1, 7).
11. Bracknell and Barwick (2020, 71).
12. Mbembe defines "Westernized" higher education institutions as "local instantiations of a dominant academic model based on a Eurocentric epistemic canon." By "Eurocentric epistemic canon," he means "a canon that attributes truth only to the Western way of knowledge production" (2016, 32). I follow his usage.
13. Boal (1984, 96), as cited in Dalaqua (2020, 9).
14. Chávez and Skelchy (2019, 120). Hil, Lyons, and Thompsett (2021, section 1) call this process of intensification the "neoliberal takeover" of higher education. See also Mbembe (2016) and Bhambra, Gebrial, and Kerem (2018).
15. Hebert (2022, 180). See also Docherty (2014) and Hil, Lyons, and Thompsett (2021).
16. Miranda Fricker (2007) coined the term *epistemic injustice*; other scholars have expanded and elaborated on its meanings. See for example Bhargava (2013) and the edited volume by Kidd, Medina, and Pohlhaus Jr (2017).
17. De Sousa Santos (2016, 2018). De Sousa Santos (2016) refers to "cognitive injustice" largely in the way other scholars refer to epistemic injustice. On epistemicide, see also Grosfoguel (2013).
18. Lomax (1972). See also Carvalho, Cohen, et al. (2016, 129).
19. Lomax (1972, 9).
20. Lomax (1972, 13). Lomax's conviction about the roles and responsibilities of music institutions in matters of cultural sustainability reverberate today in the professed commitment of the International Society for Music Education (ISME) not only to education and culture, but also to "conservation and the durable development of our cultural heritage" (ISME n.d., "History" section). ISME proclaims that music education programs should be

founded on a paradigm of cultural equity, whereby a wide variety of musics are taught and learnt, and all musics are worth of study and respect.

21. Around 7,100 languages are spoken in the world (Eberhard, Simons, and Fennig 2022). My estimate of the global number of musical practices uses language as a proxy for culture, and assumes that each culture, on average, has more than one associated musical practice.
22. Indigenous studies and educational research scholars Eve Tuck and K. Wayne Yang warn about educational initiatives that "dress up" as decolonization, but instead serve as "moves to innocence" that assuage colonial guilt, recenter White people, and fail to address settler colonial power and privilege (2012). See also Ahmed (2012), Maldonado-Torres (2020), and Diamond and Castelo-Branco (2021, 15).
23. Leung (2018, 261).
24. On the last of these points, see Nzewi (2006) on the "ignorant expert." Also Hess (2018, 576); Bracknell and Barwick (2020).
25. Robinson (2019, 137).
26. Among the many recent critiques of prevailing music education pedagogies, and calls for anti-oppressive and decolonial change, are Hess (2015, 2018, 576–577); Kallio et al. (2021, 4–5); Nzewi (2006, 2019); Nzewi and Omolo-Ongati (2014); and several chapters in edited volumes by Benedict et al. (2015); Coppola, Hebert, and Campbell (2020); and Southcott, Sutherland, and De Bruin (2022). AEC-SMS Diversity, Identity, Inclusiveness Working Group (2022) provides further examples from Europe and beyond. A growing raft of initiatives around the world strive for more educationally, epistemically, and culturally just educational approaches. Carvalho and Florez (2014, 134–135) provide examples from India, Nigeria, Ecuador, Spain, Colombia, and Mexico; the New School of the Anthropocene (nsota.org) is a recent UK-based example. Student actions dating back to at least the 1960s have called for the "formal desegregation" of higher education, and its meaningful participation in "a project of social, economic, and cognitive decolonization" (Maldonado-Torres, 2016, 4). See also several chapters in Bhambra, Gebrial, and Kerem (2018).
27. Described in Travae (2013) and Vieira and Arends-Kuenning (2019).
28. Carvalho (2023c, 68).
29. The English word "Master" does not capture the rich meanings of the Portuguese words *Mestres* (female) and *Maestros* (male), which refer to people who know, lead, research, and who are wise. I (Jorge) talk about this further in International Society for Ecological Economics (2021, 14:28–14:50); see also Carvalho et al. (2016, 114).
30. Carvalho (2018, 2021, 2023a, 2023b, 2023c), Carvalho and Florez (2014), Carvalho et al. (2016).
31. Afro-Brazilian musical genres abound in some states, such as Rio de Janeiro, Minas Gerais, Bahia, Pernambuco, and Maranhão, whereas in the Amazonian states of the center-west and north of Brazil, Indigenous music is highly present.
32. Carvalho (2023a, 2023b, 2023c).
33. Carvalho (2018, 87), Carvalho (2023a, 16), Carvalho (2023c, 69).
34. Carvalho (2018).
35. See Carvalho (2023a and 2023b). The latter source presents a proposal to transform the curriculum of King's College, London.
36. Acton et al. (2017).
37. Bengala (personal communication, August 25, 2023).
38. For more on this, see Carvalho (2023a, 11–12).

39. In this regard, Nzewi refers to the "ignorant expert" (2006).
40. Asea (2022, 2).
41. Brown (2020, paras. 6 and 5, respectively).
42. Mbembe (2016, 32).
43. Education philosopher Burke Stanton calls music-making "a locality ripe for decolonial activity" (2018, 4, 15) by dint of its profound connection with embodied experience. See also Acton et al. (2017, 1319–1320). *Musicking* is Small's term (1998) that emphasizes the social and performative aspects of music.
44. Hess (2018, 579).
45. After French theorists Deleuze and Guattari, Hess calls such a curriculum structure "rhizomatic" (2015, 342, 345).
46. Acton et al. (2017, 1318).
47. Diamond and Castelo-Branco (2021, 20).
48. Qualitative methodologist Pranee Liamputtong notes the value of enabling partnerships with, between, and among researcher-practitioners of indigenous and other historically excluded groups, who are then empowered to work together toward decoloniality (2010, 23).
49. Freire (1970), Darder (2017).
50. Australia-New Zealand Regional Committee of the ICTM (2011, paras. 1 and 3); see also Corn and Bracknell (2020).
51. Acton et al. (2017, 1317). Acton and colleagues caution against homogenizing "Indigenous ways of knowing," emphazizing diverse localized articulations (2017, 1315, 1318).
52. Bracknell and Barwick (2020, 77).
53. Bengala (personal communication, August 25, 2023). "The privileged cannot empathize with inhabitants of a contrasting lifeworld," writes ethnomusicologist Michael Frishkopf, "so long as they only experience the 'other' in aggregate, mediated by a dehumanizing system" (2021, 56).
54. Bengala (personal communication, August 25, 2023).
55. Carvalho (2023c, 74).
56. See Carvalho (2023a, 16; 2023b, 8).
57. Carvalho (2018, 87, 89).
58. Saberes Tradicionais UFMG (2022, para. 1).
59. Bengala (personal communication, August 25, 2023).
60. Saberes Tradicionais UFMG (2022, para. 1).
61. Bengala (personal communication, August 25, 2023).
62. Bengala (personal communication, August 25, 2023). Congado is a relatively strong cultural practice among Afro-Brazilian communities; Dempsey refers to "thousands of Congadeiros [practitioners of Congado] all over urban and rural Brazil, notably in the states of São Paulo and Goiás" (2017, 1).
63. Bengala (personal communication, August 25, 2023).
64. Asea (2022, 11).
65. Mbembe (2016, 32). The term has been used by other scholars and in other settings. Mignolo traces its development (2018, ix).
66. Carvalho (2023c, 67).
67. Maldonado-Torres (2016, 7, 10). On decoloniality, see Mignolo and Walsh (2018). Chávez and Skelchy (2019, 130) and Asea (2022, 5) use the term to refer to the action-oriented processes of dismantling colonial systems and structures of power.

68. Elsewhere, Jorge sets out a blueprint for decolonizing and rebuilding universities, involving radical institutional and epistemic reorganization (Carvalho 2023b).
69. Maldonado-Torres (2016, 31, 30).
70. See also Carvalho (2023b).
71. McDermott (2017, 44).

4 Music for Life and Livelihood

1. Ahmed (2022).
2. *Bhatiyali* or *bhatiali*. *Folk songs* and *folk music*, and more broadly *folk practices* and *folk traditions*, are terms used by the Rural Craft and Cultural Hub (RCCH) project to refer to local, vernacular, intangible expressions of culture, typically transmitted aurally over generations. Following RCCH, I use these terms in this way throughout this chapter, while recognizing—like ethnomusicologist Anna Morcom (2013, Introduction, footnote 30)—that terms like these are both problematic and approximate, and that boundaries often blur between "classical," "popular," and "folk" practices in India. Parts of this chapter are adapted from Grant (2020), with permission from the publisher Springer Nature.
3. Women occasionally sing *bhatiyali* (Banglanatak 2020, 16), though the genre is mostly sung by men, who are most likely to own and use boats on the river (Saurav Moni, personal communication, 28 October, 2022).
4. Banglanatak (2022, para. 1 and "Musical Instruments" section).
5. Banglanatak (2020, 14).
6. Saurav Moni (personal communication, 28 October, 2022). Morita and Jensen (2017) refer to ways of being in delta environments, where life moves fluidly between land and water, as 'delta ontologies.' The Sundarbans are not the only striking geographical feature of West Bengal: the state also encompasses the massive Ganges delta and the Darjeeling Himalayan hills in the north.
7. Ganguly (2020, 12).
8. Bengal Info (2021).
9. Global Data Lab (2022).
10. NITI Aayog (2021).
11. Government of West Bengal (2022, "Facts and Figures" section).
12. Government of West Bengal (2022, "Our Culture" section) (Banglanatak 2020).
13. Saurav Moni (personal communication, October 28, 2022).
14. Government of West Bengal (2022, "Our Culture" section).
15. Banglanatak (2022, "History of Bhatiyali" and "Status" sections).
16. Bhattacharya (2014, 344–345).
17. Morcom (2013, Introduction, footnote 31).
18. Banglanatak (2020, 16).
19. Saurav Moni (personal communication, October 28, 2022).
20. Banglanatak (2022, "Status" section).
21. Pier (2021, "Amitava Bhattacharya on How Creative Skills Can Alleviate Rural Poverty" section).
22. UNESCO (2021b, para. 1).
23. Bhattacharya (2014, 341).
24. Bhattacharya (2014, 341).

25. Banglanatak (2020, 2–3).
26. Banglanatak (2020, 1).
27. Banglanatak (2020, 1).
28. Bhava (2021).
29. Banglanatak (2020).
30. Saurav Moni (personal communication, December 17, 2022).
31. Touch TD (2020, February).
32. Banglanatak (2020, 32, 33).
33. Dirksen (2015, 52).
34. Pier (2021, "How Banglanatak's Art For Life Works" section).
35. UNESCO (1980/2022).
36. Banglanatak (2020, 33). Nearly two-thirds of crafts-persons involved with the Hubs are women; for performing artists, the figure is much lower (a little over one in five), reflecting historical sociocultural norms relating to gender in performance practices. For more on women and the performing arts in India, see Morcom (2013).
37. Banglanatak (2020, 32).
38. Contact Base internal note to UNESCO (June 29, 2022); see also Rural Craft and Cultural Hubs (2023, "Background" section, para. 3).
39. United Nations (2024, SDG 1, "Facts and Figures" section).
40. United Nations (2024, SDG 1, "Why It Matters: No Poverty" section).
41. United Nations (2024, para. 1).
42. $2.15USD per person per day at 2017 purchasing power parity. United Nations (2024, SDG 1, paras. 1, 3).
43. United Nations (2024, SDG 1, para. 2).
44. Engberg-Pedersen and Ravnborg (2010).
45. Sen (2001).
46. Dirksen (2015, 45).
47. Frankenhuis and Nettle (2020).
48. The UN's SDGs (2022) refer to the role of arts and culture in reaching targets 2.5, 4.7, 8.3, 8.9, and 11.4, for example.
49. UNESCO (2024).
50. Smithsonian Center for Folklife and Cultural Heritage (2022).
51. See for example Osnes (2013), Grant (2016), Harrison (2020b), and several chapters in the *Oxford Handbook of Economic Ethnomusicology* (Morcom and Taylor 2020). Increasingly, researchers are employing participatory and action research methodologies in attempts to improve socioeconomic conditions of the people and communities they work with. See, for example, Burns (2016), who describes a collaborative commercial recording initiative to ameliorate socioeconomic challenges confronting Southern Ewe dance-drummers in Ghana; and Araújo and Cambria's (2013) long-term participatory ethnography with *favela* residents in Maré, Brazil.
52. Pier (2021, "How Banglanatak's Art For Life Works" section).
53. Touch TD (2020, February, 5, 33, 34).
54. Baker (2014); Baker, Bull, and Taylor (2018).
55. Touch TD (2020, February, 23).
56. HIPAMS (2018–2021, "About" and "Resources" pages). The project was funded by the British Academy's Sustainable Development Programme.
57. Titon (2021, 26).

58. Harnish (2016).
59. Rees (2009, 56–61).
60. Dirksen (2015, 43). In the context of her study of cultural wealth and material poverty in Haiti, Dirksen's answer to all three questions is a qualified "yes."
61. Hebert (2022, 175–176).
62. Harrison (2013).
63. Schippers and Grant (2016, 13).
64. Harnish (2016).
65. Grant (2016, 17).
66. Fiol (2013).
67. UNESCO (2022a, 5).
68. Hall (2020, "Distribution" section).
69. Burns (2016).
70. Throsby and Petetskaya (2017).
71. See for example Posada and Solana Moreno (2015, 42), who describe how the relatively low social status of the *iggâwen* (hereditary musicians) of Western Sahara (see Chapter 5) is partly due to a common interpretation of Islam as prohibiting string instruments, and partly due to the perception that artistic talent is a God-bestowed gift that should not be used for economic gain. Burns (2016) and Moisala (2013) offer further examples from Ghana and Nepal respectively.
72. Grant and Chhuon (2016).
73. UNESCO (2022b). The full name of the instrument is *chapei dang weng* (or *chapei dong veng*), often abbreviated to *chapei*.
74. Saurav Moni (personal communication, December 17, 2022). For further on the relationship between music, culture, and the caste system in India, see Ajotikar (2022).
75. See Touch TD (2020, February).
76. Banglanatak (2020, 32).
77. Banglanatak (2020, 17).
78. Banglanatak (2020, 17).
79. Banglanatak (2020, 17).
80. Dirksen (2015, 54).
81. Weintraub and Yung (2009). See also Moisala (2013), who explores links between poverty reduction, cultural rights, and cultural sustainability.
82. Banglanatak (2021).
83. United Nations World Tourism Organization (2013, 9).
84. Grant (2022a, 118).
85. Nussbaum (2011).
86. Grant (2016, 16).
87. Titon (2008–2022).

5 Music for a Desert Homeland

1. Violeta Ruano Posada (personal communication, March 27, 2023).
2. Mohamed Sleiman Labat (personal communication, July 1, 2023).
3. Motif Art Studio (2023, "Who We Are" section). For this chapter, the challenges associated with poor phone and internet connectivity in the refugee camps prevented collaboration

with a Saharawi musician who had participated in the *Portraits of Saharawi Music* project. Mohamed's relationship to this chapter therefore differs slightly from those of the other Story Holders to their respective chapters, in that he was not directly involved in the music project this chapter describes. The chapter owes much to his lived experience, knowledge, and insights as a Saharawi artist. I am also grateful to Kamal Fadel, Polisario Front representative of the Saharawi Arab Democratic Republic (SADR) to Australia and New Zealand, for feedback on this chapter.

4. Fynn (2011, 44). The event is known as the Green March. Mauritania invaded from the south as Morocco invaded from the north, though the former would withdraw within four years.
5. Also romanized as Sahrawi. Romanization of Saharawi names and terms is not standardized. Mohamed Sleiman Labat notes the contention around the English spelling of Saharawi terms, which tends to reflect Spanish or French spelling conventions (invoking colonial powers Spain and Morocco) (personal communication, July 1, 2023). In this chapter, romanization follows Mohamed's guidance, informed by usage in key English-language sources.
6. Ruano Posada (2019, 3), citing https://eacnur.org/blog/refugiados-saharauis-40-anos-de-vida-en-los-campos/. The five camps, spread over 180 kilometers, are Laayoune (El-Aaiún), Awserd, Smara, Dakhla, and Cape Boujdour.
7. Ruano Posada (2016, 41).
8. Fynn (2011, 41, 44, 57). See Boukhars and Roussellier (2014) and Kingsbury (2016) regarding the role of Western Sahara's natural resources in the Saharawi efforts towards decolonization.
9. Minder (2022, para. 12), United Nations General Assembly (1990).
10. MINURSO (2022), Amnesty International (2024).
11. Fynn (2011).
12. United Nations Department of Economic and Social Affairs (2022a, "Western Sahara" data).
13. Fynn (2011), Amnesty International (2024, "Repression of Dissent" section), Azkue et al. (2022, 8).
14. OCHA (2022, para. 1).
15. The SADR is recognized by forty-one UN Member States, though the UN officially recognizes the sovereignty over Western Sahara of neither the SADR nor Morocco.
16. Smith and Ruano (2021, "Seeking Opportunities and Protection in Europe" section). Giménez Amorós (2018) and Caruso (2021) describe some of the procedural challenges of seeking asylum, Giménez Amorós specifically in relation to the Saharawi people.
17. King (2014, 101).
18. Whitehead (2022, para. 7).
19. Lovatt and Mundy (2021).
20. Kulkarni (2022, para. 6).
21. Smith and Ruano (2021, "A New and Uncertain Era" section).
22. Azkue et al. (2022, 8).
23. Whitehead (2022, para. 7), Amnesty Internation (2024).
24. UNICEF Algeria (2022).
25. Personal communication (June 28, 2023). Historically and to a lesser extent still today, poets and musicians would collaborate, poets providing the lyrics for songs. Sometimes poets and musicians would perform together, maintaining the distinction of their art forms: poets would recite, for example, then musicians pick up certain of their lines—a

tradition Mohamed describes as a "disappearing practice" (personal communication, June 28, 2023).

26. Smith and Ruano (2022, 91), where the word is romanized as *adlal*. Mohamed Sleiman Labat suggests the spelling given here. As a Saharawi musical practice, Mohamed also describes "a kind of humming" that functioned to establish an intimate connection with goats and camels (personal communication, June 28, 2023).
27. Giménez Amorós (2015, 34, 39).
28. *Aardin* was historically more common in present-day Mauritania (in the south of Trab el-Bidhân region) but has come to be closely associated with Saharawi music (Violeta Ruano Posada, personal communication, March 28, 2023).
29. Mohamed Sleiman Labat (personal communication, June 28, 2023). Mohamed believes that at a time when "this crazy materialistic world" is "desperately in need of sustainable practices," the minimalistic lifestyles of nomadic peoples may offer useful insights into what it means to live sustainably and responsibly (June 28, 2023).
30. McConnell (2020) explores the social role of the griot, including in conflict mediation and political engagement. As composers, performers, orators, and retainers of memory, *iggâwen* played an important social role despite their low social status (Kamal Fadel, personal communication, August 23, 2023).
31. Ruano Posada (2016, 42), Giménez Amorós (2015, 41).
32. Violeta Ruano Posada (personal communication, March 28, 2023). Violeta notes that performing for money is more common (and more accepted) in Mauritania than it is in the camps, where music has become primarily about the political cause. Thus, some Saharawi musicians may feel freer to earn income from performances abroad, whether in Mauritania or elsewhere.
33. Violeta Ruano Posada (personal communication, March 28, 2023); see also Smith and Ruano (2022, 92). Violeta notes that this shift eventually led to tensions between those "political" musicians and those who wanted to charge money for performing in weddings and other private events. By the 1990s, functional shifts in music associated with the revolution had all but ended the *iggâwen* system. At least in theory, by then, any Saharawi person could access musical training (e.g., through the Ministry of Culture) and start their own music "business" in the camps or abroad. Today, many musicians in the camps combine working for the Ministry with working independently.
34. Ruano Posada (2016, 44–45).
35. Shumba (2015, para. 2), Ruano Posada (2016, 44).
36. Giménez Amorós (2015, 39).
37. Ruano Posada (2019, 4).
38. Ruano Posada (2016, 46).
39. Giménez Amorós (2015, 42).
40. Shumba (2015, para. 4).
41. Giménez Amorós (2018), Ruano Posada (2016, 51). See also Prada Bianchi and Magid (2024), who trace the "shapeshifting entity" that is the Saharawi band El Wali, active since the 1970s.
42. Saharawi Voice (2023).
43. Baz (2015). My thanks to Mohamed Sleiman Labat for sharing with me information and resources on Suilma Aali and Yslem Hijo del Desierto.
44. Refugee Radio (2011).

45. Hassan (2012). El Aaiún is the largest city in Moroccan-occupied Western Sahara. Giménez Amorós (2018) examines the promotion of the Saharawi political cause via Hassan's performances in 2012 and 2013, including Hassan's "stage talk" that introduced the political message of the songs to her audiences.
46. Africa Beats (2014).
47. Terminology relating to forced displacement varies widely and is often inconsistent. *Forced migration* usually refers to displacement across geopolitical borders, whereas *forced displacement* refers more generally to people being compelled to move, whether within or outside of their home country. The office of the United Nations High Commissioner for Refugees (UNHCR) describes the following groups: *refugees*, who flee their country due to conflict or persecution; *internally displaced people*, who seek safety in other parts of their country; and *people seeking asylum*, those refugees who seek international protection (UNCHR 2001–2022). A related group is *stateless people*—those without a nationality—whose human rights are also often jeopardized or unrealized.
48. UNHCR (1951/1967).
49. United Nations (1948).
50. UNHCR (2021, 2). Correlatedly, in that same decade, the number of countries affected by medium- or high-level conflict also doubled, to twenty-three in 2021 (UNHCR 2021, 5).
51. UNHCR (2021, 9).
52. The first part of Lettau, Mtaku, and Otchere's edited volume *Performing Sustainability in West Africa* (2022) examines the implications for cultural sustainability of internal forced displacement, such as those persons internally displaced by the Boko Haram insurgency in Northeast Nigeria.
53. UNHCR defines protracted forced displacement as lasting at least five years (2021, 20). Geopolitical conflicts last thirty-seven years on average (Milliband 2016, 12). In 2016, refugees fleeing across geopolitical borders were displaced for an average of seventeen years; those internally displaced, for twenty-three (Milliband 2016, 19).
54. Reyes (2019, 46).
55. Giménez Amorós (2015, 32) writes that such syncretic exchange has been relatively limited in the case of the Tindouf camps: since Algerian people do not generally live in the camps, Saharawi and Algerian people have had relatively little opportunity to share their musical lives. Giménez Amorós notes that financial aid provided by the Algerian government has helped fund a range of cultural activities and resources in the camps, including the purchase of electronic instruments for the practice of *nidal* and other contemporary Saharawi styles.
56. Personal communication (28 June, 2023). Mohamed elaborates: although young musicians enjoy *raï* and its incorporation into their music, "a lot of us [Saharawi] don't like it [laughs] . . . but those musicians have the right to do so—and they can still call it Saharawi music, because they are Saharawi" (personal communication, June 28, 2023).
57. Mohamed Sleiman Labat (personal communication, June 28, 2023).
58. In Ruano Posada (2016, 114).
59. Ruano Posada (2016, 121). Mohamed Sleiman Labat refers to the slow and subtle processes of Moroccan control over the version of Hassānīya spoken by Saharawi people in occupied Western Sahara, processes that aim to normalize the Moroccan presence in the occupied territory and obscure a distinct Saharawi identity (personal communication, June 28, 2023). Saharawi Polisario Front representative Kamal Fadel notes that Morocco has been prohibiting Saharawi people from establishing tents in the occupied area, having

recognized that the tent is an important symbol of Saharawi culture and cultural resistance (personal communication, August 23, 2023; see also Artikel2 n.d., paras. 15–16).

60. Ruano Posada (2019, 4).
61. Ruano Posada (2019). Violeta comments that the over-politicization of practices like *nidal* can jeopardize the international support those practices and their practitioners are given, since international bodies may be wary of being seen to "take sides" in any international conflict (personal communication, June 19, 2022).
62. Freemuse (2008, "Interview with Aziza Brahim" section). See also "Life is Waiting," a documentary film about a young Saharawi rapper from the occupied territories who was repeatedly attacked by the Moroccan police (Lee 2015).
63. Sandblast (2012); see also Chatty (2010).
64. Ruano Posada believes that the "over-politicization" of music, such as is represented by the rise of *nidal*, has caused "the disappearance of many traditional songs that were once essential for the recognition of an independent Saharawi identity, at least on a collective level" (2016, 121).
65. Sleiman Labat (2022a, 29).
66. Sleiman Labat (2022a, 29); see also the series of three oral essays by Sleiman Labat, *New Practices, New Narratives* (2022b).
67. Sleiman Labat (2022a, 30).
68. For examples, see Frishkopf (2022), Ogut and Sulun (n.d.), and Sechehaye and Martiniello (2019). International NGO Musicians without Borders, mentioned in Chapter 1, runs music programs with and for refugee populations (and those others affected by war, genocide, or mass violence) (Musicians Without Borders 2022).
69. For example, Shao writes of the risk, in music programs in refugee camps, of "merely reinforc[ing] uneven relations of power, justifying the restrictive dimensions of [refugee] encampment and the normalization of the unequal treatment of certain bodies over others" (2021, 88).
70. Sandblast (2021); see also Smith and Ruano (2022).
71. Ruano Posada (2019, 6).
72. British Library (n.d.(a)). The British Museum's blog on the project is available at https://blogs.bl.uk/music/2014/05/saharawi-music-in-the-refugee-camps-in-sw-algeria.html. Violeta's personal blog about project fieldwork is at https://violetaruanomusic.blogspot.com/.
73. Regarding remuneration, Ruano Posada writes that some (mostly older) musicians viewed their participation in the project as activism for the Saharawi cause and so were reluctant to accept payment, while other (often younger) musicians who viewed music as a possible career did expect payment. The Ministry oversaw fair payment of participating musicians, where requested by the musicians (Ruano Posada 2019, 7).
74. Ruano Posada (2019, 7).
75. Ruano Posada (2016, 121).
76. Ruano Posada (2016, 120).
77. Smith and Ruano (2022, 101).
78. British Library (n.d.(b)).
79. Seminal studies on these intersections include those of Reyes (1999) and Diehl (2002). More recent scholarship includes that of Urbain (2007), O'Connell and Castelo-Branco (2010), Levi and Scheding (2010), Alajaji (2015), and a special issue of the journal *Music and Minorities* (Hemetek 2021).

80. O'Connell (2010, 10).
81. O'Connell (2010, 12).
82. Ruano Posada (2016, 122).

6 Weaving Sound through Ocean and Land

1. In line with common usage, the demonym and adjective *ni-Vanuatu* is used in this chapter to refer to the Indigenous peoples of Vanuatu; the adjective *Vanuatuan* refers to being from, of, or relating to Vanuatu more generally.
2. Personal communication (November 11, 2017).
3. Parts of this chapter are adapted from Grant (2019), first published in *Asia Pacific Journal of Anthropology*. Copyright: Taylor and Francis. Used with permission.
4. Roberts and Selmen (2020).
5. Tahana (2020, para. 1).
6. Milano (2020, para. 4).
7. World Vision (2020, para. 1).
8. Milano (2020, para. 4).
9. United Nations Children's Fund (2016).
10. World Bank Group (2021), Klint et al. (2012).
11. World Bank Group (2021).
12. Spickett, Katscherian, and McIver (2013), World Bank Group (2021).
13. Perumal (2018). Perumal critiques what she calls over-simplistic and sensationalized representations in media and policy discourse of "climate refugees" in the Pacific Islands, noting that at least in the medium-term, most climate-related migration in Vanuatu is unlikely to be cross-border.
14. Spickett, Katscherian, and McIver (2013, 48).
15. Bündnis Entwicklung Hilft (2021, 6).
16. Paul and Ahmed (2022, 6). Excess emissions are those that exceed an established baseline or permitted levels for a monitoring period.
17. Hamill (2021, abstract).
18. Consider the case of the Saharawi people in the Tindouf refugee camps, presented in Chapter 5, whose lives in forced displacement are made more difficult by extreme weather conditions.
19. Pörtner et al. (2022, 12, section B.2.4).
20. Orlove et al. (2022).
21. Eckersley (2009, 100), Bond (2012), Thorp (2014). Climate justice can be understood as a subcategory of *environmental justice*—matters relating to the inequitable exposure of marginalized peoples to environmental hazards and ecological destruction (Paul and Ahmed 2022, 5).
22. World Bank (2024, para. 2).
23. Rimon and Tong (2021).
24. Behrman and Kent (2022), Pörtner et al. (2022).
25. Aktürk and Lerski (2021).
26. Silvers (2018, 6).
27. Silvers (2018, 5).
28. Lohmann (2008, 364), Purdy (2015).

29. Paul and Ahmed (2022, 7).
30. Lele et al. (2019).
31. Sherman and Ford (2014), Warrick (2007, 5).
32. Warrick (2009, 59–60), Conway and Mustelin (2014, 339); see also Grant (2019, 5).
33. Davies (2015, 56).
34. Davies (2015, 58).
35. Paul and Ahmed (2022), Thorp (2014).
36. Schippers and Grant (2016).
37. See Vanuatu National Statistics Office (2020, v) for population and housing data on Luganville.
38. Forsyth and Dick (2021, 7); see also Tabani (2017). Vanuatu became independent from French-British colonial rule in 1980.
39. Eberhard, Simons, and Fennig (2022, Mwerlap entry).
40. Hayward (2014, 115).
41. Hayward (2014, 114).
42. Davies (2015, 52).
43. Dick (2014).
44. Wessergo (2014, 1).
45. Wessergo (2014).
46. In Hayward (2014, 119).
47. Diettrich, Moulin and Webb (2011, 131).
48. Ratuva (2010, 41). Tabani (2017) traces the commercialization of *kastom* in Vanuatu.
49. Hamill (2021, 116–117). Writing of *forró* music of northeastern Brazil, Silvers (2018) proposes that the music creates the environment, just as the environment creates the music. These concepts build on seminal work of ethnomusicologists Anthony Seeger and Stephen Feld, among other scholars.
50. Steinberg and Peters (2015).
51. Hayward (2014, 121).
52. Personal communication (November 11, 2017).
53. Feld (2012).
54. Hamill (2021, 115–116).
55. See several chapters in Cooley (2019a).
56. Hamill (2021, 115).
57. Personal communication (November 11, 2017).
58. Ballard et al. (2020).
59. Ratuva (2010, 53–54).
60. Allen and Dawe (2015); these scholars comment that the field might better be called *ecomusicologies*, as it constitutes diverse and sometimes divergent views.
61. See, for example, Post (2018), Impey (2018), Dirksen (2019), McConnell (2019).
62. Maffi and Woodley (2012).
63. Malvatumauri National Council of Chiefs (2012, x).
64. Dick (2015, 53).
65. Warrick (2007, 8).
66. Marett (2010).
67. Davies (2015, 62).
68. Holmes McDowell et al. (2021).

69. See, for example, Cooley (2019a), Hamill (2021), and Holmes McDowell et al. (2021). Silvers writes how in northeastern Brazil, music has become a "vehicle" through which people combat drought in various ways: music is used to protest against specific drought-related policies and circumstances, to raise awareness and funds to cope with it, to sustain and disrupt certain beliefs about drought and drought vulnerability, and, quite simply, to "fill drought-plagued landscapes with sound" (2018, 9). Aktürk and Lerski (2021) describe how intangible cultural expressions can bolster the resilience and adaptiveness of communities following climate displacement.
70. Bolton (2003), Dick and Meltherorong (2011). Relatedly, and with reference to Vanuatu and Australia in particular, Sunderland et al. (2023) explain how musical activity is a cultural determinant of health for First Nations people.
71. Central Intelligence Agency (2022, Economy section).
72. Hayward (2014).
73. Trip Advisor (2022).
74. Sunderland et al. (2023). Performer and matriarch Cecelia Wari asks rhetorically: "Say you couldn't do water music anymore, what kind of jobs would the women have to go and do?"; performer Celia Lulumle comments: "The water music helps me. I can pay for my school, like my children's school fees" (both in Sunderland et al., 2023, 7).
75. In an illustration of climate injustice: the carbon emissions generated by the economy return flight of a tourist to Vanuatu from Australia roughly equals those generated by the average ni-Vanuatu person in a year (0.7 metric tons, according to the most recent available data on average per capita emissions in Vanuatu) (Climate Watch 2024).
76. Loehr, Addinsall, and Weiler (2019), Loehr (2020).
77. Personal communication (November 11, 2017).
78. Spickett, Katscherian, and McIver (2013), Central Intelligence Agency (2022, "Economy" section).
79. Klint et al. (2012, 254), Central Intelligence Agency (2022, "Environment—Current Issues" section).
80. Personal communication (November 11, 2017).
81. Forsyth and Dick (2021, 140–141).
82. See Tabani (2017), who explores contestations relating to the commercialization of *kastom* practices in Vanuatu.
83. Dick (2014), Hayward (2014, 125).
84. Cole (2014).
85. Personal communication (November 11, 2017).
86. As do both Hayward (2014, 123,125) and Dick (2015, 54).
87. Diettrich, Moulin and Webb (2011, 109).
88. The 2015 iteration of *Balance-Unbalance* in Arizona, USA.
89. Personal communication (January 15, 2023).
90. Hamill (2021). In another example, ecomusicologist Jennifer Post (2019) describes how seminomadic Kazakh pastoralists residing in western Monoglia have managed to moderate and adapt, and thereby maintain, their musical and other cultural practices in challenging environments threatened by the climate crisis.
91. (Dick 2015, 54)

7 The Eyes of All Future Generations

1. Vice (2019, 5:13). Thunberg gave this speech at COP24, the 2018 Conference of the Parties to the United Nations Framework Convention on Climate Change in Katowice, Poland.
2. NPR (2019, paras. 2–3, 12).
3. Carrington (2019). Thunberg's advocacy successes have attracted plenty of criticism too, including that despite years of spirited climate advocacy by children and youth from Pacific nations and across the Global South, it took a White European girl to attain a global platform on the matter.
4. Jewkes and Piovaccari (2021, title).
5. Monbiot (2019, 49).
6. World Future Council˙ (2019, "Why Should We Recognise Crimes against Future Gnerations?" section).
7. Sensoy and DiAngelo (2019).
8. World Future Council (2019).
9. Alwin (2000, "Perceiving Justice" section). Emphasis in original.
10. Alwin (2000, "Perceiving Justice" section).
11. For more on "futures thinking," see Sandford and Cassar (2020) and several further chapters in Holtorf and Högberg's edited volume *Cultural Heritage and the Future* (2020).
12. McDermott (2017, xii).
13. Clammer (2015).
14. UNESCO (1997, Article 7).
15. Harvey (2001, 320).
16. Mason and Turner (2020, 93).
17. See for example Grant (2014a), Titon (2008–2022, 2009), and Schippers and Grant (2016).
18. See Grant (2022a, 117), Auclair and Fairclough's (2015) edited volume, and Holtorf and Högberg's (2020) edited volume. In 2017, a *UNESCO Chair in Heritage Futures* was established, with an objective to promote futures thinking in the heritage sector (see https://lnu.se/en/unescochair).
19. Turino (2008, 18).
20. Harris (2022, 229–230).
21. Marett (2010, 251).
22. Mason and Turner (2020, 88).
23. DeNora and Ansdell (2014, 9).
24. Hess (2018, 585–586).
25. Patel (2016, 79).
26. Opara (2022); Grant, Opara and Dyck (2024).
27. Silvers (2018, 25).
28. Dyck (2016); Grant, Opara, and Dyck (2024).
29. See for example Kent (2008, 107) and several chapters in the *Routledge Companion to Music and Human Rights* (Fifer et al. 2022). As general categories, protest songs and slave songs are further examples of inversely correlated relationships between cultural sustainability and social justice: social injustices spur their vitality as cultural practices, whereas advances in social justice may lead to their weakened vitality and viability.
30. Grant (2022b, 3).

31. See, for example, Galloway (2009), who examines these issues of correlations versus causality in the social impact of arts-based interventions, and Pedelty (2016, 18), who contends that it is impossible to draw direct links between musical activity and policy outcomes (or, it could be argued by extension, between music and social justice outcomes).
32. McLean (1996).
33. Sen (2001).
34. Sen (2004, 55).
35. Tan (2021, 135).
36. Seeger (2019, 26).
37. UNESCO (2022a).
38. Among the raft of recent sources underscoring the importance of culture in sustainable development are #Culture2030Goal (2020), Hesser and Bartleet (2020), and Mason and Turner (2020, 87).
39. United Nations (2024).
40. Sen (2001).
41. UNESCO (2001, Article 4). The notion of sustainable development is not without its critics. One objection has been an apparent contradiction in the term itself, which invokes the idea of continual growth on "a planet with limits" (Allen 2019, 47). Leitão Pereira observes a certain tension between intangible cultural heritage frameworks, which hold people and communities at their core, and those of sustainable development—for sustainability, she argues, "must no longer be just a process of change that satisfies human needs or aspirations . . . it needs to be posthumanist" (2022, xxiii). I leave further examination of these important debates for another time.
42. United Nations Department of Economic and Social Affairs (2022b).
43. On the relationship between Intangible Cultural Heritage and sustainable development, see Orr (2023, chapter 5) and Bortolotto and Skounti (2024). In relation to music, Hesser and Bartleet (2020) offer a compendium of examples from around the world.
44. UNESCO (2021a, "Culture for Sustainable Development" section).
45. #Culture2030Goal (2020). See also IFACCA (2014).
46. UNESCO (2021a, "Culture for Sustainable Development" section).
47. Mason and Turner (2020, 82).
48. McDonald (2021, 84); see also Wong (2021, 189), Diamond and Castelo-Branco (2021, 7–8) and several further chapters that volume.
49. Tan (2021, abstract).
50. Hemetek, Kölbl and Sağlam (2019, 8). See also Frishkopf (2021).
51. Diamond and Castelo-Branco (2021, 7–8).
52. McDonald (2021, 76).
53. McDonald (2021, 74–75).
54. hooks (2000, 33).
55. Nussbaum (2000).
56. Friere (1970, 89).
57. hooks (1994, 250). On love in the pursuit of social justice, see also McDonald (2022, 4–5).
58. McDermott (2017, 6).
59. Pedelty (2016, 237).
60. Miller (1999, 265).

References

Acton, Renae, Peta Salter, Max Lenoy, and Robert Stevenson. 2017. "Conversations on Cultural Sustainability: Stimuli for Embedding Indigenous Knowledges and Ways of Being into Curriculum." *Higher Education Research and Development* 36 (7): 1311–1325.

AEC-SMS [Association of European Conservatoires—Strengthening Music in Society] Diversity, Identity, Inclusiveness Working Group. 2022. "Artistic Plurality and Inclusive Institutional Culture in HME [Higher Music Education]." Brussels, Belgium: Association Européenne des Conservatoires. Accessed July 17, 2023. https://aec-music.eu/publication/artistic-plurality-and-inclusive-institutional-culture-in-hme/.

Afghanistan National Institute of Music. 2021. "About ANIM." Accessed February 2, 2022. https://www.anim-music.org/.

Africa Beats. 2014. "Africa Beats: Aziza Brahim Voices Western Sahara Blues." *BBC News*, September 21, 2014. Accessed August 18, 2022. https://www.bbc.com/news/av/world-africa-29020181.

Ahmed, Sara. 2012. *On Being Included: Racism and Diversity in Institutional Life*. Durham, NC: Duke University Press.

Ahmed, Sara. 2022. "Using Art and Song to Help Bring the World's Largest Mangrove Swamp Back from the Brink." *The Conversation*, December 8, 2022. Accessed March 9, 2024. https://theconversation.com/using-art-and-song-to-help-bring-the-worlds-largest-mangrove-swamp-back-from-the-brink-193816.

AIATSIS [Australian Institute of Aboriginal and Torres Strait Islander Studies]. 2022. *Ethical Research.* Accessed March 15, 2023. https://aiatsis.gov.au/research/ethical-research.

AIATSIS. n.d.(a) "Indigenous Australians: Aboriginal and Torres Strait Islander People." Accessed February 4, 2022. https://aiatsis.gov.au/explore/indigenous-australians-aboriginal-and-torres-strait-islander-people.

AIATSIS. n.d.(b) "To Remove and Protect." Accessed February 4, 2022. https://aiatsis.gov.au/collection/featured-collections/remove-and-protect.

AIATSIS. n.d.(c) "Missions, Stations and Reserves." Accessed February 4, 2022. https://aiatsis.gov.au/explore/missions-stations-and-reserves.

Ajotikar, Rasika. 2022. "Sounds of a Caste-ending Cultural Movement in Western India." In *Routledge Companion to Music and Human Rights*, edited by Julian Fifer, Angela Impey, Peter G. Kirchschlaeger, Manfred Nowak, and George Ulrich, 365–378. Abingdon: Routledge.

Aktürk, Gül, and Martha Lerski. 2021. "Intangible Cultural Heritage: A Benefit to Climate-Displaced and Host Communities." *Journal of Environmental Studies and Sciences* 11 (3): 305–315.

Alajaji, Sylvia Angelique. 2015. *Music and the Armenian Diaspora: Searching for Home in Exile.* Bloomington, IN: Indiana University Press.

Alfaro Rotondo, Santiago. 2020. "Piracy as Media Practice: The Informal Market of Music and Videos in Peru." In *Piracy and Intellectual Property in Latin America: Rethinking Creativity and the Common Good*, edited by Víctor Goldgel-Carballo and Juan Poblete, 70–89. New York: Routledge.

Allam, Lorena, Calla Wahlquist, Nick Evershed, and Miles Herbert. 2021. "The 474 Deaths Inside: Tragic Toll of Indigenous Deaths in Custody Revealed." *The Guardian*, April 9, 2021.

Accessed February 18, 2022. https://www.theguardian.com/australia-news/2021/apr/09/the-474-deaths-inside-rising-number-of-indigenous-deaths-in-custody-revealed.

Allen, Aaron S. 2019. "Sounding Sustainable; Or, the Challenges of Sustainability." In *Cultural Sustainabilities: Music, Media, Language, Advocacy*, edited by Timothy J. Cooley, 43–60. Illinois: Illinois University Press.

Allen, Aaron S., and Kevin Dawe. 2015. "Ecomusicologies." In *Current Directions in Ecomusicology: Music, Culture, Nature*, edited by Aaron S. Allen and Kevin Dawe, 1–15. Abingdon: Routledge.

Alwin, Duane. 2000. "Social Justice." In *Encyclopedia of Sociology*, 2nd ed., edited by Edgar F. Borgatta and Rhonda J. V. Montgomery, 2695–2711. New York: Macmillan Reference USA.

Amnesty International. 2021. "Does Australia Have a Racism Problem?" *Amnesty International*, October 6, 2021. Accessed March 30, 2022. https://www.amnesty.org.au/does-australia-have-a-racism-problem-in-2021/.

Amnesty International. 2024. "Morocco and Western Sahara 2023." Accessed July 3, 2024. https://www.amnesty.org/en/location/middle-east-and-north-africa/morocco-and-western-sahara/report-morocco-and-western-sahara/.

Anderson, Sue, Agnes Rigney, and Richard Hunter. 1997. "Mission Life Unearthed: An Aboriginal Perspective on Swan Reach." *Oral History Association of Australia Journal* 19: 45–48.

Anonymous. 2021. "You Shall Sing and Dance: Contested 'Safeguarding' of Uyghur Intangible Cultural Heritage." *Asian Ethnicity* 22 (1): 121–139.

Anti-Discrimination Commission Queensland. 2017 (updated 2018, July 25). "Aboriginal People in Queensland: A Brief Human Rights History." *Queensland Human Rights Commission*. Accessed March 25, 2023. https://www.qhrc.qld.gov.au/__data/assets/pdf_file/0013/10606/Aboriginal-timeline-FINAL-updated-25-July-2018.pdf.

Araújo, Samuel, and Vincenzo Cambria. 2013. "Sound Praxis, Poverty, and Social Participation: Perspectives from a Collaborative Study in Rio de Janeiro." *Yearbook for Traditional Music* 45 (1): 28–42.

Artikel2 n.d. "The Saharawi Art of Resistance." Accessed 6 September, 2023. https://emmausstockholm.se/the-sahrawi-art-of-resistance/.

Asai, Susan M. 2022. "Raising the Imperative for Direct Action." In *At the Crossroads of Music and Social Justice*, edited by Brenda M. Romero, Susan M. Asai, David A. McDonald, Andrew G. Snyder and Katelyn E. Best, 277–281. Bloomington: Indiana University Press.

Asea, Wilson B. 2022. "Epistemic Decoloniality of Westernised Higher Education: A Discourse on Curriculum Justice and Knowledge Integration at Historically White Universities in South Africa." *Arts and Humanities in Higher Education* 21 (4): 1–19.

Auclair, Elizabeth, and Graham Fairclough, eds. 2015. *Theory and Practice in Heritage and Sustainability: Between Past and Future*. Abingdon: Routledge.

Australia-New Zealand Regional Committee of the International Council for Traditional Music. 2011. "Statement on Indigenous Australian Music and Dance." Accessed February 4, 2022. https://www.ictmusic.org/sites/default/files/ICTM%20Statement%20on%20Indigenous%20Music&Dance.pdf.

Australian Curriculum, Assessment and Reporting Authority. n.d. "Aboriginal and Torres Strait Islander Histories and Cultures (Version 8.4)." *Australian Curriculum*. Accessed March 30, 2022. https://www.australiancurriculum.edu.au/f-10-curriculum/cross-curriculum-priorities/aboriginal-and-torres-strait-islander-histories-and-cultures/.

Australian Human Rights Commission. 1997. "Bringing Them Home: The 'Stolen Children' Report (1997)." April 1, 1997. Accessed February 4, 2022. https://humanrights.gov.au/our-work/aboriginal-and-torres-strait-islander-social-justice/publications/bringing-them-home.

Australian Human Rights Commission. 2018. "Commission Welcomes Palm Island Decision." *Australian Human Rights Commission*. May 2, 2018. Accessed March 25, 2023. https://humanrights.gov.au/about/news/commission-welcomes-palm-island-decision.

Azkue, Irantzu Mendia, Gloria Guzmán Orellana, Tatiana Montenegro Garay, El Ghalia Djimi, Mina Baali, Salha Boutanguiza, Salka Leili, and Nassra Dah. 2022. *Let Everything Come to Light: Human Rights Violations of Women in Occupied Western Sahara (1975–2021)*. Bilbao, Spain: UPV/EHU.

Bakan, Michael B., with Mara Chasar, Graeme Gibson, Elizabeth J. Grace, Zena Hamelson, Dotan Nitzberg, Gordon Peterson, Maureen Pytlik, Donald Rindale, Amy Sequenzia, and Addison Silar. 2018. *Speaking for Ourselves: Conversations on Life, Music, and Autism*. New York: Oxford University Press.

Baker, Geoffrey. 2014. *El Sistema: Orchestrating Venezuela's Youth*. New York: Oxford University Press.

Baker, Geoffrey, Anna Bull, and Mark Taylor. 2018. "Who Watches the Watchmen? Evaluating Evaluations of El Sistema." *British Journal of Music Education* 35 (3): 255–269.

Ballard, Chris, Meredith Wilson, Yoko Nojima, Richard Matanik, and Richard Shing. 2020. "Disaster as Opportunity? Cyclone Pam and the Transmission of Cultural Heritage." *Anthropological Forum* 30 (1–2): 91–107.

Banglanatak. 2020. "Rural Craft & Cultural Hubs of West Bengal." *Banglanatak*. Accessed October 17, 2022. https://cms.banglanatak.com/wp-content/uploads/2021/03/RCCH-project-brochure.pdf.

Banglanatak. 2021. "IIWG Campaign Promoting Cultural Tourism in Rural Bengal." YouTube. January 31, 2021. Accessed September 22, 2022. https://youtu.be/aAJpjKVUbHA.

Banglanatak. 2022. "Bhatiyali." Accessed October 17, 2022. https://bncmusical.co.in/genre/20.

Bartleet, Brydie-Leigh, and Lee Higgins, eds. 2018. *Oxford Handbook of Community Music*. New York: Oxford University Press.

Baz, Chris, director and producer. 2015. "Yslem Hijo del Desierto: Universal Justice (Official Video) El Profesoul & DJ Sunshine." YouTube. June 25, 2015. Accessed July 7, 2023. https://www.youtube.com/watch?v=BC06OAsVwzA.

Behrman, Simon, and Avidan Kent, eds. 2022. *Climate Refugees*. Cambridge: Cambridge University Press.

Bell, Lee Anne, and Dipti Desai. 2011. "Imagining Otherwise: Connecting the Arts and Social Justice to Envision and Act for Change." *Equity and Excellence in Education* 44 (3): 287.

Bendrups, Dan. 2019. *Singing and Survival: The Music of Easter Island*. New York: Oxford University Press.

Benedict, Cathy, Gary Spruce, Patrick Schmidt, and Paul Woodford, eds. 2015. *Oxford Handbook of Social Justice in Music Education*. New York: Oxford University Press.

Bengal Info. 2021. "Bengal Info: Information about West Bengal, India." Accessed December 18, 2022. https://bengalinfo.com/economy.php.

Bhambra, Gurminder K, Dalia Gebrial, and Nişancıoğlu Kerem, eds. 2018. *Decolonising the University*. London: Pluto Press.

Bhargava, Rajeev. 2013. "Overcoming the Epistemic Injustice of Colonialism." *Global Policy* 4 (4): 413–417.

Bhattacharya, Ananya. 2014. "Integrating Culture in Planning and Action for Sustainable Development: The Role of ICH NGOs." *Volkskunde* 3: 339–437.

Bhava, Atithidevo. 2021. "India: Tourism Statistics at a Glance." *Ministry of Tourism, Government of India*. Accessed October 17, 2022. https://tourism.gov.in/sites/default/files/2022-09/India%20Tourism%20Statistics%20at%20a%20Glance%202021%20%281%29.pdf.

Bingley, Kate. 2011. "Bambeh's Song: Music, Women and Health in a Rural Community in Post-Conflict Sierra Leone." *Music & Arts in Action* 3 (2): 59–78.

Birtles, Dora. 1935. *North-West by North: A Journal of a Voyage*. London: Jonathan Cape.

Boal, Augusto. 1984. *Técnicas Latino-Americanas de Teatro Popular: Uma Revolução Copernicana ao Contrário* [*Latin American Popular Theater Techniques: A Copernican Revolution in Reverse*]. São Paulo: Hucitec.

Bolton, Lissant. 2003. *Unfolding the Moon: Enacting Women's Kastom in Vanuatu*. Honolulu: University of Hawai'i Press.

Bond, Patrick. 2012. *Politics of Climate Justice: Paralysis Above, Movement Below*. Scottsville, South Africa: University of KwaZulu-Natal Press.

Bortolotto, Chiara, and Ahmed Skounti, eds. 2024. *Intangible Cultural Heritage and Sustainable Development: Inside a UNESCO Convention*. London and New York, Routledge.

Boukhars, Anouar, and Jacquies Roussellier, eds. 2014. *Perspectives on Western Sahara: Myths, Nationalisms, and Geopolitics*. Lanham, MD: Rowman & Littlefield.

Bracknell, Clint, and Linda Barwick. 2020. "The Fringe or the Heart of Things? Aboriginal and Torres Strait Islander Musics in Australian Music Institutions." *Musicology Australia* 42 (2): 70–84.

Brisbane Times. 2016. "Queensland Police Breached Discrimination Act on Palm Island, Court Finds." *Brisbane Times*, December 5, 2016. Accessed March 25, 2023. https://www.brisbanetimes.com.au/national/queensland/queensland-police-breached-discrimination-act-on-palm-island-court-finds-20161205-gt487s.html.

British Library. n.d.(a). "Violeta Ruano Portraits of Saharawi Music [Digital Collection]." *British Library*. Accessed May 17, 2023. https://www.bl.uk/collections/violeta-ruano-posada-collection [archived].

British Library. n.d.(b). "Violeta Ruano Portraits of Saharawi Music: Continue the Struggle." *British Library*. Accessed August 8, 2022. https://sounds.bl.uk/World-and-traditional-music/Violeta-Ruano-portraits-of-Saharawi-Music/025M-C1640X0052XX-0001V0 [archived].

Bromham, Lindell, Russell Dinnage, Hedvig Skirgård, Andrew Ritchie, Marcel Cardillo, Felicity Meakins, Simon Greenhill, and Xia Hua. 2021. "Global Predictors of Language Endangerment and the Future of Linguistic Diversity." *Nature Ecology & Evolution* 6 (2): 163–173.

Brooks, Bonny. 2018. "How Contemporary Capitalism Drives Hysterical Wokeness." Medium, August 14, 2018. Accessed February 2, 2022. https://medium.com/arc-digital/how-contemporary-capitalism-drives-hysterical-wokeness-9fb206158aad.

Brown, Danielle. 2020. "An Open Letter on Racism in Music Studies—Especially Ethnomusicology and Music Education." June 12, 2020. Accessed July 17, 2023. https://www.mypeopletellstories.com/blog/open-letter.

Bündnis Entwicklung Hilft. 2021. "World Risk Report 2021." *Relief Web*. Accessed February 21, 2022. https://reliefweb.int/sites/reliefweb.int/files/resources/2021-world-risk-report.pdf.

Burns, James. 2016. "Southern Ewe Dance-Drumming: An Ethnographic Study of Performing Musicians in Contemporary Contexts." In *Sustainable Futures for Music Cultures: An Ecological Perspective*, edited by Huib Schippers and Catherine Grant, 43–75. New York: Oxford University Press.

Cambodian Living Arts. 2017. "About Us." Accessed February 2, 2022. https://www.cambodianlivingarts.org/about-us/ [archived].

Capeheart, Loretta, and Dragan Milovanovic. 2007. *Social Justice: Theories, Issues and Movements*. Piscataway, NJ: Rutgers University Press.

Carrington, Damian. 2019. "School Climate Strikes: 1.4 Million People Took Part, Say Campaigners." *The Guardian*, March 19, 2019. Accessed March 22, 2022. https://www.theguardian.com/environment/2019/mar/19/school-climate-strikes-more-than-1-million-took-part-say-campaigners-greta-thunberg.

Caruso, Fulvia. 2021. "Experiencing and Crossing Borders Through Music." In *Borders, Migration and Globalization: An Interdisciplinary Perspective*, edited by Anna Rita Calabrò, 363–373. London: Routledge.

Carvalho, José Jorge de. 2018. "Transculturality and the Meeting of Knowledges." In *Transkulturelle Erkundungen*, edited by Ursula Hemetek, Daliah Hindler, Harald Huber, Therese Kaufmann, Malmberg Isolde, and Hande Saglam, 79–94. Vienna, Austria: Böhlau Verlag.

Carvalho, José Jorge de. 2021. "Ethnomusicology and the Meeting of Knowledges in Music: The Inclusion of Masters of Traditional Musics as Lecturers in Higher Education Institutions." In *Transforming Ethnomusicology Volume II: Political, Social & Ecological Issues*, edited by Beverley Diamond and Salwa El-Shawan Castelo-Branco, 185–206. New York: Oxford University Press.

Carvalho, José Jorge de. 2023a. "Meeting of Knowledges: A Model to Decolonize the Eurocentric Curriculum of Universities in Latin America (first draft)." In *Cadernos de Inclusão* 19: 1–20. Brasília: Instituto de Nacional de Ciência e Tecnologia de Inclusão no Ensino Superior e na Pesquisa.

Carvalho, José Jorge de. 2023b. "A Proposal to Transform the Curriculum of Universities: Towards a Multilingual, Multicultural and Pluriepistemic Academic Institution." In *Cadernos de Inclusão* 21: 1–13. Brasília: Instituto de Nacional de Ciência e Tecnologia de Inclusão no Ensino Superior e na Pesquisa.

Carvalho, José Jorge de. 2023c. "The Meeting of Knowledges in the Universities: A Movement to Decolonise the Eurocentric Academic Curriculum in Latin America." In *Routledge Companion to Architectural Pedagogies of the Global South*, edited by Harriet Harriss, Ashraf M. Salama, and Ane Gonzalez Lara, 67–76. Abingdon: Routledge.

Carvalho, José Jorge de, Liliam Barros Cohen, Antenor Ferreira Corrêa, Sonia Chada, and Paula Nakayama. 2016. "The Meeting of Knowledges as a Contribution to Ethnomusicology and Music Education." *The World of Music (New Series)* 5 (1): 111–133.

Carvalho, José Jorge de, and Juliana Florez. 2014. "The Meeting of Knowledges: A Project for the Decolonization of Universities in Latin America." *Postcolonial Studies* 17 (2): 122–139.

Central Intelligence Agency. 2022. "Vanuatu." *World Factbook*, November 15, 2022. Accessed November 28, 2022. https://www.cia.gov/the-world-factbook/countries/vanuatu/.

Charmaz, K. 2014. *Constructing Grounded Theory*. Thousand Oaks, CA: Sage.

Chatty, Dawn. 2010. *Deterritorialized Youth: Sahrawi and Afghan Refugees at the Margins of the Middle East*. Oxford: Berghahn Books.

Chávez, Luis, and Russell P. Skelchy. 2019. "Decolonization for Ethnomusicology and Music Studies in Higher Education." *Action, Criticism, and Theory for Music Education* 18 (3): 115–143.

Chen, David. 2018. "Palm Island Riots: Queensland Government to Pay $30m in Class Action Case." *ABC News*, May 1, 2018. Accessed March 25, 2023. https://www.abc.net.au/news/2018-05-01/palm-island-riots-qld-government-pay-$30m-class-action-decision/9714640.

Chorn-Pond, Arn, and Michael Ungar. 2012. "An Interview with Arn Chorn-Pond: Helping Children in Cambodia through the Revival of Traditional Music and Art." In *The Social Ecology of Resilience: A Handbook of Theory and Practice*, edited by Michael Ungar, 99–108. New York: Springer.

Clammer, John A. 2015. *Art, Culture and International Development: Humanizing Social Transformation*. London: Routledge.

Clayton, Martin. n.d. "Entrainment in Congado Music." *Experience and Meaning in Music Performance*. The Open University. Accessed August 29, 2023. https://fass.open.ac.uk/research/projects/experience-meaning-in-music-performance/congado-music.

Climate Watch. 2024. "Historical GHG Emissions." Accessed July 5, 2024. https://www.climatewatchdata.org/ghg-emissions?end_year=2021&start_year=1990.

Cohen, Cynthia E. 2008. "Music: A Universal Language?" In *Music and Conflict Transformation: Harmonies and Dissonances in Geopolitics*, edited by Olivier Urbain, 26–39. London: I.B. Tauris.

Cohen, Cynthia E. 2020. "Reimagining Transitional Justice." *International Journal of Transitional Justice* 14 (1): 1–13.

Cohen, Patricia. 2005. "If Cambodia Can Learn to Sing Again." *New York Times*, December 18, 2005. Accessed July 17, 2023. https://www.nytimes.com/2005/12/18/arts/music/if-cambodia-can-learn-to-sing-again.html.

Cole, Tim, director. 2014. *Vanuatu Women's Water Music* [documentary]. Melbourne, Australia: Wantok Music.

Conway, Declan, and Johanna Mustelin. 2014. "Strategies for Improving Adaptation Practice in Developing Countries." *Nature Climate Change* 4 (5): 339–342.

Cooley, Timothy, ed. 2019a. *Cultural Sustainabilities: Music, Media, Language, Advocacy*. Illinois: University of Illinois Press.

Cooley, Timothy. 2019b. "Sustainability, Resilience, Advocacy, and Activism: Introduction." In *Cultural Sustainabilities: Music, Media, Language, Advocacy*, edited by Timothy Cooley, xxiii–xxxiv. Illinois: University of Illinois Press.

Coppola, William J., David G. Hebert, and Patricia Shehan Campbell, eds. 2020. *World Music Pedagogy, Volume VII: Teaching World Music in Higher Education*. Abingdon: Routledge.

Corn, Aaron. 2011. "National Recording Project for Indigenous Performance in Australia." *Aboriginal Artists Agency*. Accessed March 13, 2023. http://www.aboriginalartists.com.au/NRP_vision.htm.

Corn, Aaron, and Clint Bracknell. 2020. "Editorial." *Musicology Australia* 42 (2): 65–69.

Cronin-Furman, Kate. 2018. "China Has Chosen Cultural Genocide in Xinjiang—For Now." *Foreign Policy*, September 19, 2018. Accessed May 15, 2022. https://foreignpolicy.com/2018/09/19/china-has-chosen-cultural-genocide-in-xinjiang-for-now/.

#Culture2030Goal. 2020. "#Culture2030Goal Statement on Culture and the CoVid19 Pandemic." April 20, 2020. Accessed January 8, 2023. http://culture2030goal.net/culturecovid19-statement.

Dalaqua, Gustavo H. 2020. "Aesthetic Injustice." *Journal of Aesthetics and Culture* 12 (1): 1–12.

Darder, Antonia. 2017. *Reinventing Paulo Freire: A Pedagogy of Love*. Abingdon: Routledge.

Davies, Kirsten. 2015. "Kastom, Climate Change and Intergenerational Democracy: Experiences from Vanuatu." In *Climate Change in the Asia-Pacific Region*, edited by Walter Leal Filho, 49–66. Cham, Switzerland: Springer.

Dempsey, Genevieve. 2016. *The Sacred Sound of Congado: Performing Songs of Devotion, Race, and Gender in Afro-Brazilian Religious Communities*. PhD diss., University of Chicago. Accessed August 29, 2023. https://knowledge.uchicago.edu/record/482.

Dempsey, Genevieve E. 2017. "The Acoustics of Justice: Music and Myth in Afro-Brazilian Congado." *Yale Journal of Music & Religion* 3 (2): 1–25. https://elischolar.library.yale.edu/yjmr/vol3/iss2/1/.

DeNora, Tia, and Gary Ansdell. 2014. "What Can't Music Do?" *Psychology of Well-Being: Theory, Research and Practice* 4 (23): 1–10.

De Sousa Santos, Boaventura. 2016. *Epistemologies of the South: Justice against Epistemicide*. Abingdon: Routledge.

De Sousa Santos, Boaventura. 2018. *The End of the Cognitive Empire: The Coming of Age of Epistemologies of the South*. Durham, NC: Duke University Press.

Diamond, Beverley, and Salwa El-Shawan Castelo-Branco. 2021. "Ethnomusicological Praxis: An Introduction." In *Transforming Ethnomusicology Volume II: Political, Social & Ecological Issues*, edited by Beverley Diamond and Salwa El-Shawan Castelo-Branco, 1–25. New York: Oxford University Press.

Dick, Thomas. 2014. "Vanuatu Water Music and the Mwerlap Diaspora: Music, Migration, Tradition, and Tourism." *AlterNative: An International Journal of Indigenous Peoples* 10 (4): 392–407.

Dick, Thomas. 2015. "Alternative Approaches to Well-being and Engagement in Vanuatu." *Australasian Psychiatry* 23 (6): 52–54.

Dick, Thomas, and Marcel Meltherorong. 2011. "Dovetailing Discourses of Emergent Resilience in Vanuatu." In *Songs of Resilience*, edited by Andy Brader, 97–120. Newcastle: Cambridge Scholars Press.

Diehl, Keila. 2002. *Echoes from Dharamsala: Music in the Life of a Tibetan Refugee Community*. Berkeley: University of California Press.

Diettrich, Brian, Jane Freeman Moulin, and Michael Webb. 2011. *Music in Pacific Island Cultures: Experiencing Music, Expressing Culture*. New York: Oxford University Press.

Diouf, Sylviane A. 2016. *Slavery's Exiles: The Story of the American Maroons*. New York: New York University.

Dirksen, Rebecca. 2015. "Surviving Material Poverty by Employing Cultural Wealth: Putting Music in the Service of Community in Haiti." *Yearbook for Traditional Music* 45 (1): 43–57.

Dirksen, Rebecca. 2019. "Haiti's Drums and Trees: Facing the Loss of the Sacred." *Ethnomusicology* 63 (1): 43–77.

Docherty, Thomas. 2014. *Universities at War*. Los Angeles: Sage Publications.

Dyck, Kirsten. 2016. *Reichsrock: The International Web of White-Power and Neo-Nazi Hate Music*. New Brunswick, New Jersey, and London: Rutgers University Press.

Eberhard, David M., Gary F. Simons, and Charles D. Fennig, eds. 2022. *Ethnologue: Languages of the World*, 25th ed. Dallas, Texas: SIL International.

Eckersley, Robyn. 2009. "Just Carbon Trading?" In *Climate Change and Social Justice*, edited by Jeremy Moss, 99–127. Melbourne: Melbourne University Press.

Engberg-Pedersen, Lars, and Helle Munk Ravnborg. 2010. "Conceptualisations of Poverty." *Danish Institute for International Studies*. Accessed October 14, 2022. https://pure.diis.dk/ws/files/61212/RP2010_01_conceptualisations_poverty_web.pdf.

Feld, Steven. 2012. *Sound and Sentiment*. Philadelphia: University of Pennsylvania Press.

Fifer, Julian, Angela Impey, Peter G Kirchschlaeger, Manfred Nowak, and George Ulrich, eds. 2022. *Routledge Companion to Music and Human Rights*. Abingdon: Routledge.

Fiol, Stefan. 2013. "Of Lack and Loss: Assessing Cultural and Musical Poverty in Uttarakhand." *Yearbook for Traditional Music* 45 (1): 83–96.

Flexner, James L., and Matthew Spriggs. 2015. "Mission Sites as Indigenous Heritage in Southern Vanuatu." *Journal of Social Archaeology* 15 (2): 184–209.

Ford, Biranda. 2021. "From a Different Place to a Third Space: Rethinking International Student Pedagogy in the Western Conservatoire." In *The Politics of Diversity in Music Education*, edited by Alexis Anja Kallio, Kathryn Marsh, Heidi Westerlund, Sidsel Karlsen and Eva Sæther, 177–189. Cham, Switzerland: Springer.

Forsyth, Miranda, and Thomas Dick. 2021. "Liquid Regulation: The (Men's) Business of Women's Water Music?" *International Journal of Law in Context* 18 (2): 133–155.

Foster, Victoria. 2016. *Collaborative Arts-based Research for Social Justice*. Abingdon: Routledge.

Frandy, Tim. 2022. "From Sustainability to Sustainabilities: Dialogue, Crisis and Power." *Communicating Sustainability: An International Conversation with Sustainability Activists*. Baltimore, MD: Goucher College.

Frankenhuis, Willem E., and Daniel Nettle. 2020. "The Strengths of People in Poverty." *Current Directions in Psychological Science* 29 (1): 16–21.

Franklin, James. 2016. "Catholic Missions to Aboriginal Australia: An Evaluation of their Overall Effect." *Journal of the Australian Catholic Historical Society* 37 (1): 45–68.

Fraser, Nancy. 1995. "From Redistribution to Recognition? Dilemmas of Justice in a 'Post-Socialist' Age." *New Left Review* 1 (212): 68–93.

Fraser, Nancy. 2012. "On Justice." *New Left Review* no. 74: 41–51.

Freemuse. 2008. "Aziza Brahim (Western Sahara)" [blog post]. *Freemuse*, December 7, 2008. Accessed July 17, 2021. http://www.freemuse.org/sw31191.asp [archived].

Freemuse. 2020. "LGBTI Freedom of Artistic Expression: About This Report." *Freemuse: Defending Artistic Expression*, December 10, 2020. Accessed May 17, 2022. https://freemuse.org/resource-list/lgbti-freedom-of-artistic-expression/.

Freemuse. 2022. "The State of Artistic Freedom 2022." *Freemuse: Defending Artistic Freedom*, February 2022. Accessed April 25, 2023. https://freemuse.org/media/yk2paxxb/saf-report-2022.pdf.

Fricker, Miranda (2007). *Epistemic Injustice: Power and the Ethics of Knowing*. Oxford: Oxford University Press.

Freire, Paolo. 1970. *Pedagogy of the Oppressed*. New York: Seabury Press.

Frishkopf, Michael. 2021. "Music for Global Human Development." In *Transforming Ethnomusicology Volume II: Political, Social & Ecological Issues*, edited by Beverley Diamond and Salwa El-Shawan Castelo-Branco, 47–66. Oxford Scholarship Online.

Frishkopf, Michael. 2022. "Giving Voice to Hope: Music of Liberian Refugees." *Canadian Centre for Ethnomusicology, University of Alberta* [Wiki page]. February 19, 2022. Accessed August 15, 2022. https://www.artsrn.ualberta.ca/fwa_mediawiki/index.php?title=Giving_Voice_to_Hope:_Music_of_Liberian_Refugees.

Fynn, Veronica P. 2011. "Africa's Last Colony: Sahrawi People – Refugees, IDPS and Nationals?" *Journal of Internal Displacement* 1 (2): 40–58.

Galloway, Susan. 2009. "Theory-Based Evaluation and the Social Impact of the Arts." *Cultural Trends* 18 (2): 125–149.

Ganguly, Lopamudra. 2020. "Past and Present Economic Status of West Bengal: A Review." *Asian Review of Social Sciences* 9 (2): 8–13.

"Garma Statement on Indigenous Music and Performance." 2002. *Musicological Society of Australia*. Accessed March 13, 2023. https://msa.org.au/wp-content/uploads/2021/08/NRPIPA-Garma-Statement-2002.pdf.

Garrison, Cassandra. 2017. "Afghan Orchestra Puts Women's Rights Center Stage at Davos." *Reuters*, January 20, 2017. Accessed April 23, 2023. https://www.reuters.com/article/us-davos-meeting-orchestra-idUSKBN1532N2.

Gberie, Lansana. 2005. *A Dirty War in West Africa: The RUF and the Destruction of Sierra Leone*. Bloomington, IN: Indiana University Press.

Gillespie, Kirsty. 2017. "The Ethnomusicologist at the Rock Face: Reflections on Working at the Nexus of Music and Mining." In *Ethnomusicology: A Contemporary Reader*, Vol. 2, edited by Jennifer C. Post, 81–96. New York: Routledge.

Gillespie, Kirsty. 2022. "Mining for Music: Ethical Entanglements in Lihir, Papua New Guinea." In *The Routledge Companion to Ethics and Research in Ethnomusicology*, edited by Jonathan P. J. Stock and Beverley Diamond, 199–208. New York: Routledge.

Giménez Amorós, Luis. 2015. "Azawan: Precolonial Musical Culture and Saharawi Nationalism in the Refugee Camps of the Hamada Desert in Algeria." *African Music* 10 (1): 31–51.

Giménez Amorós, Luis. 2018. "Mariem Hassan, Nubenega Records and the Western Saharawi Struggle." In *Songs of Social Protest: International Perspectives*, edited by Aileen Dillane, Martin J. Power, Eoin Devereux, and Amanda Haynes, 435–453. London: Rowman & Littlefield.

Glatzer, Jocelyn, filmmaker. 2003. *The Flute Player* [documentary]. San Francisco, CA: Center for Asian American Media.

Global Data Lab. 2022. "Subnational HDI (v5.0): India." Accessed July 17, 2023. https://globaldatalab.org/shdi/table/shdi/IND/?levels=1+4&interpolation=0&extrapolation=0.

Goldbard, Arlene. 2017. "Art Became the Oxygen: An Artistic Response Guide." *US Department of Arts and Culture*. Accessed January 20, 2023. https://usdac.us/artisticresponse.

Government of West Bengal. 2022. "West Bengal State Portal." Accessed October 14, 2022. https://www.wb.gov.in/.

Grant, Catherine. 2014a. *Music Endangerment: How Language Maintenance Can Help*. New York: Oxford University Press.

Grant, Catherine. 2014b. "Perspectives of Culture-Bearers on the Vitality, Viability and Value of Traditional Khmer Music Genres in Contemporary Cambodia." *The Asia-Pacific Journal of Anthropology* 15 (1): 26–46. Grant, Catherine. 2015. "Learning and Teaching Traditional Music in Cambodia: Challenges and Incentives." *International Journal of Music Education* 35 (1): 5–16.

Grant, Catherine. 2016. "Socioeconomic Concerns of Young Musicians of Traditional Genres in Cambodia: Implications for Music Sustainability." *Ethnomusicology Forum* 25 (3): 306–325.

Grant, Catherine. 2017. "Finding New Ground: Maintaining and Transforming Traditional Music." In *The Handbook of Contemporary Cambodia*, edited by Katherine Brickell and Simon Springer, 432–441. Abingdon: Routledge.

Grant, Catherine. 2018. "Academic Flying, Climate Change, and Ethnomusicology: Personal Reflections on a Professional Problem." *Ethnomusicology Forum* 27 (2): 123–135.

Grant, Catherine. 2019. "Climate Justice and Cultural Sustainability: The Case of Etëtung (Vanuatu Women's Water Music)." *Asia Pacific Journal of Anthropology* 20 (1): 42–56.

Grant, Catherine. 2020. "Roles of Culture and Cultural Sustainability in Eliminating Poverty." In *No Poverty. Encyclopedia of the UN Sustainable Development Goals*, edited by Walter Leal Filho, Anabela Marisa Azul, Luciana Brandli, Amanda Lange Salvia, Pinar Gökçin Özuyar, and Tony Wall, 1–11. Cham, Switzerland: Springer Cham.

Grant, Catherine. 2022a. "Music Sustainability, Human Rights, and Future Justice." In *The Routledge Companion to Music and Human Rights*, edited by Julian Fifer, Angela Impey, Peter G. Kirchschlaeger, Manfred Nowak, and George Ulrich, 113–122. Abingdon: Routledge.

Grant, Catherine. 2022b. "Introduction to 'Social Justice, Human Rights, and Sustainability of Traditional Arts.'" *International Journal of Traditional Arts* 4 (1): 1–5.

Grant, Catherine, and Sarin Chhuon. 2016. "Gauging Music Vitality and Viability: Three Cases from Cambodia." *Yearbook for Traditional Music* 48: 25–47.

Grant, Catherine, Ruth Opara, and Kirsten Dyck. 2024. "Inverse Relationships Between Cultural Sustainability and Human Rights: The Counterintuitive Cases of Nigerian *Avu Udu* Dance and White-Power Music." *International Journal of Cultural Policy* [online first version]. Accessed September 16, 2024. https://doi.org/10.1080/10286632.2024.2402242.

Groemer, Gerald. 2016. *Goze: Women, Musical Performance, and Visual Disability in Traditional Japan*. Oxford: Oxford University Press.

Grosfoguel, Ramon. 2013. "The Structure of Knowledge in Westernized Universities Epistemic: Racism/Sexism and Four Genocides/Epistemicides of the Long 16th Century." *Journal of the Sociology of Self-Knowledge* 11 (1): 73–90.

Gupta, Toolika. 2021. "UNESCO Evaluation Report: Evaluation Report for Year 1 of the Project 'Promoting Intangible Cultural Heritage (ICH) and Developing Cultural Tourism in Jodphur, Barmer, Jaisalmer and Bikaner districts in Rajasthan.'" September 11, 2021. Jaipur: Indian Institute of Crafts & Design.

Hall, Stefan Brambilla. 2020. "This is How COVID-19 is Affecting the Music Industry." *World Economic Forum*, May 27, 2020. Accessed October 5, 2022. https://www.weforum.org/agenda/2020/05/this-is-how-covid-19-is-affecting-the-music-industry/.

Hamill, Chad S. 2021. "The Earth is (Still) Our Mother: Traversing Indigenous Landscapes Through Sacred Geographies of Song." In *Transforming Ethnomusicology Volume II: Political, Social & Ecological Issues*, edited by Beverley Diamond and Salwa El-Shawan Castelo-Branco, 115–126. New York: Oxford University Press.

Harnish, David. 2016. "The Challenges of Music Sustainability in Lombok, Indonesia." In *Performing Indonesia*, edited by Andy McGraw and Sumarsam. Washington, USA: Freer Sackler. Accessed July 18, 2023. https://asia-archive.si.edu/essays/article-harnish/.

Harris, Deonte L. 2022. "On Race, Value, and the Need to Reimagine Ethnomusicology for the Future." *Ethnomusicology* 66 (2): 213–235.

Harrison, Klisala. 2013. "The Relationship of Poverty to Music." *Yearbook for Traditional Music* 45: 1–12.

Harrison, Klisala. 2014. "The Second Wave of Applied Ethnomusicology." *MUSICultures* 4 (2): 15–33.

Harrison, Klisala. 2020a. "Value Alignment in Applied and Community-Based Music Research." *Artikkelit / Musiikki* 1–2: 71–87.

Harrison, Klisala. 2020b. *Music Downtown Eastside: Human Rights and Capability Development Through Music in Urban Poverty*. New York: Oxford University Press.

Harvey, David C. 2001. "Heritage Pasts and Heritage Presents: Temporality, Meaning and the Scope of Heritage Studies." *International Journal of Heritage Studies* 7 (4): 319–338.

Hassan, Mariem. 2012. "El Aaiún Egdat" (El Aaiún on Fire). Produced by Manuel Domínguez. Madrid: Nubenegra INN1137-2, CD.

Hayward, Philip. 2014. "Sounding the Aquapelago: The Cultural-Environmental Context of ni-Vanuatu Women's Liquid Percussion Performance." *Perfect Beat* 15 (2): 113–127.

Hebert, David G. 2022. "Nature Conservation and Music Sustainability: Fields with Shared Concerns." *Canadian Journal of Environmental Education* 25: 175–189.

Hemetek, Ursula, ed. 2021. "Music and Forced Migration" [special issue]. *Music and Minorities* 1.

Hemetek, Ursula, Marko Kölbl, and Hande Sağlam. 2019. "Introduction." In *Ethnomusicology Matters: Influencing Social and Political Realities*, edited by Ursula Hemetek, Marko Kölbl, and Hande Sağlam, 7–14. Vienna: Böhlau Verlag.

Hess, Juliet. 2015. "Decolonizing Music Education: Moving beyond Tokenism." *International Journal of Music Education* 33 (3): 336–347.

Hess, Juliet. 2018. "Challenging the Empire in Empir(e)ical research: The Question of Speaking in Music Education." *Music Education Research* 20 (5): 573–590.

Hesser, Barbara, and Bartleet Brydie-Leigh, eds. 2020. *Music as a Global Resource: Solutions for Cultural, Social, Health, Educational, Environmental, and Economic Issues*, 5th ed. New York: Music as a Global Resource.

Hil, Richard, Kristen Lyons, and Fern Thompsett. 2021. *Transforming Universities in the Midst of Global Crisis: A University for the Common Good*. London: Routledge.

Hilder, Thomas. 2015. *Sámi Musical Performance and the Politics of Indigeneity in Northern Europe*. Lanham, MD: Rowman & Littlefield.

HIPAMS [Heritage-Sensitive Intellectual Property & Marketing Strategies]. 2018–2021. "Heritage-Sensitive Intellectual Property & Marketing Strategies." Accessed October 5, 2022. https://hipamsindia.org/about.

Hofman, Ana. 2010. "Maintaining the Distance, Othering the Subaltern: Rethinking Ethnomusicologists' Engagement in Advocacy." In *Applied Ethnomusicology: Historical and Contemporary Approaches*, edited by Klisala Harrison, Elizabeth Mackinlay, and Svanibor Pettan, 22–35. Newcastle upon Tyne, UK: Cambridge Scholars Publishing.

Holmes McDowell, John, Katherine Borland, Rebecca Dirksen, and Sue Tuohy, eds. 2021. *Performing Environmentalisms: Expressive Culture and Ecological Change*. Champaign: University of Illinois Press.

Holtorf, Cornelius, and Anders Högberg, eds. 2020. *Cultural Heritage and the Future*. Abingdon: Routledge.

hooks, bell. 1994. *Teaching to Transgress: Education as the Practice of Freedom*. New York: Routledge.

hooks, bell. 2000. *All About Love: New Visions*. New York: William Morrow.

Hooper, Chloe. 2006. "Who Let the Dogs Out?" *The Monthly*, November. Accessed March 25, 2023. https://www.themonthly.com.au/issue/2006/november/1246441718/chloe-hooper/who-let-dogs-out#mtr.

Hopgood, Stephen. 2014, July. "The Endtimes of Human Rights." In *Debating the Endtimes of Human Rights: Institutions and Activism in a Neo-Westphalian World*, edited by Doutje Lettinga and Lars van Troost, 11–18. Amsterdam: Amnesty International.

Howell, Gillian. 2018. "Community Music Interventions in Post-Conflict Contexts." In *Oxford Handbook of Community Music*, edited by Brydie-Leigh Bartleet and Lee Higgins, 43–70. New York: Oxford University Press.

IFACCA [International Federation of Arts Councils and Culture Agencies]. 2014. "Declaration on the Inclusion of Culture in the Sustainable Development Goals." May 1, 2014. Accessed February 2, 2022. https://www.ifla.org/wp-content/uploads/2019/05/assets/hq/topics/libraries-development/documents/declaration_culture_and_sdgs_post2015_-_1_may_2014_-_eng.pdf.

IFACCA. 2023. "9th World Summit Discussion Paper." *9th World Summit on Arts & Culture*. Accessed April 23, 2023. www.artsummit.org/discussionpaper.

Impey, Angela. 2014. "Dinka Ox-songs (Cattle Songs)." *Music Endangerment*. Accessed May 8, 2023. http://www.musicendangerment.com/portfolio/dinka-ox-songs-cattle-songs/ [archived].

Impey, Angela. 2018. *Song Walking: Women, Music, and Environmental Justice in an African Borderland*. Chicago: University of Chicago Press.

Impey, Angela. 2021. "Performing Transitional Justice: Song, Truth-telling, and Memory in South Sudan." In *Transforming Ethnomusicology Volume I: Methodologies, Institutional Structures, and Policies*, edited by Beverley Diamond and Salwa El-Shawan Castelo-Branco, 169–186. New York: Oxford University Press.

International Society for Ecological Economics. 2021. "'Meeting of Knowledges' in Brazil." YouTube. May 6, 2021. Accessed April 10, 2022. https://www.youtube.com/watch?v=ZbmECKdFn64.

International Society for Music Education. n.d. "International Society for Music Education." Accessed April 6, 2022. https://www.isme.org/.

Jeffery, Renee. 2021. "The Role of the Arts in Cambodia's Transitional Justice Process." *International Journal of Politics, Culture, and Society* 34: 335–358.

Jewkes, Stephen, and Giulio Piovaccari. 2021. "'30 Years of Blah Blah Blah: Thunberg Questions Italy Climate Talks." *Reuters*, September 29, 2021. Accessed January 19, 2022. https://www.reuters.com/world/europe/protests-proposals-activists-face-climate-talks-test-2021-09-28/.

Kallio, Alexis Anja, and Heidi Westerlund. 2016. "The Ethics of Survival: Teaching the Traditional Arts to Disadvantaged Children in Post-Conflict Cambodia." *International Journal of Music Education* 34 (1): 90–103.

Kallio, Alexis Anja, Kathryn Marsh, Heidi Westerlund, Sidsel Karlsen, and Eva Sæther. 2021. "The Politics of Diversity in Music Education: Introduction." In *The Politics of Diversity in Music Education*, edited by Alexis Anja Kallio, Kathryn Marsh, Heidi Westerlund, Sidsel Karlsen, and Eva Sæther, 1–11. Cham, Switzerland: Springer.

Kent, George. 2008. "Unpeaceful Music." In *Music and Conflict Transformation: Harmonies and Dissonances in Geopolitics*, edited by Olivier Urbain, 104–111. London: I.B. Tauris.

Khalil, Shaimaa. 2015. "Afghanistan's First Female Conductor." *BBC*, November 10, 2015. Accessed April 23, 2023. https://www.bbc.com/news/magazine-34581264.

Khmer Magic Music Bus. 2019. "Khmer Magic Music Bus." Accessed January 15, 2022. http://kmmb.cambodianlivingarts.org/.

Khmer Magic Music Bus. 2022. "The Khmer Magic Music Bus." Accessed August 27, 2024. https://magicmusicbus.org/index.html.

Kidd, Ian James, José Medina, and Gaile Pohlhaus Jr., eds. (2017). *Routledge Handbook of Epistemic Injustice*. Abingdon: Routledge.

King, Ashley. 2021. "Taliban Government Will Ban Music in Public in Afghanistan." *Digital Music News*, August 26, 2021. Accessed May 17, 2022. https://www.digitalmusicnews.com/2021/08/26/taliban-gov-ban-music-afghanistan/.

King, Stephen J. 2014. "The Emergence and Politics of the Polisario Front." In *Perspectives on Western Sahara: Myths, Nationalisms, and Geopolitics*, edited by Anouar Boukhars and Jacquies Roussellier, 87–105. Lanham, MD: Rowman & Littlefield.

Kingsbury, Damien, ed. 2016. *Western Sahara: International Law, Justice and Natural Resources*. Abingdon: Routledge.

Klint, Louise Munk, Emma Wong, Min Jiang, Terry DeLacy, David Harrison, and Dale Dominey-Howes. 2012. "Climate Change Adaptation in the Pacific Island Tourism Sector: Analysing the Policy Environment in Vanuatu." *Current Issues in Tourism* 15 (3): 247–274.

Koehler, Robert. 2019. "The Music That's in All of Us." *La Progressive*, February 14, 2019. Accessed May 6, 2022. https://www.laprogressive.com/musicians-without-borders/.

Koger, Susan, and Deborah Du Nann Winter. 2010. *The Psychology of Environmental Problems: Psychology for Sustainability*, 3rd ed. New York: Psychology Press.

Kulkarni, Pavan. 2022. "Ahead of UN Session, Sahrawis Recollect Decades of Betrayal that Enabled Moroccan Colonization." *People's Dispatch*. October 10, 2022. Accessed February 19, 2023. https://peoplesdispatch.org/2022/10/10/ahead-of-un-session-sahrawis-recollect-decades-of-betrayal-that-enabled-moroccan-colonization/.

Lee, Iara, director. 2015. "Life is Waiting: Referendum and Resistance in Western Sahara." *Cultures of Resistance Films*. YouTube. Accessed March 28, 2023. https://www.youtube.com/watch?v=9QzRzm4uFxU.

Leitão Pereira, Mariana Pinto. 2022. "Introduction. Situating Intangible Cultural Heritage and Sustainable Development: A Challenging Partnership?" In *Sustaining Support for Intangible Cultural Heritage*, edited by Shihan de Silva Jayasuriya, Mariana Pinto Leitão Pereira, and Gregory Hansen, xvii–xxx. Newcastle upon Tyne, UK: Cambridge Scholars Publishing.

Lele, Sharachchandra, Eduardo S. Brondizio, John Byrne, and Georgina M. Mace, eds. 2019. *Rethinking Environmentalism: Linking Justice, Sustainability, and Diversity*. Cambridge, MA: MIT Press.

Lettau, Meike, Christopher Yusufu Mtaku, and Eric Debrah Otchere, eds. 2022. *Performing Sustainability in West Africa: Cultural Practices and Policies for Sustainable Development*. New York: Routledge.

Leung, Bo-Wah. 2018. "Coda: Current Trends and Future Development in Transmitting Traditional Music." In *Traditional Musics in the Modern World: Transmission, Evolution, and Challenges*, edited by Bo-Wah Leung, 261–272. Cham, Switzerland: Springer.

Levi, Erik, and Florian Scheding. 2010. *Music and Displacement: Diasporas, Mobilities and Dislocations in Europe and Beyond*. Lanham, MD: Scarecrow Press.

Levy, Denise L., and Daniel C. Byrd. 2011. "Why Can't We Be Friends? Using Music to Teach Social Justice." *Journal of the Scholarship of Teaching and Learning* 11 (2): 64.

Liamputtong, Pranee. 2010. *Performing Qualitative Cross-Cultural Research*. Cambridge, UK: Cambridge University Press.

Lloyd, Jessie. 2017a. "Songs Give Insight into Life in Aboriginal Missions" [interview by M Schafter]. Sydney: ABC-TV. YouTube. May 4, 2017. Accessed March 23, 2023. https://www.youtube.com/watch?v=1qeegyQqQAI.

Lloyd, Jessie, producer. 2017b. *The Songs Back Home: Mission Songs Project*. Melbourne, Australia: Jessie Lloyd Music MSP002, CD.

Lloyd, Jessie. n.d. *Mission Songs Project*. Accessed March 23, 2023. https://www.missionsongsproject.com/.

Loehr, Johanna, Cherise Addinsall, and Betty Weiler. 2019. "Understanding How Context Affects Resilience and its Consequences for Sustainable Tourism." In *A Research Agenda for Sustainable Tourism*, edited by Stephen F. McCool and Keith Bosak, 39–52. Cheltenham, UK: Edward Elgar.

Loehr, Johanna. 2020. "The Vanuatu Tourism Adaptation System: A Holistic Approach to Reducing Climate Risk." *Journal of Sustainable Tourism* 28 (4): 515–534.

Lohmann, Larry. 2008. "Carbon Trading, Climate Justice and the Production of Ignorance: Ten Examples." *Development* 51 (3): 359–365.

Lomax, Alan. 1972. "An Appeal for Cultural Equity." *World of Music* 14 (2): 3–17. Accessed July 17, 2023. https://www.culturalequity.org/alan-lomax/appeal.

Lorde, Audre. 1984. *Sister Outsider: Essays and Speeches by Audre Lorde*. Berkeley, CA: Crossing Press.

Lovatt, Hugh, and Jacob Mundy. 2021. "Free to Choose: A New Plan for Peace in Western Sahara." *European Council on Foreign Relations*, May 2021. Accessed February 19, 2023. https://ecfr.eu/wp-content/uploads/Free-to-choose-A-new-plan-for-peace-in-Western-Sahara.pdf.

Lucas, Glaura, 2002. "Musical Rituals of Afro-Brazilian Religious Groups Within the Ceremonies of Congado." *Yearbook for Traditional Music* 34: 115–128.

Maffi, Luisa, and Ellen Woodley. 2012. *Biocultural Diversity Conservation: A Global Sourcebook*. Abingdon: Routledge.

Maldonado-Torres, Nelson. 2016. "Outline of Ten Theses on Coloniality and Decoloniality." *Fondation Frantz Fanon*. Accessed June 28, 2023. https://fondation-frantzfanon.com/outline-of-ten-theses-on-coloniality-and-decoloniality/.

Maldonado-Torres, Nelson. 2020. "Interrogating Systemic Racism and the White Academic Field." *Fondation Frantz Fanon*. Accessed June 20, 2023. https://fondation-frantzfanon.com/interrogating-systemic-racism-and-the-white-academic-field/.

Malvatumauri National Council of Chiefs. 2012. "Alternative Indicators of Wellbeing for Melanesia: Vanuatu Pilot Study Report." Port Vila, Vanuatu: Vanuatu National Statistics Office. Accessed November 20, 2022. https://www.toksavepacificgender.net/wp-content/uploads/2021/03/Vanuatu-National-Statistics-Office_2012.pdf.

Marett, Allan. 2010. "Vanishings Songs: How Musical Extinctions Threaten the Planet: The Laurence Picken Memorial Lecture 2009." *Ethnomusicology Forum* 19 (2): 249–262.

Mason, Michael Atwood, and Rory Turner. 2020. "Cultural Sustainability: A Framework for Relationships, Understanding and Action." *Journal of American Folklore* 133 (527): 81–99.

Mbembe, Achille Joseph. 2016. "Decolonising the University: New Directions." *Arts & Humanities in Higher Education* 15 (1): 29–45.

McClary, Susan. 2001. *Conventional Wisdom: The Content of Musical Form*. Berkeley: University of California Press.

McConnell, Bonnie B. 2019. *Music, Health, and Power: Singing the Unsayable in the Gambia*. Milton: Taylor & Francis.

McConnell, Bonnie B. 2020. "Jali Popular Song and Conflict Mediation in the Aftermath of The Gambia's 2016 Election." *Ethnomusicology Forum* 29 (2): 213–229.

McDermott, Veronica. 2017. *We Must Say No to the Status Quo: Educators as Allies in the Battle for Social Justice*. Thousand Oaks, CA: Corwin.

McDonald, David A. 2021. "Sincerely Outspoken: Toward a Critical Activist Ethnomusicology." In *Transforming Ethnomusicology Volume I: Methodologies, Institutional Structures, and Policies*, edited by Beverley Diamond and Salwa El-Shawan Castelo-Branco, 73–86. New York: Oxford University Press.

McDonald, David A. 2022. "Introduction: Pathways toward a Justice-Oriented Ethnomusicology." In *At the Crossroads of Music and Social Justice*, edited by Brenda M. Romero, Susan M. Asai, David A. McDonald, Andrew G. Snyder, and Katelyn E. Best, 1–19. Bloomington: Indiana University Press.

McLean, Mervyn. 1996. *Maori Music*. Auckland: Auckland University Press.

Mignolo, Walter D. 2018. "Foreword: On Pluriversity and Multipolarity." In *Constructing the Pluriverse*, edited by Bernd Reiter, ix–xv. Durham, NC and London: Duke University Press.

Mignolo, Walter D., and Catherine E. Walsh. 2018. *On Decoloniality: Concepts, Analytics, Praxis*. Durham, NC: Duke University Press.

Milano, Alannys. 2020. "Cyclone Harold's Impact on Vanuatu." *Borgen Magazine*, December 5, 2020. Accessed November 14, 2022. https://www.borgenmagazine.com/cyclone-harolds-impact/.

Miller, David. 1999. *Principles of Social Justice*. Cambridge, MA: Harvard University Press.

Milliband, David. 2016. "The Best Ways to Deal with the Refugee Crisis." *International Rescue Committee*. October 13, 2016. Accessed July 28, 2022. https://www.rescue.org/press-release/best-ways-deal-refugee-crisis.

Minder, Raphael. 2022. "Spain, Seeking Better Ties with Morocco, Shifts Stance on Western Sahara." *New York Times*. March 20, 2022.

MINURSO [United Nations Mission for the Referendum in Western Sahara]. 2022. "Security Council Resolutions and Statements." *MINURSO*. Accessed August 8, 2022. https://minurso.unmissions.org/security-council-resolutions-and-statements.

Moisala, Pirkko. 2013. "'Nobody Should be Forced to Make a Living by Begging': Social Exclusion and Cultural Rights of Gāine/Gandharva Musicians of Nepal." *Yearbook of Traditional Music* 45 (1): 13–27.

Monbiot, George. 2019. "Future Lives Should Not Be Sacrificed to Fuel Our Greed." *The Guardian Weekly*, March 22, 2019, 48–49.

Morcom, Anna. 2013. *Illicit Worlds of Indian Dance: Cultures of Exclusion*. New York: Oxford University Press.

Morcom, Anna, and Timothy D. Taylor, eds. 2020. *The Oxford Handbook of Economic Ethnomusicology*. Oxford: Oxford University Press.

Morita, Atsuro and Casper Bruun Jensen. 2017. "Delta Ontologies: Infrastructural Transformations in the Chao Phraya Delta, Thailand." *Social Analysis* 61 (2): 118–133.

Motif Art Studio. 2023. "Who We Are." *Motif Art Studio: A Temple of Art in the Middle of the Desert*. Accessed June 22, 2023. https://motifartstudio.com/.

Musicians Without Borders. 2022. "Musicians without Borders." Accessed February 12, 2023. https://www.musicianswithoutborders.org/.

National Archives of Australia. n.d. "Royal Commission into Aboriginal Deaths in Custody." *National Archives of Australia*. Accessed March 30, 2023. https://www.naa.gov.au/explore-collection/first-australians/royal-commission-aboriginal-deaths-custody#reports.

NITI [National Institution for Transforming India] Aayog. 2021. "SDGs India Index 2021–2022." June 13, 2021. Accessed December 18, 2022. https://sdgindiaindex.niti.gov.in/#/ranking.

Nothling, Lily. 2018. "Palm Island Riots Class Action Payout 'Slap in Face' to Police, Union Says." *The Courier Mail*, May 2, 2018. Accessed March 25, 2023. https://www.abc.net.au/news/2018-05-02/riot-class-action-payout-prompts-police-union-anger/9717084.

NPR. 2019. "Transcript: Greta Thunberg's Speech at the U.N. Climate Action Summit." *NPR*, September 23, 2019. Accessed January 22, 2022. https://www.npr.org/2019/09/23/763452863/transcript-greta-thunbergs-speech-at-the-u-n-climate-action-summit.

Nussbaum, Martha C. 2000. *Women and Human Development: The Capabilities Approach*. Cambridge: Cambridge University Press.

Nussbaum, Martha. 2003. "Capabilities as Fundamental Entitlements: Sen and Social Justice." *Feminist Economics* 9 (2–3): 33–59.

Nussbaum, Martha. 2011. *Creating Capabilities: The Human Development Approach.* Cambridge, MA: Harvard University Press.

Nzewi, Meki. 2006. "Growing in Musical Arts Knowledge Versus the Role of the Ignorant Expert." In *Centering on African Practice in Musical Arts Education*, edited by Minette Mans, 49–60. Cape Town: African Minds.

Nzewi, Meki. 2019. "Pertinent Concepts for Advancing Indigenous Epistemological Integrity for African Musical Arts Education." In *Music Education in Africa: Concept, Process, and Practice*, edited by Emily Achieng' Akuno, 76–91. Abingdon: Routledge.

Nzewi, Meki and Rose Omolo-Ongati. 2014. "Injecting the African Spirit of Humanity into Teaching, Learning and Assessment of Musical Arts in the Modern Classroom." *Journal of the Musical Arts in Africa* 11 (1): 55–72.

O'Connell, John Morgan, and Salwa El-Shawan Castelo-Branco. 2010. *Music and Conflict.* Urbana: University of Illinois Press.

OCHA [United Nations Office for the Coordination of Humanitarian Affairs]. 2022. "ACAPS Briefing Note: Algeria: Sahrawi Refugees in Tindouf (19 January 2022)." *Relief Web*, January 19, 2022. Accessed February 19, 2023. https://reliefweb.int/report/algeria/acaps-briefing-note-algeria-sahrawi-refugees-tindouf-19-january-2022.

Office for the Arts. 2023. "Indigenous Arts and Languages Program." Australian Government. Accessed March 13, 2023. https://www.arts.gov.au/what-we-do/indigenous-arts-and-languages/indigenous-languages-and-arts-program.

Office of the High Commissioner for Human Rights. 1966. "International Covenant on Economic, Social and Cultural Rights." December 16, 1966. Accessed May 10, 2023. https://www.ohchr.org/en/instruments-mechanisms/instruments/international-covenant-economic-social-and-cultural-rights.

Office of the High Commissioner for Human Rights. 2007. "United Nations Declaration on the Rights of Indigenous Peoples." September 13, 2007. Accessed May 10, 2023. https://www.ohchr.org/EN/Issues/IPeoples/Pages/Declaration.aspx.

Office of the High Commissioner for Human Rights. 2019. "Cultural Rights: Tenth Anniversary Report. Report of the Special Rapporteur in the Field of Cultural Rights." February–March 2019. Accessed May 18, 2022. https://www.ohchr.org/EN/Issues/CulturalRights/Pages/AnnualReports.aspx.

Office of the High Commissioner for Human Rights. 2023. "Transitional Justice and Human Rights." Accessed May 6, 2023. https://www.ohchr.org/en/transitional-justice.

Office of the High Commissioner for Human Rights. n.d. "Mapping Cultural Rights: Nature, Issues at Stake and Challenges." Accessed April 23, 2023. https://www.ohchr.org/EN/Issues/CulturalRights/Pages/MappingCulturalRights.aspx.

Ogut, Evrim Hikmet, interviewer, and Umut Sulun, videographer. n.d. *Sınırın Ötesinden Sesler / Sounds Beyond the Border.* YouTube. Accessed August 6, 2022. https://www.youtube.com/watch?v=ZgOBGgFJTCc.

Opara, Ruth. 2022. "Music and the African Girl Child: Gender-based Violence, Resistance, and Sustainability in Pot Drum Dance." *International Journal of Traditional Arts* 4 (1): 1–18.

Orlove, Ben, Neil Dawson, Pasang Sherpa, Ibidun Adelekan, Wilfredo Alangui, Rosario Carmona, Deborah Coen, et al. 2022. "ICSM CHC White Paper I: Intangible Culture Heritage, Diverse Knowledge Systems and Climate Change" [discussion paper]. Charenton-le-Pond and Paris, France: ICOMOS & ISCM CHC. Accessed July 17, 2023. https://openarchive.icomos.org/id/eprint/2717/.

Orr, Joanne. 2023. *Practitioner Perspectives on Intangible Cultural Heritage.* London: Routledge.

Osnes, Beth. 2013. *Theatre for Women's Participation in Sustainable Development.* Oxford: Routledge.

Our Race. n.d. "Power to the Story Holder." Accessed August 27, 2024. https://www.ourrace.com.au/ .

Pacelli, Shirley. 2019. "In Black Consciousness Month, Get to Know the Quilombola Community of Arturos." *O'tempo*, November 19, 2019. Accessed August 29, 2023. https://www.otempo.com.br/turismo/no-mes-da-consciencia-negra-conheca-a-comunidade-quilombola-dos-arturos-1.2263325.

Painter, Nell Irvin. 2020. "Why 'White' should be Capitalized, too." *Washington Post*, July 22, 2020. Accessed May 28, 2023. https://www.washingtonpost.com/opinions/2020/07/22/why-white-should-be-capitalized/.

Pann, Rethea. 2019. "Preserving Cambodia's Cultural Heritage with the Magic Music Bus." *Phnom Penh Post*, June 18, 2019. Accessed May 15, 2023. https://www.phnompenhpost.com/lifestyle-around-ngos/preserving-cambodias-cultural-heritage-magic-music-bus.

Pann, Rethea. 2022. "Khmer Instrument Added to Music Curriculum." *Phnom Penh Post*, August 23, 2022. Accessed May 15, 2023. https://www.phnompenhpost.com/lifestyle-arts-culture/khmer-instrument-added-music-curriculum.

Patel, Leigh. 2016. *Decolonizing Educational Research: From Ownership to Answerability*. New York: Routledge.

Paul, Harpreet Kaur, and Farah Ahmed. 2022. "Creative Climate Justice Guide." *Julie's Bicycle*. Accessed November 19, 2022. https://juliesbicycle.com/wp-content/uploads/2022/04/Creative-Climate-Justice-Final.pdf.

Pedelty, Mark. 2016. *A Song to Save the Salish Sea: Musical Performance as Environmental Activism*. Bloomington and Indianapolis: Indiana University Press.

Perumal, Nikita. 2018. "'The Place Where I Live is Where I Belong: Community Perspectives on Climate Change and Climate-Related Migration in the Pacific Island Nation of Vanuatu." *Island Studies Journal* 13 (1): 45–64.

Pettan, Svanibor, and Jeff Todd Titon, eds. 2015. *The Oxford Handbook of Applied Ethnomusicology*. New York: Oxford University Press.

Phillips-Hutton, Ariana. 2020. *Music Transforming Conflict*. Cambridge: Cambridge University Press.

Pier, Meg. 2021. "Interview with Amitava Bhattacharya, Founder of Banglanatak.com." April 21, 2021, updated October 7, 2022. Accessed October 20, 2022. https://www.peopleareculture.com/amitava-bhattacharya/.

Porsdam, Helle. 2019. *The Transforming Power of Cultural Rights*. Cambridge: Cambridge University Press.

Pörtner, Hans-Otto, Debra C. Roberts, Melinda M.B. Tignor, Elvira Poloczanska, Katja Mintenbeck, Andrés Alegría, Marlies Craig, Stefanie Langsdorf, Sina Löschke, Vincent Möller, Andrew Okem, and Bardhyl Rama, eds. 2022. "Climate Change 2022: Impacts, Adaptation and Vulnerability." Contribution of Working Group II to the Sixth Assessment Report of the Intergovernmental Panel on Climate Change, Cambridge: Cambridge University Press. Accessed July 17, 2023. https://report.ipcc.ch/ar6/wg2/IPCC_AR6_WGII_FullReport.pdf.

Posada, Violeta Ruano, and Vivian Solana Moreno. 2015. "The Strategy of Style: Music, Struggle, and the Aesthetics of Sahrawi Nationalism in Exile." *Transmodernity* (Winter): 40–61.

Post, Jennifer C. 2018. "Climate Change and Cultural Heritage in Western Mongolia." *Leonardo* 51 (3): 285–286.

Post, Jennifer C. 2019. "Climate Change, Mobile Pastoralism, and Cultural Heritage in Western Mongolia." In *Cultural Sustainabilities: Music, Media, Language, Advocacy*, edited by Timothy J. Cooley, 75–86. Illinois: University of Illinois Press.

Prada Bianchi, Andrea, and Pesha Magid. 2024. "This Music Survived in a Network of Phones': El Wali, the Shapeshifting Voice of Saharan Struggle." *The Guardian*, March 13, 2024.

Accessed August 30, 2024. https://www.theguardian.com/music/2024/mar/13/el-wali-the-shapeshifting-voice-of-saharan-struggle.

Purdy, Jedediah. 2015. "Environmentalism's Racist History." *The New Yorker*, August 13, 2015. Accessed November 20, 2022. https://www.newyorker.com/news/news-desk/environmentalisms-racist-history.

Queensland Government. 1958. "Location of Government Settlements, Church Missions and Torres Strait Island Reserves Shown" [map]. *Annual Report of the Director of Native Affairs for the Year Ending 30 June 1958.* Accessed March 15, 2023. https://aiatsis.gov.au/sites/default/files/docs/digitised_collections/remove/82200.pdf.

Queensland Government. 2018. "Palm Island." March 18, 2018. Accessed February 4, 2022. https://www.qld.gov.au/firstnations/cultural-awareness-heritage-arts/community-histories/community-histories-n-p/community-histories-palm-island.

Queensland State Parliament. 1897. "Aboriginal Protection and Restriction of the Sale of Opium Act 1897." *To Remove and Protect.* Accessed February 4, 2022. https://aiatsis.gov.au/collection/featured-collections/remove-and-protect.

Race Forward: The Center for Racial Justice Innovation. 2014. *Moving the Race Conversation Forward.* Accessed January 16, 2022. https://www.raceforward.org/research/reports/moving-race-conversation-forward.

Ratuva, Steven. 2010. "Back to Basics: Towards Integrated Social Protection for Vulnerable Groups in Vanuatu." *Pacific Economic Bulletin* 25 (3): 40–64.

Rawls, John. 1971. *A Theory of Justice*. Cambridge, MA: Harvard University Press.

Rees, Helen. 2009. "Use and Ownership: Folk Music in the People's Republic of China." In *Music and Cultural Rights*, edited by Andrew Noah Weintraub and Bell Yung, 42–85. Illinois: University of Illinois Press.

Refugee Radio. 2011. "Tiris: Saharawi Refugee Camp Band" [podcast]. *Refugee Radio*, December 8, 2011. Accessed August 18, 2022. https://refugeeradio.org.uk/2011/12/08/tiris/ [archived].

Reigersberg, Muriel Swijghuisen. 2017. "The Songs Back Home: The Missions Songs Project" [review]. May 3, 2017. http://musictrust.com.au/loudmouth/the-songs-back-home-the-mission-songs-project/.

Reisch, Michael, ed. 2014. *Routledge International Handbook of Social Justice*. Abingdon: Routledge.

Reyes, Adelaida. 1999. *Songs of the Caged, Songs of the Free: Music and the Vietnamese Refugee Experience*. Philadelphia, PA: Temple University Press.

Reyes, Adelaida. 2019. "The Beneficence and the Tyranny of Paradigms: Kuhn, Ethnomusicology and Migration." In *Ethnomusicology Matters, Vol. 1: Influencing Social and Political Realities*, edited by Ursula Hemetek, Marko Kölbl, and Hande Sağlam, 35–52. Vienna: Böhlau Verlag.

Rimon, Akka, and Anote Tong. 2021. "The Seas are Coming For Us in Kiribati. Will Australia Rehome Us?" *The Conversation*, November 23, 2021. Accessed January 10, 2023. https://theconversation.com/the-seas-are-coming-for-us-in-kiribati-will-australia-rehome-us-172137.

Rinehart, Robert E., Karen N. Barbour, and Clive C Pope. 2014. "Proem: Engaging Contemporary Ethnography across the Disciplines." In *Ethnographic Worldviews: Transformations and Social Justice*, edited by Robert E. Rinehart, Karen N. Barbour, and Clive C Pope, 1–11. Dordrecht: Springer.

Roberts, Anita, and Harrison Selmen. 2020. "Luganville Mayor Pleads for Urgent Help." *Daily* Post, April 8, 2020. Accessed February 21, 2022. https://www.dailypost.vu/news/luganville-mayor-pleads-for-urgent-help/article_43abe1da-791c-11ea-9c4d-3bce13ffdb85.html.

Roberts, Rhoda. 2021. "The Modernity of the Songlines." In *Transforming Ethnomusicology Volume II: Political, Social & Ecological Issues*, edited by Beverley Diamond and Salwa El-Shawan Castelo-Branco, 126–132. New York: Oxford University Press.

Robinson, Dylan. 2019. "To All Who Should Be Concerned." *Intersections* 39 (1): 137–144.

Robinson, Dylan. 2020. *Hungry Listening: Resonant Theory for Indigenous Sound Studies*. Minneapolis: University of Minnesota Press.

Romero, Brenda M., Susan M. Asai, David A. McDonald, Andrew G. Snyder, and Katelyn E. Best, eds. 2022. *At the Crossroads of Music and Social Justice*. Bloomington: Indiana University Press.

Rowatt, Christina. 2022. "Aboriginal Australian Songkeeper Jessie Lloyd." *Music Industry Insights Podcast*, July 5, 2022. Accessed March 9, 2023. https://aim.edu.au/news/aboriginal-australian-songkeeper-jessie-lloyd-music-industry-insights-podcast/.

Ruano Posada, Violeta. 2016. "Portraits of Saharawi Music: When Cultural Preservation Meets Political Activism." *African Music* 10 (2): 108–125.

Ruano Posada, Violeta. 2019. "International Archives and National Music Competitions: The Preservation of an 'Endangered' Musical Heritage in the Saharawi Refugee Camps (Southwest Algeria)." *Transposition: Musique et Sciences Sociales* 8: 1–22.

Rural Craft and Cultural Hubs. 2023. "About the Project." Accessed February 9, 2023. https://www.rcchbengal.com/about-the-project.

Rush, Peter D., and Olivera Simić. 2014. *The Arts of Transitional Justice: Culture, Activism, and Memory after Atrocity*. New York: Springer.

Saharawi Voice. 2023. "The Full Story: Suilma Aali." *The Full Story*, YouTube. June 27, 2023. Accessed July 7, 2023. https://www.youtube.com/watch?v=Jo1oWX6_SP8.

Sam, Sam-Ang. 2016. "Cambodia." In *Bloomsbury Encyclopedia of Popular Music of the World: Locations: Asia and Oceania*, edited by John Shepherd, David Horn and Dave Liang, 167–171. London: Continuum.

Sandblast. 2012. "Studio Live: Promoting Saharawi Voices through Music." *The Communication Initiative Network*, July 13, 2012. Accessed February 8, 2023. https://www.comminit.com/global/content/studio-live-promoting-saharawi-voices-through-music.

Sandblast. 2021. "Desert Voicebox." *Sandblast*. Accessed August 20, 2022. http://www.sandblast-arts.org/desert-voicebox.html.

Sandford, Richard, and May Cassar. 2020. "Heritages of Futures Thinking: Strategic Foresight and Critical Futures." In *Cultural Heritage and the Future*, edited by Cornelius Holtorf and Anders Högberg, 245–263. Abingdon: Routledge.

Saberes Tradicionais UFMG [Federal University of Minas Gerais] (2022). "José Bonifácio da Luz / Bengala." Accessed September 3, 2023. https://www.saberestradicionais.org/jose-bonifacio-da-luz-bengala/.

Scheidel, Arnim. 2015. "Stung Cheay Areng Hydroelectric Dam in Koh Kong, Cambodia." *Environmental Justice Atlas*. Accessed May 15, 2023. https://www.ejatlas.org/conflict/stung-cheay-areng-hydroelectric-dam-development-at-the-cost-of-indigenous-communities-koh-kong-cambodia.

Schmidt-Pirro, Julia, and Karen McCurdy. 2005. "Employing Music in the Cause of Social Justice: Ruth Crawford Seeger and Zilphia Horton." *Voices* 31 (1–2): 32–36. www.nyfolklore.org/pubs/voic31-1-2/socjust1.html.

Schippers, Huib, and Anthony Seeger, eds. 2022. *Music, Communities, Sustainability: Developing Policies and Practices*. New York: Oxford University Press.

Schippers, Huib, and Catherine Grant, eds. 2016. *Sustainable Futures for Music Cultures*. New York: Oxford University Press.

Sechehaye, Hélène, and Marco Martiniello. 2019. "Refugees for Refugees: Musicians Between Confinement and Perspectives." *Arts* 8 (14): 1–16.

Seeger, Anthony. 2019. "How Does Ethnomusicology Matter? The Socio-Political Relevance of Ethnomusicology in the 21st Century." In *Ethnomusicology Matters: Influencing Social and Political Realities*, edited by Ursula Hemetek, Marko Kölbl and Hande Sağlam, 15–32. Vienna: Böhlau Verlag.

Sen, Amartya. 2001. *Development as Freedom*, 2nd ed. New York: Oxford University Press.

Sen, Amartya. 2004. "How Does Culture Matter?" In *Culture and Public Action: A Cross-Disciplinary Dialogue on Development Policy*, edited by Michael Walton and Vijayendra Rao, 37–58. Redwood, CA: Stanford University Press.

Sensoy, Ozlem, and Robin DiAngelo. 2019. "What Is a Social Justice Framework?" Accessed July 17, 2023. https://education.csuci.edu/justice-conference/faq.htm.

Sethi, Rajeev. 2001. "A Seed is not Shy of Germination." In *Safeguarding Tradtitional Cultures: A Global Assessment*, edited by Peter Seitel, 83–86. Washington DC: Center for Folklife and Cultural Heritage, Smithsonian Institution.

Shao, Oliver Y. 2021. "'How Is That Going To Help Anyone?': A Critical Activist Ethnomusicology." In *Transforming Ethnomusicology Volume I: Methodologies, Institutional Structures, and Policies*, edited by Beverley Diamond and Salwa El-Shawan Castelo-Branco, 87–100. New York: Oxford University Press.

Sherman, Mya, and Hames Ford. 2014. "Stakeholder Engagement in Adaptation Interventions: An Evaluation of Projects in Developing Nations." *Climate Policy* 14 (3): 417–441.

Shumba, Ano. 2015. "Portraits of Saharawi Music (British Library)." September 30, 2015. Accessed August 8, 2022. https://www.musicinafrica.net/directory/violeta-ruano-portraits-saharawi-music-british-library.

Silvers, Michael B. 2018. *Voices of Drought: The Politics of Music and Environment in Northeastern Brazil*. Urbana: University of Illinois Press.

Skelchy, Russell, and Jeremy Taylor. 2022. "Introduction." In *Sonic Histories of Occupation: Experiencing Sound and Empire in a Global Context*, edited by Russell Skelchy and Jeremy Taylor, 1–22. New York: Bloomsbury.

Sleiman Labat, Mohamed. 2022a. "A Temple of Art in the Middle of the Desert: Reflections on Creating *Motif Art Studio* and the Role of Art in the Sahrawi refugee camps." *Arts and Culture in Global Development Practice: Expression, Identity and Empowerment*, edited by Cindy Maguire and Ann Holt, 17–33. Abingdon: Routledge.

Sleiman Labat, Mohamed. 2022b. "New Practices, New Narratives: Oral Essays by Mohamed Sleiman Labat." Soundcloud. Accessed June 20, 2023. https://soundcloud.com/motif_art_studio.

Small, Christopher. 1998. *Musicking: The Meanings of Performing and Listening*. Middletown, CT: Wesleyan University Press.

Smith, Danielle, and Violeta Ruano. 2021. "Political Limbo and Statelessness in Africa's Last Colony." *European Network on Statelessness: Blog*, April 1, 2021. Accessed June 23, 2023. https://www.statelessness.eu/updates/blog/political-limbo-and-statelessness-africas-last-colony.

Smith, Danielle, and Violeta Ruano. 2022. "Creative Teaching through Solidarity Networks in the Sahrawi Refugee Camps." In *Arts and Culture in Global Development Practice: Expression, Identity and Empowerment*, edited by Cindy Maguire and Ann Holt, 86–103. London: Routledge.

Smithsonian Center for Folklife and Cultural Heritage. 2022. "Cultural Heritage Tourism Initiative." Accessed October 14, 2022. https://folklife.si.edu/cultural-heritage-tourism?mc_cid=4c01247981&mc_eid=4bbea55744.

Snyder, Andrew G., and Katelyn E. Best 2022. "Preface." In *At the Crossroads of Music and Social Justice*, edited by Brenda M. Romero, Susan M. Asai, David A. McDonald, Andrew G. Snyder, and Katelyn E. Best, ix–xii. Bloomington: Indiana University Press.

Society for Ethnomusicology. n.d. *Music and Social Justice Resources Project.* Accessed January 15, 2022. https://ethnomusicology.site-ym.com/general/custom.asp?page=Resources_Social.

Southcott, Jane, Andrew Sutherland, and Leon De Bruin, eds. 2022. *Revolutions in Music Education: Historical and Social Explorations*. Lanham, MD: Rowman & Littlefield.

Spickett, Jeffrey, Dianne Katscherian, and Lachlan McIver. 2013. "Health Impacts of Climate Change in Vanuatu: An Assessment and Adaptation Action Plan." *Global Journal of Health Science* 5 (3): 42–53.

Stanton, Burke. 2018. "Musicking in the Borders toward Decolonizing Methodologies." *Philosophy of Music Education Review* 26 (1): 4–23.

Steinberg, Philip and Kimberley Peters. 2015. "Wet Ontologies, Fluid Spaces: Giving Depth to Volume through Oceanic Thinking." *Society and Space* 33 (2): 247–264.

Stillman, Amy Ku'uleialoha. 2009. "Access and Control: A Key to Reclaiming the Right to Construct Hawaiian History." In *Music and Cultural Rights*, edited by Andrew Noah Weintraub and Bell Yung, 86–109. Illinois: University of Illinois Press.

Stobart, Henry. 2017. "'Justice With My Own Hands': The Serious Play of Piracy in Bolivian Indigenous Music Videos." In *Ethnomusicology: A Contemporary Reader*, edited by Jennifer C. Post, 35–52. New York: Routledge.

Sunderland, Naomi, Phil Graham, Brydie-Leigh Bartleet, Darren Garvey, Clint Bracknell, Kristy Apps, Glenn Barry, Rae Cooper, Brigitta Scarfe, and Stacey Vervoort. 2023. "First Nations Music as a Determinant of Health in Australia and Vanuatu: Political and Economic Determinants." *Health Promotion International* 38: 1–14.

Tabani, Marc. 2017. "Development, Tourism, and Commodification of Cultures in Vanuatu." In *Tides of Innovation in Oceania: Value, Materiality and Place*, edited by Elisabetta Gnecchi-Ruscone and Anna Paini, 225–260. Canberra, Australia: ANU Press.

Tahana, Jamie. 2020. "Close to 70 Percent of Vanuatu's Luganville Destroyed by Cyclone Harold." RNZ, April 9, 2020. Accessed November 14, 2022. https://www.rnz.co.nz/international/pacific-news/413890/close-to-70-percent-of-vanuatu-s-luganville-destroyed-by-cyclone-harold.

Taket, Ann, and Fiona McKay, eds. 2020. *Health Equity, Social Justice and Human Rights*. Abingdon: Routledge.

Tan, Sooi Beng. 2008. "Activism in Southeast Asian Ethnomusicology: Empowering Youths to Revitalize Traditions and Bridge Cultural Barriers." *Musicological Annual* 44 (1): 69–84.

Tan, Sooi Beng. 2021. "Engaged Activist Research: Dialogical Interventions toward Revitalizing the Chinese Glove Puppet Theater in Penang." In *Transforming Ethnomusicology Volume I: Methodologies, Institutional Structures, and Policies*, edited by Beverley Diamond and Salwa El-Shawan Castelo-Branco, 131–150. New York: Oxford University Press.

Thaiday, Willie. 1981. *Under the Act*. Townsville, Australia: N.Q. Black Publishing Company.

Thorp, Teresa M. 2014. *Climate Justice: A Voice for the Future*. London: Palgrave Macmillan.

Throsby, Charles, and Katya Petetskaya. 2017. "Making Art Work: An Economic Study of Professional Artists in Australia." *Australia Council for the Arts*, November 2017. Accessed December 19, 2022. https://australiacouncil.gov.au/advocacy-and-research/making-art-work/.

Titon, Jeff Todd, ed. 2009. *World of Music* [special issue] 51 (1).

Titon, Jeff Todd. 2008–2022. "Sustainable Music" [blog]. Accessed January 15, 2022. https://sustainablemusic.blogspot.com/.

Titon, Jeff Todd. 2020. *Toward a Sound Ecology: New and Selected Essays*. Indiana: Indiana University Press.

Titon, Jeff Todd. 2021. "A Sound Economy." In *Transforming Ethnomusicology Volume II: Political, Social & Ecological Issues*, edited by Beverley Diamond and Salwa El-Shawan Castelo-Branco, 26–46. New York: Oxford University Press.

Touch TD. 2020, February. "Final Evaluation of the Project 'Development of Rural Craft and Cultural Hubs in West Bengal to Support Intergenerational Transmission of Rural Craft and Performing Arts (RCCH)'." Report commissioned by UNESCO Cluster Office. New Delhi and London: Touch TD.

Townsville Bulletin. 2015. "Long-Awaited Apology Overshadowed by Trial." *Townsville Bulletin*, March 5, 2015.

Travae, Marques. 2013. "10 Years of Affirmative Action at the University of Brasília: Black Student Enrollment Increases by 71.5% and Quota Students Outperform Non-quota Students." *Black Brazil Today: Analyzing Brazil from the Perspective of Race*. June 10, 2013. Accessed June 19, 2023. https://blackbraziltoday.com/10-years-of-affirmative-action-at-the-university-of-brasilia/.

Treloyn, Sally, and Rona Goonginda Charles. 2021. "Music Endangerment, Repatriation, and Intercultural Collaboration in an Australian Discomfort Zone." In *Transforming Ethnomusicology*, Vol. 2, edited by Beverley Diamond and Salwa El-Shawan Castelo-Branco, 133–147. New York: Oxford University Press.

Trip Advisor. 2022. "Magical Water Music Experience." *Trip Advisor*. Accessed February 22, 2022. https://www.tripadvisor.com.au/Attraction_Review-g1207993-d4756137-Reviews-Magical_Water_Music_Experience-Luganville_Espiritu_Santo.html.

Truth and Reconciliation Commission of Canada. 2015. "Honouring the Truth, Reconciling for the Future: Summary of the Final Report of the Truth and Reconciliation Commission of Canada." *National Centre for Truth and Reconciliation*. Accessed March 21, 2023. https://ehprnh2mwo3.exactdn.com/wp-content/uploads/2021/01/Executive_Summary_English_Web.pdf.

Tuck, Eve, and K. Wayne Yang. 2012. "Decolonization is Not a Metaphor." *Decolonization: Indigeneity, Education & Society* 1 (1): 1–40.

Turino, Thomas. 2008. *Music as Social Life: The Politics of Participation*. Chicago: University of Chicago Press.

UNESCO [United Nations Educational, Scientific and Cultural Organization]. 1980 / 2022. "Recommendation Concerning the Status of the Artist." Accessed October 4, 2022. https://en.unesco.org/creativity/governance/status-artist.

UNESCO. 1997. "Declaration on the Responsibilities of the Present Generations towards Future Generations." November 12, 1997. Accessed January 4, 2023. https://en.unesco.org/about-us/legal-affairs/declaration-responsibilities-present-generations-towards-future-generations.

UNESCO. 2001. "Universal Declaration on Cultural Diversity." November 2, 2001. Accessed January 8, 2023. https://en.unesco.org/about-us/legal-affairs/unesco-universal-declaration-cultural-diversity.

UNESCO. 2003. "Text of the Convention for the Safeguarding of the Intangible Cultural Heritage." Accessed January 15, 2022. https://ich.unesco.org/en/convention.

UNESCO. 2005. "Convention on the Protection and Promotion of the Diversity of Cultural Expressions." Accessed May 17, 2022. https://en.unesco.org/creativity/convention.

UNESCO. 2019. "Artistic Freedom." *UNESCO Diversity of Cultural Expressions*. Accessed April 23, 2023. https://en.unesco.org/creativity/sites/creativity/files/artistic_freedom_pdf_web.pdf.

UNESCO. 2021a. "Culture and Sustainable Development: Powering Culture across Public Policies." Accessed January 8, 2023. https://en.unesco.org/culture-development.

UNESCO. 2021b. "Development of Rural Craft and Cultural Hubs in West Bengal for Inter-generational Transmission." Accessed October 20, 2022. https://en.unesco.org/fieldoffice/newdelhi/projects/ruralcraft_westbengal.

UNESCO. 2022a. "Re/Shaping Policies for Creativity: Addressing Culture as a Global Public Good." February 8, 2022. Accessed January 5, 2023. https://www.unesco.org/reports/reshaping-creativity/2022/en.

UNESCO. 2022b. "Chapei Dang Veng." Accessed October 4, 2022. https://ich.unesco.org/en/USL/chapei-dang-veng-01165.

UNESCO. 2024. "Establishing A Community-Driven Alliance for Sustainable Cultural Development Planning in Lautem." Accessed July 2, 2024. https://www.unesco.org/creativity/en/articles/establishing-community-driven-alliance-sustainable-cultural-development-planning-lautem-0.

UNESCO. n.d.(a). "Dive into Intangible Cultural Heritage." Accessed February 14, 2022. https://ich.unesco.org/en/dive.

UNESCO. n.d.(b). "Ethics and Intangible Cultural Heritage." Accessed March 29, 2022. https://ich.unesco.org/en/ethics-and-ich-00866.

UNHCR [United Nations High Commissioner for Refugees]. 1951/1967. "Convention and Protocol Relating to the Status of Refugees." Accessed July 17, 2022. https://www.unhcr.org/3b66c2aa10.

UNHCR. 2001–2022. "Who We Help." Accessed August 15, 2022. https://www.unhcr.org/en-au/who-we-help.html.

UNHCR. 2021. "Global Trends: Forced Displacement in 2021." Accessed July 21, 2022. https://www.unhcr.org/62a9d1494/global-trends-report-2021.

UNICEF [United Nations Children's Fund] Algeria. 2022. "With Higher Food Prices and Pressing Needs, UN Team in Algeria Calls for Support for Sahrawi Refugees." August 24, 2022. Accessed February 19, 2023. https://www.unicef.org/algeria/en/press-releases/higher-food-prices-and-pressing-needs-un-team-algeria-calls-support-sahrawi-refugees.

United Nations. 1948. "Universal Declaration of Human Rights." Accessed January 15, 2022. https://www.un.org/en/about-us/universal-declaration-of-human-rights.

United Nations. 2024. "Sustainable Development Goals." Accessed July 2, 2024. https://www.un.org/sustainabledevelopment/.

United Nations Children's Fund. 2016. "Cyclone Pam: One Year On." *Relief Web*, March 12, 2016. Accessed February 21, 2022. https://reliefweb.int/report/vanuatu/unicef-fast-facts-cyclone-pam-one-year-march-2016.

United Nations Department of Economic and Social Affairs. 2022a. "World Population Prospects 2022." Accessed August 15, 2022. https://population.un.org/wpp/.

United Nations Department of Economic and Social Affairs. 2022b. "The 17 goals." Accessed January 8, 2023. https://sdgs.un.org/goals.

United Nations Development Programme. 2020. "Human Development Reports: Cambodia." December 15, 2020. Accessed April 4, 2022. https://www.hdr.undp.org/en/countries/profiles/KHM#.

United Nations General Assembly. 1990. "Question of Western Sahara: Resolution / Adopted by the General Assembly, A/RES/45/21." *Refworld*, November 20, 1990. Accessed August 15, 2022. https://www.refworld.org/docid/3b00efe510.html.

United Nations General Assembly. 2016. "Report of the Special Rapporteur in the Field of Cultural Rights." February 3, 2016. Accessed January 16, 2022. https://www.ohchr.org/EN/HRBodies/HRC/RegularSessions/Session31/Documents/A.HRC.31.59_E.docx.

United Nations World Tourism Organization. 2013. "Summary: Study on Tourism and Intangible Cultural Heritage." January 13, 2013. Accessed December 15, 2022. https://www.unwto.org/archive/global/publication/study-tourism-and-intangible-cultural-heritage.Urbain, Olivier, ed. 2007. *Music and Conflict Transformation: Harmonies and Dissonances in Geopolitics*. London: I.B. Tauris.

Vanuatu National Statistics Office. 2020. "National Population and Housing Census: Basic Tables Report Volume 1." Accessed December 30, 2022. https://pacificdata.org/data/dataset/spc_vut_2020_phc_v01_m.

Vice. 2019. "The 16 Year Old Calling Out Global Leaders on Climate Change." YouTube. May 24, 2019. Accessed January 15, 2022. https://www.youtube.com/watch?v=oCVQdr9QFwY&feature=youtu.be.

Vieira, Renato Schwambach, and Mary Arends-Kuenning. 2019. "Affirmative Action in Brazilian Universities: Effects on the Enrollment of Targeted Groups." *Economics of Education Review* 73: 1–12.

Visiting Arts. 2001. *South East Asia Regional Arts Profile: Cambodia Arts Directory*. London: Visiting Arts.

Walker, Darren. 2015. "On the Art of Change." April 21, 2015. Accessed January 15, 2022. https://medium.com/@FordFoundation/on-the-art-of-change-cef0864c4930.

Walzer, Michael. 1983. *Spheres of Justice: In Defense of Pluralism and Equality*. New York: Basic Books.

Ware, Vicki-Ann, and Kim Dunphy. 2020. "How Do Arts Programmes Contribute in International Development? A Systematic Review of Outcomes and Associated Processes." *Progress in Development Studies* 20 (2): 140–162.

Warrick, Olivia. 2007. "Development, Forest Conservation and Adaptation to Climate Change: A Case for Integrated Community-Based Sustainability in Rural Vanuatu." Paper presented at 2007 ANZSEE Conference: Reinventing Sustainability: A Climate for Change, July 3–6, 2007, Queensland, Australia. Australia-New Zealand Society for Ecological Economics.

Warrick, Olivia. 2009. "Ethics and Methods in Research for Community-Based Adaptation: Reflections from Rural Vanuatu." *Participatory Learning and Action* 60: 76–87.

Watson, Joanne. 1995. "'We Couldn't Tolerate Any More': The Palm Island Strike of 1957." *Labour History* 69: 149–170.

Watson, Joanne. 2010. *Palm Island, Through a Long Lens*. Canberra: Aboriginal Studies Press.

Weaver, Hilary N. 2014. "Indigenous Struggles for Justice." In *Routledge International Handbook of Social Justice*, edited by Michael Reisch, 111–122. Abingdon: Routledge.

Webb, Michael. 2019. "Melanesian Worlds of Music and Dance." In *The Melanesian World*, edited by Eric Hirsch and Will Rollason, 455–470. Abingdon: Routledge.

Webb, Michael. 2023. "Ol Sing Blong Plantesen" [digital album and booklet]. *Wantok Music*. Accessed March 13, 2023. https://wantokmusik.bandcamp.com/album/ol-sing-blong-plantesen.

Weintraub, Andrew Noah, and Bell Yung, eds. 2009. *Music and Cultural Rights*. Chicago: University of Illinois Press.

Weintraub, Andrew Noah. 2009. "Introduction." In *Music and Cultural Rights*, edited by Andrew Noah Weintraub and Bell Yung, 1–17. Chicago: University of Illinois Press.

Wessergo, Warren Wevat. 2014. "The History of the Magical Water Music." *Vanuatu Women's Watern Music*. Melbourne, Australia: Wantok Music.

Whitehead, Alex. 2022. "'Sons of the Clouds': Oral Tradition and Resistance in Africa's Last Colony." *Honi Soit*, August 7, 2022. Accessed February 19, 2023. https://honisoit.com/2022/08/sons-of-the-clouds-oral-tradition-and-resistance-in-africas-last-colony/.

Whitmarsh, Lorraine, and Agnes Kreil. 2022. "Challenging the Values of the Polluter Elite: A Global Consequentialist Response to Evensen and Graham's (2022) 'The Irreplaceable Virtues of In-Person Conferences.'" *Journal of Environmental Psychology* 83: 1–2.

Wight, Emily. 2013. "The Magic Music Bus: Carpeting Cambodia with Music, not Bombs." *Phnom Penh Post*, November 22, 2013. Accessed January 16, 2022. https://www.phnompenhpost.com/7days/magic-music-bus-carpeting-cambodia-music-not-bombs.

Wong, Chuen-Fung. 2017. "Modernist Reform, Virtuosity, and Uyghur Instrumental Music in Chinese Central Asia." In *Ethnomusicology: A Contemporary Reader*, edited by Jennifer C. Post, 53–64. New York: Routledge.

Wong, Deborah. 2021. "Witnessing: A Methodology." In *Transforming Ethnomusicology Volume I: Methodologies, Institutional Structures, and Policies*, edited by Beverley Diamond and Salwa El-Shawan Castelo-Branco, 187–201. New York: Oxford University Press.

Wood, Geoff. 2017. "NAIDOC: Jessie Lloyd on Mission to Reclaim Indigenous Cultural Heritage Through Song." *ABC News*, July 2, 2017. Accessed February 7, 2022. https://www.

abc.net.au/news/2017-07-02/jessie-lloyd-mission-to-reclaim-indigenous-heritage-through-song/8667454.

World Bank. 2015. "Girls Find Their Place in Afghanistan's Music Institute." September 2, 2015. Accessed April 23, 2023. https://www.worldbank.org/en/news/feature/2015/09/01/girls-find-place-afghanistan-music-institute.

World Bank. 2019. "Rural Population (% of Total Population): Cambodia." Accessed April 22, 2023. https://data.worldbank.org/indicator/SP.RUR.TOTL.ZS?locations=KH.

World Bank. 2023. "Life Expectancy at Birth, Male (Years)—Cambodia." Accessed April 22, 2023. https://data.worldbank.org/indicator/SP.DYN.LE00.MA.IN?locations=KH.

World Bank. 2024. "Social Dimensions of Climate Change." Accessed July 5, 2024. https://www.worldbank.org/en/topic/social-dimensions-of-climate-change.

World Bank Group. 2021. "Climate Risk Country Profile: Vanuatu." *World Bank Group*. Accessed February 21, 2022. https://climateknowledgeportal.worldbank.org/sites/default/files/country-profiles/15825-WB_Vanuatu%20Country%20Profile-WEB.pdf.

World Economic Forum. 2022. *Global Risks Report 2022*. January 22, 2022. Accessed February 2, 2022. https://www.weforum.org/reports/global-risks-report-2022/digest.

World Future Council. 2019. "Future Justice." Accessed July 17, 2023. https://www.worldfuturecouncil.org/future-justice/.

World Vision. 2020. "Cyclone Harold Leaves 160,000 Homeless: CAT II Disaster Declared." April 11, 2020. Accessed February 21, 2022. https://www.worldvision.com.au/media-centre/resource/cyclone-harold-leaves-160-000-homeless-cat-ii-disaster-declared?utm_source=miragenews&utm_medium=miragenews&utm_campaign=news.

Yale University. 2019. "Cambodian Genocide Program." Accessed April 22, 2023. https://gsp.yale.edu/case-studies/cambodian-genocide-program.

Zemaryalai, Parniyan, and John Geddie. 2021. "The Day the Music Died: Afghanistan's All-Female Orchestra Falls Silent." *Reuters*, September 4, 2021. Accessed April 23, 2023. https://www.reuters.com/world/asia-pacific/day-music-died-afghanistans-all-female-orchestra-falls-silent-2021-09-03/.

Index

For the benefit of digital users, indexed terms that span two pages (e.g., 52–53) may, on occasion, appear on only one of those pages.

Figures are indicated by an italic *f* following the page number.